RECORDS
OF THE
EVANGELICAL REFORMED CHURCH
IN
FREDERICK, MARYLAND
1746–1800

TRANSLATIONS

BY

William J. Hinke
AND E. W. Reinecke

HERITAGE BOOKS
2019

HERITAGE BOOKS
AN IMPRINT OF HERITAGE BOOKS, INC.

Books, CDs, and more—Worldwide

For our listing of thousands of titles see our website
at
www.HeritageBooks.com

Published 2019 by
HERITAGE BOOKS, INC.
Publishing Division
5810 Ruatan Street
Berwyn Heights, Md. 20740

Originally published by Family Line Publications
1986

International Standard Book Numbers
Paperbound: 978-1-58549-095-0
Clothbound: 978-0-7884-6818-6

INTRODUCTION

The registers of the Evangelical Reformed Church of Frederick constitute a major source of vital records of that area in the 18th century. The original and a translation by E. W. Reinecke, in 1861, are held by the State Archives, Annapolis. A later translation was made by William J. Hinke in 1941, from which this book is primarily based. (Microfilm copies of the Hinke translation may be obtained from the Historical Society of the Evangelical and Reformed Church, Philip Schaff Library, Lancaster Theological Seminary, Lancaster, Pennsylvania.)

Reinecke claimed to have devoted painstaken hours in the careful interpretation of these records, sometimes several hours on a single name. A brief screening of the original seems to bear this out. Nevertheless his translation is incomplete on two counts. He omits the names of the few black persons, freed blacks and slaves, contained in the original registers and he does not include the names of the god parents. In making the translations, Reinecke rearranged them in alphabetical groupings, losing the original sequence of entries. Thus it appears that the Hinke translation is to be preferred. Included in the Reinecke translation are death records that he found in loose papers, not included in the Hinke translation, and are included here. (These deaths records were also published in Western Maryland Genealogy, vol. 2, no. 4, Oct. 1986.)

In using these records one must consider that inconsistent variations in the spelling of German names were introduced by persons intending to Anglicize them. Reinecke noted that the following letters were used interchangeably: B and P; C, G and K; D and T; F and V; and J and Y. The reader will experience countless other variations.

An extensive history of this church is given in "A History of the Evangelical Reformed Church, Frederick, Maryland: Unto Us," by James B. and Dorothy S. Ranck, Margaret R. Motter and Katharine E. Dutrow. 1964. Also see Frederick Sheely Weiser, "Frederick Maryland Lutheran Marriages and Burials, 1743 - 1811," published by The National Genealogical Society, 1972. In his introduction Pastor Weiser briefly describes both Reformed and Lutheran congregations of this region and their records.

F. Edward Wright
13405 Collingwood Terrace
Silver Spring, Maryland 20904

CONTENTS

Records of the Evangelical Reformed Church in Frederick, Maryland
1746 - 1800

The following records were taken from the translation made by William J. Hinke in 1941. Baptisms have been arranged chronologically, in the following format: Parents/Children/Sponsors/

Baptisms by Visiting Ministers, 1746-1752.

Georg Becker, Anna Maria/Joh. Peter bapt Jul 10 1746/Peter Arnd & wf.
Thomas Schley, Maria Margaretha/Maria Barbara b May 27 1746, bapt Oct 31 1746/Jacob Brunner, Maria Barbara
George Laye, Elisabetha/Adam bapt Dec 15 1746/Adam Stoll, Barbara
Melchior Stehely, Barbara/Susanna Barbara b Feb 3 1747/Heinrich Bechdolt & wf.
Adam Stoll, Barbara/Elisabetha b Feb 6 1747/George Laye, Maria Elisabetha
Gottfried Ledermann, Elizabetha/Elisabetha b Feb 9 1747/George Laye, Elisabetha
Gilbert Kâmpff, Margaretha/Friedrich, b Feb 11 1747/Friedrich Kâmpff
Frantz Weiss, Anna Barbara/Catharina b Feb -- 1747/Jacob Behny, Catharina
Christian Kämpff, Elisabetha/Catharina b Feb 14 1747/Catharina Kämpff
Peter Berg, Anna Catharina/Johannes b Mar 10 1747/Johannes Berg, Anna Gertraut
Peter Schuhmacher, Eva/Maria Apollonia b Jun 24 1747/Peter Hoffman, Maria Apollonia
Jacob Stahely, Margaretha/Heinrich b May 18 1747/Heinrich Roth, Catharina
Gabriel Thomas, Anna Margaretha/Catharina b Jul 22 1747/Heinrich Sinn & wf.
Sebastian Shaub, Anna/Catharina b Oct 9 1747/Stephan Romesperger, Anna Catharina
Caspar Duebelbies, Anna/Johan Georg b Oct 9 1747/Johannes Hoffman
Abraham Weiss, Anna/Maria Barbara b (1747)/Jacob Brunner, Maria Barbara
Stephan Romesperger, Anna Catharina/Elias b Mar 20 1748/Elias Brunner, Albertina
Valentin Usselmann, Eva Barbara/Maria Margaretha b Mar 5 1748/Thomas Schley, Maria Margaretha
Johannes Brunner, Anna Maria/Elisabetha b May 22 1748/Catharina Götzendanner
Martin Cuntz, Susanna/Anna Maria b May 23 1748/Anna Maria Storm
Jacob Storm, Maria Benedicta/Maria Catharina b Sep 6 1748/Catharina Brunner
Martin Adam, Anna Maria/Jacob b Sep 26 1748/Jacob Brunner, Maria Barbara
Michael Thomas, Barbara/Jacob b -- 1748/Jacob Götzdanner
Gilbert Kämpff, Margaret Gabriel bapt May 7 1749/Gabriel Götzendanner
Michael Thomas, Barbara/Michael bapt May 7 1749/Gabriel Thomas, Margaretha
Gabriel Thomas, Anna Margaretha/Barbara bapt May 7 1749/Christian Götzendanner, Anna Barbara
Elias Brunner, Albertina/Stephan bapt May 7 1749/Stephan Romesperger, Anna Catharina
Friedrich Unselt, Maria Apollonia/Abraham bapt May 7 1749/Johannes Hoffman, Anna Barbara
Jacob Schley, Anna Maria/Johannes bapt May 7 1749/Johannes Brunner, Anna Maria
Caspar Wenderod, Anna Margretha/Johan Peter bapt May 7 1749/Peter Brunner, Anna Maria
Thomas Schley, Maria Margaretha/Eva Catharina b Mar 13 1749, bapt May 7 1749/Anna Catharina Schley

Baptisms of the Evangelical Reformed Church in Frederick, Maryland

David De Latere, Anna Barbara/Johannes b Aug 6 1749, bapt Nov 1 1749/ Johannes Brunner, Maria
Conrad Köhler, Barbara/Maria Magdalena b Mar 29 1749, bapt Nov 1 1749/ Heinrich Brunner, Magdalena
Johannes Neff, Susanna/Sarah Cöpp b Dec 2 1748, bapt Nov 1 1749/Sarah Neff
Christoph Michel, Catharina/Michael b Oct 1749, bapt Nov 1 1749/Georg Michel Brunner, Margaretha Schwartz
Johannes Berg, Juliana/Cath. Margretha b Aug 19 1749, bapt Nov 1 1749/ Barthel Jeserany, Cath. Margretha
Peter Berg, Anna Catharina/Philippus b Jul 5 1749, bapt Nov 1 1749/Philip Schmidt, Gertraut Dick
Godfried Lederman, Anna Elisabeth/Godfried bapt Jun 2 1750/Friedrich Unselt, Maria Apollonia
Jean Compere, Rahel/Heinrich bapt Jun 2 1750/Heinrich Schober, Anna Vock
Adam Romesperger, Catharina/Catharina Elisabeth bapt Jun 2 1750/Cath. Elisabeth Romersperger
Jacob Alt, Maria Elisabetha/Johannes bapt Jun 2 1750/Johannes Tropff
Gilbert Kämpff, Margaretha/Catharina bapt Aug 11 1751/Cath. Kämpff
George Laye, Elisabeth/George Friedrich bapt Aug 11 1751/Friedrich Hoffman, Anna Maria Dieter
Melchior Steheli, Barbara/Jacob bapt Aug 11 1751/Jacob Steheli, Margaretha
Peter Schuhmacher, Eva/Eva Elisabetha bapt Aug 11 1751 Elisabetha Hoffmann
Thomas Schley, Maria Margaretha/Johann Jacob b Jul 12 1751, bapt Aug 11 1751/Johan Jacob Brunner, Maria Barbara
Jacob Storm, Maria Benedicta/Charlotta bapt Aug 11 1751/Michel Romer, Charlotta
Godfried Ledermann, Anna Elisabetha/Maria Elisabetha bapt Aug 11 1751/Jacob Storm, Maria Benedicta
Wendel Storm, Magdalena/Michael bapt Aug 11 1751/Michael Eberle, Catharina Sinn
Peter Brunner, Anna Maria/Johannes bapt Aug 11 1751/Johannes Brunner, Maria Barbara Storm
Jacob Köhler, Eva/Eva Maria bapt Aug 11 1751/Rudolph Köhler, Eva Maria Berg
Jacob Köhler & wf./Anna Barbara bapt Aug 11 1751/Jacob Brunner, Maria Barbara
Mattheus Seyler, Magdalena/Anna Maria bapt Aug 11 1751/Heinrich Schober, Anna
Martin Wetzel, Catharina/Magdalena Elisabetha bapt Aug 11 1751/Leonhard Hoffman, Magdalena Elisabetha
Johannes Stall, Elis. Margaretha/Anna Catharina bapt Aug 11 1751/George Deubelbiss, Anna Catharina
Georg Däubelbiss, Anna Catharina/Johan Adam bapt Aug 11 1751/Johan Adam Stoll
Jacob Crämer, Anna Catharina/Johannes bapt Aug 11 1751/Johannes Berg, Juliana Catharina
Heinrich Bechtoldt, Anna Barbara/Georg Heinrich bapt Aug 11 1751/Conrad Kemff, Anna Maria
Christian Thomas, Magdalena/Anna Maria bapt Aug 11 1751/Johannes Brunner, Anna Maria
Christian Cuhn, Anna Elisabetha/Cath. Elisabetha bapt Aug 11 1751/Cath. Elisabetha Baitzel

Baptisms of the Evangelical Reformed Church in Frederick, Maryland

Joseph Doltrich, Elisabetha/Elisabetha bapt Aug 11 1751/N.N. (nomen nescio)
Abraham Weiss, Margaretha/Johann Peter bapt Aug 11 1751/John Bell, Elisabetha
Heinrich Camrer, Anna Catharina/Johannes bapt Aug 11 1751/Johannes Storm
Friedrich Kämpff, Regina/Maria Sophia bapt Aug 11 1751/Maria Sophia Kämpff
same parents/Peter bapt Jun 28 1749/Peter Kämpff
Joh. Georg Kroneiss, Anna Maria/Eva bapt Sep 10 1751/Leonhard Eberle, Eva Eberle
Adam Romesperger, Catharina/Georg Adam bapt Mar 23 1752/Johann Georg Romesperger
Paul Wolff, Margaretha/Maria Cathrina bapt April 5 1752, b May 30 1750/ Rudolph Cöller, Catharina Berg
Peter Bergmann, Ursula/Johann Peter b Sep -- 1751, bapt Aug 30 1752/Michael Thomas, Barbara
Peter Baltzell, Anna Maria/Maria Magdalena b Apr 17 1752, bapt Aug 29 1752/ Heinrich Brunner, Maria Magdalena
Peter Weiss, Anna Maria/Susanna b Sep 15 1752, bapt Sep 17 1752/Johannes Weymer, Susanna
Vallentin Thomas, Margaretha/Gabriel bapt Sep 24 1752/Gabriel Thomas, Margaretha

Baptisms by the Rev. Theodore Franckenfeldt, 1752-1755.

(The minutes of Coetus imply, that Frenkenfeld had begun his ministry at Frederick by October 1752. There is also a change in the handwriting of the baptismal entries at that time.)

Joh. Adam Eberle, Anna Catharina/Eva Maria bapt Oct 8 1752/Eva Maria Beckebach, Leonhard Eberle, Married people
Nicolaus Back, Odilia/Rosina b Apr 12 1752/Peter Scheffer, Rosina Scheffer
Christoph Michel, Catharina/Anna Maria b Aug 3 1752/Peter Brunner, Anna Maria
Will. Berg, Eva Maria/Johann Jacob b Aug 10 1752/Jacob Kraemer
Georg Henr. Weiss, Anna Maria/Anna Margaretha bapt Oct 28 1752/Maria Margaretha Hildebrand & Hieronimy Hildebrand
Jacob Jung, Eleonore/Maria Anna b Apr 8 1752/Georg Mich. Jessem., Charlotta Romer
Georg Deubelbiss, Catharina/Barbara b Sept 2 1752/Barbara Schober & Simon Schober
Christian Berg, Anna Gerdraut/Maria Catharina b Jun 6 1752/Wilhelm Berg, Maria Catharina
Leonhard Eberle, Eva Maria/Anna Barbara b Dec 2 1752/Georg Michael Brunner, Anna Barbara
Gabriel Thomas, Anna Margaretha/Gabriel b Mar 8 1753/Andreas Paullus, Anna Maria
Caspar Deubelbiss, Anna/Anna Elisabetha b Dec 4 1752, bapt -- 1753/Valentin Schreiner, Anna Elisabeth
Elias Brunner, Albertina/Johann Peter b Mar 31 1753/Peter Kampff, Catharina
Jacob Storm, Maria Benedicta/Anna Maria b Feb 12 1753/Johannes Brunner, Anna Maria
Jean Compere, Rahel/Eva Margaretha b Mar 27 1753/Valentin Usselmann, Eva Barbara
Christian Thomas, Magdalena/Anna Barbara b Jan 6 1753/Michael Thomas, Catharina Barbara

Baptisms of the Evangelical Reformed Church in Frederick, Maryland

Joh. Georg Kroneiss, Anna Maria/Juliana b Jan 11 1753/Michael Heffner, Juliana
Jacob Huber, Catharina/Carolus b -- 1753/Carl ---
Jacob Hoffmann, Elisabetha/Leonhardus b Nov 9 1752, bapt Jan 11 1753/ Leonhard Hoffmann, Magdalena
Ludwig Herbach, Christina/Christian Thomas b Jan 14 1753/Thomas Schley, Maria Margaretha
Henrich Brunner, Magdalena/Anna Maria b Jan 18 1753/Peter Balsel, Anna Maria Balsel
Anton Dentlinger, Catharina/Henrich b Nov 27 1752, bapt -- 1753/Henrich Schober, Anna
Peter Kempff, Catharina/Elisabetha b Mar 20 1753/Christian Kampff, Elisabeth
Johan Stoll, Elisab. Margaretha/Joh. Lorentz b Feb 5 1753/Joh. Lorentz Haffner, Catharina Margaretha
Jacob Ambrosy, Catharina/Maria Sophia b Jan 12 1753/Maria Sophia Kämpff
Peter Schaeffer, Anna/Johann Martin b Apr 5 1752, bapt -- 1753/Peter Kempff, Anna Catharina
same parents/Elisabetha b Jul 9 1745/Maria Elisabetha Lay
Jacob Wüst, Eva/Johannes b Feb 4 1753/Johannes Lingenfelder, Anna Catharina
Rudolph Rohr, Eva Margaretha/Georg Michael b Apr 26 1753/--
Jacob Delater, Elisabetha/Anna Barbara b Dec 28 1752, bapt -- 1753/Anna Barbara Brunner
Henr. Alexander & wf./Anna Maria b Aug 27 1753/Peter Balsel, Anna Maria
Johan Philip Berg, Juliana/Catharina b Jan 13, 1753/Christian Berg, Catharina Hetsch
Abraham Weiss, Anna Margaretha/Anna Maria b Apr 7 1753/Peter Weiss, Anna Maria
Bernhard Kessler, Anna Catharina/Margaretha b Jun 18 1753/Thomas Sley, Margaretha
Michael Brunner, Anna Barbara/Georg Leonhard b Jun 10 1753/Anna Maria Beckebach
Rudolph Keller, Barbara/Friedrich b Jul 10 1753/Friedrich Wittmann, Catharina
Christian Rotenbach, Elisabetha/Johann Adam b Jun 15 1753/Martin Adam, Anna Maria
Jacob Mayer, Susanna/Friedrich b Jun 3 1753/Johan Friedr. Doubber, Margaretha Bell
Felde (Valentin) Adam, Anna Margaretha/Peter b Jul 16 1753/Peter Kreppel, Anna Elisabeth
Wilhelm Ritschi, Maria Magdalena/Wilhelm b Mar 27 1753/Peter Kreppel, Anna Elisabeth
Simon Schober & wf./Susanna b --- 1753/Theodore Franckenfeld, Susanna
Jacob Dorner, Maria Barbara/Johan Jacob b 1753/Joh. Jacob Sturm, Maria Benedicta
Johan Jacob Krämer, Anna Catharina/Maria b May 14 1753/Peter Berg, Maria Dick
Philip Jacob Lehmann, Barbara/Susanna b 1753/Johan Neef, Susanna
Adam Oster, Anna Maria/Casper b Sep 18 1753/Casper Schaaf, Georg Oster, Eva Cath. Schis
Johann Jung, Susanna/Maria Magdalena b Aug 1 1753/Henr. Brunner, Maria Magdalena
Conrad Jung, Maria Magdalena/child b Oct 15 1753/---

Baptisms of the Evangelical Reformed Church in Frederick, Maryland

Bernhard Wurtenbecher, Maria Catharina/Jacob b 1753/Jacob Dörner, Maria Barbara
Andreas Eberhard, Barbara/Maria Margaretha b Oct 22 1753/Georg Jacob Gertenhauer & Maria Margaretha
Daniel Matthis, Anna Catharina/Maria Barbara b 1753/Jacob Dörner, Maria Barbara
Jacob Holtz, Catharina/Rudolph b Nov 30 1753/Rudolph Rohr, Eva
Johan Lingenfelder, Anna Maria/Eva Margaretha b Dec 26 1753/Valentin Adam, Eva Margaretha
Thomas Schley, Maria Margaretha/Sibylla b Aug 11 1753, bapt Apr 20 1754/ Sibylla Stocklin
Adam Romesperger, Catharina/Philip Henrich b Aug 1 1754/Philip Henry Thomas, Anna Catharina
Peter Brunner, Anna Maria/Charlotta b Mar 27 1754/Barbara Brunner
Friedrich Kämpff, Regina/Ludwig b Jul 3 1754/Christian Kampff, Elisabeth
Peter Baltzel, Anna Maria/Maria Margaretha b Aug 29 1754, bapt Oct 6 1754/ Thomas Schley, Maria Marg.
Johan Adam Eberle, Anna Catharina/Catharina Elisabeth bapt Nov 9 1754/Johann Stoll, Elisabetha
Nicolaus Back, Odilia/Anna Maria bapt Oct 12 1754/Johan Peter Dicker, Anna Maria
Jacob Jung, Eleonora/Maria Anna b Feb 16 1754/Johan Adam Mang, Cath. Barb. Hoffman
Jacob Hoffmann, Elisabetha/Johannes b Nov 17 1754/Johann Gebel, Mar. Marg. Bader
Peter Schaeffer, Anna/Joh. Jacob b Jul 25 1754/---
Jacob Delater, Elisabetha/David b Apr 15 1754/David Delater, Barbara
Jacob Clemens, Margretha/Johann Valentin b Jan 7 1754/Valentin Schwartz, Anna Elisabeth Lay
Michael Deubelbiss, Maria Catharina/Anna Maria b Oct 8 1753 bapt Jan 18 1754/Christian Muller, Anna Maria
Peter Kreppel, Anna Elisabetha/Eva Elisabetha b Dec 22 1753, bapt Jan 22 1754/Valentin Adam, Eva Margretha
Johann David Albrecht, Catharina/Eva Catharina b Aug 6 1754/Daniel Madis, Eva Cath. Frosch Adam
Georg Peter Gist, Catharina/Jacob b Jul 22 1754/Jacob Henrich, Anna Barbara
Wilhelm Humbert, Barbara/Catharina b Aug 16 1754/Henrich Funck, Catharina Traut
Friedrich Jacob Hoffman, Anna Clara/Anna Maria b Sep 2 1754/Abraham Gibson, Anna Maria
Philip Badmann, Maria Elisabeth/Johannes b Nov 22 1754/Johannes Combeer, Rahel
Johan Georg Bell, Elisabetha/Henrich Thomas b Apr 17 1754/Thomas Sley, Margaretha
Valentin Sommer, Juliana/Juliana b Aug 11 1754/Christian Schreyner, Juliana
Abraham Lingenfelder, Barbara/Georg Valentin b Oct 1 1754/Valentin Adam, Margaretha
Melcher Häffner, Catharina/Johannes b Oct 9 1754/Johannes Brunner, Catharina Brunner
Georg Clemens, Margaretha/Johann Georg b Jul 21 1754/Georg Hutzel, Magdalena
Georg Kurtz, Esther/Michael b Jan 1 1755/Michael Heffner, Juliana

Baptisms of the Evangelical Reformed Church in Frederick, Maryland

Georg Hoffmann, Eva Margaretha/Maria Apollonia b Mar 5 1755/Friedrich Unselt, Maria Apollonia

Gabriel Thomas, Anna Margaretha/Elisabetha b Mar 22 1755/Philip Henry Thomas, Catharina

Mattheus Seyler, Magdalena/Johannes b Mar 18 1755/Johannes Brunner, Anna Maria

Friedrich Häffner, Anna Maria/Johann Michael b Apr 15 1755/Johann Michael Häffner, Juliana

Johann Thomas, Catharina/Anna Maria b Mar 7 1755/Anna Maria Götzedanner

Balthasar Kern, Magdalena/child b May 11 1755/---

Edward Beatty, Susanna/Edward b ---1775/The Mother

Martin Schaub, Maria Sophia/Johan Georg b Feb 12 1755/Conrad Kämpff, Maria

Jacob Zimmet, Susanna/Eva Margaretha b Mar 29 1755/Valentin Adam, Eva Margaretha

Georg Mehn, Elisabetha/Johann Friedrich b Aug 9 1754/Friedr. Haeffner

Valentin Adam, Eva Margaret/Georg Valentin b -- 1755/Georg Lingefelder, Eva Magdalena

Daniel Weiss, Margaretha/Valentin b Apr 18 1754/Valentin Weiss, Barbara Keiser

Nicolaus Rab, Margaretha/Christian b May 14 1755/Christian Müller, Anna Maria

(This is the last baptism entered by Franckenfeldt.)

George Ber, Magdalena/Susanna b Sep 1 1754/Theodor Frankenfeld, Susanna

Georg Ber, Magdalena/Johannes b Mar 26 1756/Johann Brunner, Anna Maria

(As the death of Frankenfeld is reported in the minutes of June 1756 (p. 145), the next baptism of October 1756 could not have been performed by him.)

Johannes Schonefeld, Catharina/Maria Margaretha b Sep 25 1756, bapt Oct 3 1756/Georg Schley, Maria Margaretha

Baptisms by the Rev. John Conrad Steiner, 1756-1759

Conrad Schneider, Maria Susanna/Georg Jacob bapt Oct 24 1756/George Jacob Trautwein, Elisabeth

Andreas Eberhard, Barbara/Maria Magdalena bapt Oct 27 1756/Hieronimus Hildebrand, Margaretha

Hieronimus Hildebrand, Margaretha/Anna Maria Barbara bapt Oct 27 1756/ Andreas Eberhard, Barbara

Johannes Jons, Catharina/Johann Peter bapt Oct 31 1756/David Jons, Dianna Louis

Bernhard Wirtenbecher, Catharina/Anna Christina bapt Nov 7 1756/Nicolaus König, Anna Christina

Jacob Holtz, Catharina/Eleonora bapt Nov 7 1756/Nicolaus Bucher, Eleonora

Martin Schaub, Maria Sophia/Maria Catharina bapt Nov 15 1756, b Sep 13 1756/ Jacob Ambrosi, Maria Catharina

Johann Conrad Steiner, Ursula/Anna Steiner, adult, bapt Nov 12 1756/bapt in manse, then confirmed and admitted to the H. Communion.

Jacob Baum, Margaretha/Jacob Friedrich bapt Nov 21 1756/Friedrich Häfner, Anna Maria

Georg Oster, Anna Barbara/Jacob bapt Nov 21 1756/Jacob Brunner, Catharina Brunner

Peter Brunner, Anna Maria/Elias bapt Nov 21 1756/Elias Brunner, Albertina

Baptisms of the Evangelical Reformed Church in Frederick, Maryland

Adam Reimensperger, Catharina/Stephan bapt Nov 28 1756, aged 14 wks./Stephan Reimensperger, Catharina
Johannes Compere, Rahel/Johannes b Dec 4 1756, bapt Dec 19 1756/Johannes Summer, Dorothea
Abraham Borrer, Anna Maria/Anna Maria bapt Jan 1 1757/Heinrich Schober, Anna
Valentin Sumer, Juliana/Valentin bapt Jan 2 1757/Valentin Scheidegger, Maria Elisabeth
Ludwig Herbach, Christina/Maria Elisabetha bapt Jan 2 1757/Johannes Scheidegger, Elisabeth Keller
Friedr. Jacob Holzman, Clara/Johann Friedrich bapt Jan 30 1757/Heinrich Schober, Anna
Peter Manz, Rosina/Anna Maria bapt Feb 15 1757/Heinrich Schober, Anna
---/Eva Margaretha bapt Feb 20 1757/Rudolph Rohr, Eva Margaretha
Johannes Widmer, Maria Elisabetha/Elias bapt Feb 20 1757/Elias Brunner, Albertina
Johannes Weimar & wf./Johannes bapt Mar 1 1757/Johannes Scheidegger, Anna Maria Weimar
Hans Georg Schaub, Anna Maria/Hans Georg bapt Mar 3 1757/Parents
Johannes Tourne, Barbara/Magdalena bapt Mar 13 1757/Leonhart Hofman, Magdalena
Hans Georg Kroneiss, Anna Maria/Stephan bapt Mar 13 1757/Stephan Reimesperger, Catharina
Johannes Thomas, Catharina/Catharina bapt Mar 13 1757/Philip Heinrich Thomas, Catharina
Hans Georg Feyer, Maria Juliana/Maria Juliana bapt Mar 27 1757/Michael Häffner, Juliana
Valentin Meyerer, Martha/Adam b 3 mos. old, when bapt Mar 29 1757/Michael Meyerer, Sarah
Peter Meyerer, Sarah/Maria b 5 mos. old, when bapt Mar 29 1757/Joh. Josua Meyerer, Maria
Peter Crebel, Anna Elisabeth/Jacob bapt Apr 1 1757/Jacob Krämer, Catharina
Peter Berg, Anna Catharina/Margaretha bapt Apr 1 1757/Margaretha Schmid
Johan Tillberg, Juliana/Heinrich bapt Apr 1 1757/Heinrich Glänz, Catharina Kramer
Jacob Wüst, Eva/Maria Barbara bapt Apr 1 1757/Simon Schober, Maria Barbara
Matthias Gassert, Anna Catharina/Johannes bapt Apr 1 1757/Johannes Hofmann, Barbara
Casper Debelbis, Anna/Barbara bapt Apr 1 1757/Johannes Hofmann, Barbara
Friedrich Kämpf, Regina/David bapt Apr 3 1757/Gilpert Kämpf, Margaretha
Gilpert Kämpf, Regina/Johan Heinrich bapt Apr 3 1757/Friedrich Kämpf, Regina
Jacob Seiler, Esther/Georg Jacob bapt Apr 5 1757/Georg Jacob Schley, Maria Lisa Bruner
Valentin Thomas, Margaretha/Valentin bapt Apr 8 1757/Valentin Weiss, Catharina Fortne
Matthias Buquet, Anna Maria/Johannes bapt Apr 10 1757/Johannes Sturm, Anna Barbara
Michael Brunner & wf./Johann Jacob bapt Apr 11 1757/Hans Jacob Brunner, Marianna Schley
Johannes Weigel, Christina/Maria Margaretha bapt Apr 14 1757/Valentin Scheidegger, Maria Elisabetha
Abraham Lingefelder, Barbara/Eva Catharina bapt Apr 17 1757/Casper Keller, Catharina Froschauer

Baptisms of the Evangelical Reformed Church in Frederick, Maryland

Samuel Berg, Maria/Johan Jacob bapt Apr 17 1757/Joh. Jacob Froschauer, Susanna Keller
Casper Meyer, Barbara/Sibylla bapt Apr 24 1757/Thomas Schley, Sibylla Stublin
Peter Neffe, Margaretha/Lorentz bapt May 3 1757/Lorentz Schnepf, Margaretha
Jacob Kebli, Elsbeth Catharina/Valentin bapt May 3 1757/Valentin Schweizer
Heinrich Siegrist, Maria Clara/Maria Margaretha bapt May 3 1757/Lorentz Neffe, Anna Maria
Lorenz Steffan, Anna Maria/Lorenz bapt May 3 1757/Peter Spiess, Anna Magdalena
Peter Spiri, Catharina Elisabeth/Peter bapt May 3 1757/Georg Schad, Catharina
George Schad, Catharina/Georg bapt May 3 1757/Peter Spiri, Catharina Elisabeth
Adam Bley, Catharina Margaretha/Johannes bapt May 8 1757/Johannes Hofmann, Catharina Barbara
Johannes Till Hen, Anna Maria/Johannes bapt May 15 1757/Johannes Näf, Maria Veronica Dick
Jacob Meyer, Susanna/Johannes Heinrich bapt May 19 1757/Johan Christ Schmit, Margaretha
Valentin Schreiner, Elisabeth/Eva Margaretha bapt May 22 1757/Valentin Adam, Eva Margaretha
Adam Schmid, Anna Veronica/Anna Catharina bapt May 24 1757/Valentin Krieger, Anna Catharina Berg
James Reis, Maria/Anna Catharina bapt May 24 1757/Jacob Krämer, Anna Maria Weber
Matthias Seiler, Magdalena/Magdalena bapt May --1757/Anna Maria Brunner
Adam Ebert, Margaretha/Elisabeth & Maria bapt May 24 1757/Elisabeth Rapp, Maria Schober
Andreas Meixel, Catharina/Jacob bapt Jun 5 1757/Georg Fux, Catharina Schneider
Nicolaus Beck, Ottilia/Johan Michael bapt Jun 26 1757/Johan Michael Häfner, Juliana
Peter Jauzen, Anna Eleonora/Anna Margaretha bapt Jun 26 1757/Johannes Schmid, Anna Margaretha
Hans Georg Baumann, Anna Maria/Isaac bapt Jun 19 1757/Lorentz Neffe, Anna Maria
Heinrich Demuth, Anna/Susanna Magdalena bapt Jun 20 1757/Lorentz Neffe & wf.
Jacob Christman, Magdalena/Sarah bapt Jun 20 1757/Hans Georg Baumann
Wilhelm Kutz, Anna Maria/Eva Catharina bapt Jul 10 1757/Johannes Froschauer, Eva Catharina
Michael Rapp, Maria Apollonia/Hans Jacob bapt July 10 1757/Andreas Boltz, Anna Maria
Christian Berg, Anna Gertrud/Eva Christina bapt Jul 17 1757/Heinrich Ziegler, Eva Christina Schmid
Michael Häfner & wf./Child bapt Aug 11 1757/Abraham Borrer
Jacob Keller, Barbara/Caspar bapt Aug 14 1757/Caspar Keller, Elisabeth Keller
Jacob Schnaurigel & wf./Peter bapt Sep 4 1757/Peter Kampf & wf.
Johannes Lingenfelder, Anna/Elisabetha bapt Sep 11 1757/--, Elisabeth Keller
Heinrich Schnauch, Elisabeth/Jacob bapt Sep 11 1757/Jacob Keller, Anna Gertrud Berg

Baptisms of the Evangelical Reformed Church in Frederick, Maryland

Georg Adam Mahler, Maria Eva/Maria Elisabetha bapt Sep 13 1757/Wilhelm Strup, Maria Elisabetha
Johannes Steiner, Catharina/Johannes bapt Sep 17 1757/Johannes Brunner & wf.
Jehn Ogle, Ruth/Sarah bapt Sep 21 1757/Joh. Jost Eigenbrodt, Maria Eva
Matthias Zacharias, Elisabeth/Matthias bapt Sep 21 1757/Matthias Ambrosi, Catharina
Philip Heinrich Thomas, Catharina/Johan Heinrich bapt Sep 25 1757/Gabriel Thomas, Margaret
Gabriel Thomas, Margaret/Johannes bapt Sep 25 1757/Valentin Thomas, Margaret
Heinrich Vollenweider, Barbara/Margaret bapt Sep 25 1757/Gilbert Kämpf, Margaret
Leonhardt Eberli, Eva Maria/Maria Elisabeth bapt Oct 9 1757/Georg Leonhart Beckenbach & Anna Maria
Heinrich Schober, Anna/Stephan bapt Nov 13 1757/Stephan Reimespreyer & wf.
Rudolph Rohr, Eva Margaretha/Heinrich bapt Dec 4 1757/Heinrich Schober, Anna
Joh. Adam Keil, Elisabeth/Johannes bapt Dec 4 1757/Johannes Sturm, Anna Barbel
Hans Georg Kurz, Esther/Maria Catharina bapt Dec 4 1757/Michael Häfner, Maria Juliana
Peter Engels, Maria Catharina/Child bapt Dec 1757/---
Heinrich Dentlinger & wf./Maria Susanna bapt Dec 29 1757/bapt on wedding day, when mar. to Joh. Scherer
--- Foland & wf. /Maria Magdalena bapt Dec 29 1757/---
Wilhelm Gutmann & wf./Anna Barbara bapt Dec 23 1757/David Delater, Anna Barbara
Johannes Sturm, Anna Barbara/Johannes bapt Dec 23 1757/Felix Suter, Apollonia Hofmann
Valentin Schwartz, Susanna/Johan Valentin bapt Jan 22 1758/Valentin Schreiner, Elisabeth
Nicolaus Raap, Margreth/Barbara bapt Jan 30 1758/Joh. Georg Jos, Barbara
Christian Müller, Anna Maria/Anna Barbara bapt Jan 30 1758/Valentin Uzelman, Barbara
Christoph Belzer, Maria Elisabeth/Clara Elisabetha bapt Feb 5 1758/Joh. Adam Maulbach, Clara Elis. Huber
Geo. Lienhart Beckenbach, Maria/Anna Maria bapt Feb 17 1758/Michael Häberly, Catharina
Jacob Zinnet, Susanna Margaret/Susanna Margaretha bapt Feb 17 1758/Heinrich Alexander, Margareth
Jacob Schmid, Elisabeth/Elisabeth bapt Feb 17 1758/Johannes Weber, Elisabeth
Andreas Gernhard, Anna Barbara/Hans Adam bapt Feb 17 1758/Hans Adam Eberli, Catharina
Johannes Stoll, Catharina/Susanna bapt Feb 19 1758/Benedict Holtz, Susanna
Georg Hinckel, Anna Maria/Maria Margaret bapt Mar 26 1758/Thomas Schley, Maria Margaret
Daniel Weiss, Margaretha/Johan Peter bapt Mar 2 1758/Peter Weiss, Anna Maria
Friedrich Häfner, Anna Maria/Apollonia bapt Mar 13 1758/Apollonia Leiny
Conrad Jung & wf./Hans Jacob bapt Mar 17 1758/Jacob Zinnet & wf.
Jacob Keller, mo. died after childbirth/Barbara bapt Mar 21 1758/Wendel Sturm, Barbara Grimm
Jacob Keller & wf./Elisabeth, twin bapt Mar 21 1758/Christoph Eberhart, Barbara

Christoph Eberhard, Barbara/Susanna bapt Mar 21 1758/Johannes Eberli, Catharina
George Weil, Elisabeth/Marianna bapt Mar 21 1758/Jacob Schmid, Elisabeth
David Stadelmeyer, Anna Magdalena/Anna Maria bapt Mar 26 1758/Heinrich Schober, Anna
Adam Wolff, Maria Clara/Johan Peter bapt Mar 26 1758/Joh. Peter Tofler, Anna Maria
Ludwig Herbach, Christina/Anna Maria bapt Mar 27 1758/Maria Elisabetha Williard
Caspar Beckenbach, Susanna/Anna Barbara bapt Mar 27 1758/Geo. Adam Beckenbach, Barbara
Jacob Stäheli, Elisabeth/Catharina bapt Mar 27 1758/Stofel Michel, Catharina
Nicolaus Fass, Catharina/Johan Jacob bapt Mar 27 1758/Jacob Türner, Barbara
Peter Beckenbach, Barbara/Maria Elisabeth bapt Mar 27 1758/Geo. Peter Beckenbach, Maria Elis. Buchner
Conrad Dick, Anna Catharina/Maria Catharina bapt Mar 28 1758/Johannes Widmer, Maria Elisabeth
Nicolaus Bucher & wf./Johan Jacob bapt Apr 2 1758/Jacob Holz & wf.
Philip Grönewald, Catharina/Margaretha bapt Mar 30 1758/Parents
Georg Wilhelm Stein, Maria Barbara/Maria Magdalena bapt Mar 30 1758/Nicolaus Leinberger, Maria Catharina
Jacob Sell, Elisabeth/Elisabeth bapt Mar 31 1758/Georg Eberli, Ottilia Humel
Philip Busch in Win. & wf./Matthias bapt Apr 9 1758/Parents
Georg Bär, Magdalena/Heinrich bapt Apr 16 1758/Heinrich Schober, Anna
Sebastian Dürr, Elisabeth/Rosina bapt Apr 16 1758/Peter Schäffer, Rosina
Adam Kiefer, Maria Elisabeth/Maria Elisabeth bapt Apr 14 1758/Wilhelm Strup, Maria Elisabeth
Georg Karcher, Elisabeth/Mattheus bapt Apr 14 1758/Mattheus Besel, Catharina Schmid
Hieronimus Hildebrand, Margaret/Andreas bapt Apr 30 1758/Andreas Eberhard, Maria Barbara
Hans Adam Eberli, Anna Catharina/Anna Barbara bapt May 4 1758/Andreas Gernant, Anna Barbara
Bernhart Würtenbecher, Eva Maria/Hans Adam bapt May 4 1758/Hans Adam Würtenbecher, Anna Maria Stempel
Carl Medard, Catharina/Maria Elisabeth bapt May 4 1758/Friedrich Graff, Elisabeth
Friedrich Kämpf, Regina/Anna Maria bapt May 7 1758/Conrad Kämpf, Anna Maria
Johannes Brunner, Christina/Maria Catharina bapt May 7 1758/Maria Catharina Bruner
Valentin Gert, Anna Maria/Maria Eva bapt May 15 1758/Nicolaus Beck, Ottilia
Jacob Delater, Elisabeth/Heinrich bapt May 16 1758/Heinrich Schober, Anna
Jacob Beck, Elisabeth/Joseph bapt May 10 1758/Georg Michel Brunner, Anna Barbara
Caspar Bonner, Anna Maria/Susanna Barbel bapt May 10 1758/Georg Heinr. Bechtold, Susanna Barbara
Daniel Schäubli, Anna Barbel/Anna Barbel bapt May 10 1758/Peter Ney, Anna Margaret
Moritz Müllhaus, dec. Canegetschick/Dorothea Müllhaus 16 yrs old, when bapt May 28 1758/Abraham Degard & mo. Maria Marg.
Melchior Leutert & wf./Anna Maria bapt May 28 1758/Georg Thomas Schley, Anna Maria

Johannes Eberli, Catharina/Catharina bapt May 28 1758/Christoph Rothermel, Juliana
Christoff Dietenhofer, Catharina/Julianna bapt May 28 1758/Jacob Wissman, Julianna
Heinrich Brunner, Barbara/Valentin bapt Jun 11 1758/Valentin Schwarz & wf.
Christian Ostertag, Juliana/Philippina Christina bapt Jun 12 1758/Andreas Berger, Philippina
Georg Michel Bruner, Barbara/Georg Peter bapt Jun 13 1758/Georg Peter Beckenbach & mo. Maria
Abraham Borrer & wf./Eva Margaret bapt Jun 18 1758/Rudolf Rohr, Eva Margaret
Paul Leschhorn, Dorothea/Catharina bapt Jun 18 1758/Peter Kämpf, Catharina
Balthasar Bach, Rosina/Michael bapt Jun 20 1758/Michael Stump & wf.
Johannes Männ & wf./Child bapt Jun 25 1758/Matheus Seiler & wf.
Joh. Georg Leu., Elisabetha/Charlotta Amalia bapt Jun 26 1758/Michael Römer, Charlotta Amalia
William Betty, Mar. Dorothy/Wilhelm bapt Jun 29 1758/Jacob Jung & wf.
Christian Brengel, Anna Barbara/Christina bapt July 2 1758/Valentin Uselman, Christina Dill
Johannes Schmid, Margaret/Johannes bapt Jul 2 1758/Johannes Doderer, Rosina Schmid
Peter Brech, Elisabetha/Eva Margaretha bapt Jul 30 1758/Rudolf Rohr, Eva Margaretha
Abraham Gips, Maria/Eva Margaret bapt Jul 30 1758/Valentin Uselman, Barbara
Johannes Lutz & wf./Juliana bapt Jul 30 1758/Jacob Keller, Juliana Berg
Peter Tofler, Maria/Stephan bapt Aug 6 1758/Stephan Reimesperger, Barbara
George Schmid, Maria Elisabeth/Maria Elisabeth bapt Aug 9 1758/Hans Adam Kiefer, Maria Elisabeth
Martin Schaub, Sophia/Johan Peter bapt Aug 20 1758/Peter Kämpf, Catharina
Georg Hofman, Rosina/Johannes bapt Aug 20 1758/Johannes Hofman & wf.
Johannes Hofman's/Negro child Maria Magdalena bapt Aug 20 1758/---
Baltasar Kron & wf./Valentin bapt Aug 20 1758/Valentin Uselman, Barbara
Johannes Sommer, Maria Dorothea/Louise bapt Aug 27 1758/Clara Huber
Jacob Hofman, Elisabeth/Elisabeth bapt Aug 27 1758/Johannes Weber, Elisabeth
Jacob Huber, Catharina/Valentin bapt Aug 27 1758//Valentin Schreiner, Anna Elisabeth
Rudolff Keller, Juliana/Jacob bapt Aug 27 1758/Jacob Eberhard, Elisabeth Keller
Johannes Mittelkauf, Maria Elisabeth/Johannes bapt Oct 8 1758/Johannes Brunner, Christina
Peter Brunner & wf./Susanna bapt Oct 8 1758/Susanna Kuenz
Hans Georg Kroneisen & wf./Heinrich bapt Dec 17 1758/Heinrich Brunner, Magdalena
Johannes Berg, Juliana/Friedrich bapt Dec 21 1758/Friedrich Rill, Eva Maria
same parents/Anna Margareth bapt Dec 21 1758/Jacob Keller, Anna Marg. Jungblut
Hans Georg Reimesperger, Maria Elisabeth/Anna Maria bapt Dec 24 1758/Anna Maria Brunner
Johannes Weber, Elisabeth/Johannes bapt Jan 1 1759/Johannes Lingefelder, Anna
Valentin Schreiner, Anna Elisabeth/Susanna bapt Jan 7 1759/Valentin Schwarz, Susanna

Baptisms of the Evangelical Reformed Church in Frederick, Maryland

Georg Michel Haller, Philippina/Marg. Philippina bapt Jan 14 1759/Margaretha Meyer, Peter Sin(n)

Jacob Steiner, Mariann/Margaretha bapt Feb 19 1759/Joh. Conrad Steiner, Margaretha Schley

Georg Tofler, Catharina/Maria Dorothea bapt Apr 8 1759/Martin Widerich, Maria Dorothea

Jacob Giezendanner, Catharina/Georg bapt Apr 13 1759/Georg Kast, Apollonia Lein

Peter Jauzer, Anna Eleonora/Hans Jacob bapt Apr 13 1759/Jacob Giezendanner, Catharina

Ulrich Mistler, Eleonora/Johannes bapt Apr 15 1759/Parents

Matthias Becki, Anna Maria/Matthias bapt Apr 15 1759/Ulrich Mistler, Eleonora

Johannes Leder, Anna Maria/Margareth bapt Apr 15 1759/Hieronimus Hildebrand, Margaret

Andreas Eberhard, Barbara/Andreas bapt Apr 15 1759/Hieronimus Hildebrand, Margaret

Valentin Sommer, Julianna/Catharina Barbara bapt Apr 15 1750/Adam Noll, Barbara

Georg Schaf, Anna Maria/Catharina bapt Apr 15 1759/Heinrich Funck, Catharina

Abraham Lingefelder, Barbara/Georg Adam bapt Apr 15 1759/Valentin Adam, Eva Margaret

Christian Focht, Anna/Wilhelm bapt Apr 16 1759/Wilhelm Krum, Anna Martha

Johan Till Berg, Juliana/Friedrich bapt Apr 16 1759/Friedrich Glabach, Gertrud Berg

Wilhelm Schmid, Agnes/Philip bapt Apr 16 1759/Philip Schmid, Gertrud Berg

Peter Kämpf, Catharine/Catharina bapt Apr 29 1759/Catharina Scheffer

Christoffel Thomas, Susanna Margaret/Catharina bapt Apr 29 1759/Catharina Thomas

Johannes Thomas, Catharina/Johannes bapt Apr 29 1759/Christian Giezentanner, Anna Barbara

Nicolaus Back, Ottilia/Maria Apollonia bapt Apr 29 1759/Apollonia Leu

Adam Reimesperger, Catharina/Johannes bapt Apr 29 1759/Johannes Steiner, Catharina

(This is the last baptism by Steiner. The next baptism was entered by Philip Otterbein.)

Gabriel Thomas, Margaretha/Georg b Sep 22 1759/Georg Reimschperger & wf.

(The baptisms from Sept. 9, 1759 to Oct 2, 1760 are entered in a fine script, most likely that of Thomas Schley. It is the same script that opened the record.)

Gilbert Kämpf, Margaretha/Joh. Heinrich bapt Sep 9 1759/Friedrich Kämpf, Regina

Heinrich Schober, Anna/Johannes bapt Sep 9 1759/Johannes Remesperger, Maria Brunner

Wilhelm Berg, Eva Maria/Georg bapt Sep 9 1759/Juliana Berg, Georg Kramer

Johannes Gomper, Rahel/Jacob bapt Sep 9 1759/Jacob Huber, Catharina

Daniel Adams, Honor./Daniel bapt Sep 9 1759/Michael Jeserong, Susanna Risner

Johannes Lingenfelder, Anna/Elisabeth bapt Sep 9 1759/Johannes Weber, Elisabetha

Christian Schott, Maria/Johan Jacob bapt Sep 9 1759/Joh. Michael Kobb, Christina Kern

Baptisms of the Evangelical Reformed Church in Frederick, Maryland

Philip Jacob Lehmann, Barbara/Clara bapt Oct 21 1759/Friedrich Holtzmann, Clara
Melchior Haffner, Catharina/Maria Margaretha bapt Oct 21 1759/Heinrich Balzel, Maria Magaretha Schley
Elias Brunner, Albertina/Johannes bapt Oct 21 1759/Johannes Brunner, Maria Brunner
Johannes Bunckely, Catharina/Joh. Friedrich, Anna Maria bapt Jun 8 1760/ Catharina Honig
Friedrich Backer, Dorothea/Rosina bapt Jun 8 1760/Samuel Backer, Rosina
Friedr. Haffner, Anna Maria/Louisa b Apr 10 bapt, Jun 8 1760/Andreas Paulus, Louisa Paulus
Jacob Huber, Catharina/Johan Michael bapt Jun 8 1760/Michael Romer, Charlotta
Jacob Krebs, Margaretha/Georg Peter bapt Jun 8 1760/Georg Peter Dick & wf.
Georg Thomas Schley, Anna Maria/Maria Margaretha bapt Jun 8 1760/Johan Thomas Schley, Maria Margaretha
Bernhard Knar, Catharina/Georg Jacob bapt Jun 22 1760/Georg Hoffman, Rosina
same parents/Christina bapt Jun 22 1760/Christian Muller, Anna Maria
Georg Bar, Magdalena/Wilhelm bapt Jun 22 1760/William Kimbel, Cath. Margaretha Grosshusch
Bartholomeus Schumacher, Barbara/Johan Peter bapt Jun 22 1760/Peter Baltzel, Maria Barbara Schley
Peter Coblentz, Susanna/Son b Jul 11 1760, bapt Oct 2 1760/Herman Coblentz, Elisabetha

Baptisms by the Rev. Philip William Otterbein, 1760-1765

Peter Schiffer, Rosina/Bastian b Sep 29 1760 bapt Nov 23 1760/Bastian Dorr & wf.
Matthaeus Backer, Anna Maria/Rosina b Sep 27 1760 bapt Nov 23 1760/Samuel Becker & wf.
Michael Trissler, Margaretha/Elisabeth b Oct 11 1760, bapt Nov 23 1760/Valentin Schreiner & wf.
Valentin Andreas, Margaretha/Johannes b Aug 26 1760, bapt Nov 23 1760/Joh. Lingefelder & wf.
Rudolf Keller, Juliana/Anna b Oct 8 1760/bapt Dec 7 1760/Joh. Lingefelder & wf.
Joh. Friedrich Riehl, Clara Elisabetha/Joh. Friedrich b Nov 20 1760, bapt Dec 7 1760/Joh. Werner Schmit, Eva Elisabeth Fleck
Joh. Pley, Elisabetha/Margaretha b Nov 18 1760, bapt Dec 24 1760/Michael Herman & wf.
Friedrich Mechtel, Anna Maria/Catharina b Nov 1 1760, bapt Dec 24 1760/ Theobald Mertz & wf.
Jacob Steiner, Marianna/Marianna b Dec 20 1760, bapt Dec 21 1760/Thomas Schley & wf.
Abraham Gips, Maria/Nicolaus b Nov 28 1760, bapt Dec 28 1760/---
Valentin Schwartz, Susanna/Johannes b Nov 26 1760, bapt Jan 1 1761/Johannes Combeer & wf.
Rudolf Rohr, Eva Margaretha/Johannes b Sep 29 1760, bapt Feb 8 1761/Johannes Lingefelder & wf.
Jacob Dorner, Anna Barbara/Elisabetha b Dec 9 1760, bapt Feb 11 1761/---
Adam Wirtenbecher, Magdalena/Johannes b Oct 26 1760, bapt Feb 15 1761/ Johannes Weber & wf.

Baptisms of the Evangelical Reformed Church in Frederick, Maryland

Thomas Bardel, Barbara/Valentin b Nov 9 1760, bapt Feb 15 1761/Valentin Hüsselman & wf.

Paul Leschhorn, Anna Dorothea/Conrad b Jun 4 1760, bapt Feb 22 1761/Conrad Kemp & wf.

Georg Remschberger, Maria Elisabetha/Johannes b Dec 15 1760, bapt Mar 23 1761/Johannes Brunner & wf.

Peter Klein, Catharina/Sarah b Nov 7 1760/bapt Mar 23 1761/---

Christophel Thomas, Susanna/Margaretha b Oct 31 1760/bapt Mar 20 1761/Wf. of Gabriel Thomas

Benedict Holtz, Susanna/Jacob b Jan 7 1761, bapt Mar 20 1761/Jacob Holtz & wf.

Philip Henrich Thomas, Catharina/Anna Maria b Oct 1 1760, bapt Mar 20 1761/ Johannes Brunner & wf.

Peter Weyer, Anna Elisabeth/2 children b Dec 20 1760, bapt Mar 31 1761/---

Abraham Lingefelder, Barbara/Anna Barbara b Dec 4 1760, bapt Mar 22 1761/ Geo. Bernhard Lingefelder & wf.

Wendel Froschauer, Eva/Philip Jacob b Feb 13 1761/bapt Mar 28 1761/Jacob Krebs & wf.

Andreas Vogel, Susanna/Johan Henrich b Jan 2 1761, bapt Mar 31 1761/Henrich Klein & wf.

Georg Mayer, Anna Maria/Susanna Catharina b Mar 10 1761, bapt Apr 15 1761/ Andreas Vogel & wf.

Friedrich Holtzman, Clara/Son b Jan 27 1761, bapt May 11 1761/---

Adam Wolff, Claudina(?)/Adam b Jan 24 1761, bapt May 11 1761/Gabriel Thomas & wf.

Johannes Riesling, Catharina/Johannes b Apr 4 1761, bapt May 11 1761/ Johannes Hoffman & wf.

Christian Vogt, Anna/Johannes b Dec 6 1760, bapt May 11 1761/Johannes Berg & wf.

Henrich Brunner, Magdalena/Anna Margaretha b Mar 16 1761, bapt May 24 1761/ Valentin Adam & wf.

Henrich Kuntz, Dorothea/Magdalena b Mar 29 1761, bapt May 31 1761/Henrich Fant & wf.

Bastian Dörr, Elisabeth/Elisabetha b Feb 16 1761, bapt May 31 1761/Peter Scheffer & wf.

Peter Brunner, Anna Maria/Maria Elisabeth b Feb 16 1761, bapt May 31 1761/ Barbara Brunner

Georg Jost, Barbara/Juliana b Jul -- 1760, bapt May 31 1761/Wf. of Jacob Lutz

Elias Brunner, Albertina/Johannes b Jun 21 1761, bapt Aug 2 1761/Johannes Brunner & wf.

Michael Alex(ander), Salome/Anna Maria b Oct 23 1760, bapt Jul 26 1761/Anna Maria Schusler

Georg Doveter, Catharina/Rosina b Jun 8 1761, bapt Aug 16 1761/Peter Scheffer & wf.

Antoni Biber, Anna Kunigunda/Friedrich b Jul 5 1761, bapt Aug 16 1761/ Friedrich Heffener & wf.

Valentin Thomas, Margaretha/Philip Henrich b May 7 1761, bapt Aug 16 1761/ Philip Henrich Thomas & wf.

Georg Dörtzenbach, Maria Magdalena/Susanna b Aug 27 1761, bapt Sep 6 1761/ Valentin Schwartz & wf.

Nicolaus Henscheler, Anna Margaretha/Johan Michael b Jul 7 1761, bapt Sep 10 1761/Joh. Michael Kolb & wf.
Joh. Michael Kolb, Catharina/Elisabeth b Aug 28 1761, bapt Sep 6 1761/Geo. Michael Jesseron & wf.
Anna Maria Betchalin/Martin b Aug 23 1761, bapt Sep 20 1761/Martin Wütterich & wf.
Georg Kunz, Esther/Susan b Sep 13 1761, bapt Sep 20 1761/Felix Sauter & wf.
Jacob Sturm, Maria Margaretha/Johan Peter b Sep 11 1761, bapt Oct 18 1761/ Peter Doveler & wf.
Adam Remschberger, Catharina/Catharina b Aug 1 1761, bapt Oct 27 1761/---
Johannes Sommer, Maria Dorthea/Friedrich b Oct 21 1761, bapt Nov 8 1761/ Friedrich Baker & wf.
Henrich Schober, Anna/Anna Maria b Sep 8 1761, bapt Sep 20 1761/Anna Maria Brunner
Thomas Schley, Anna Maria/Anna Maria b Nov 17 1761, bapt Jan 3 1762/ Christian Gotzendanner & wf.
Johannes Lingefelder, Anna Maria/Michael Nov 29 1761, bapt Jan 10 1762/ Michael Romer & wf.
Henrich Alexander, Margaretha/Johannes b Nov 22 1761, bapt Feb 7 1762/ Johannes Eberle, Jacob Frey's wf.
Peter Engel, Maria Catharina/Maria Anna b Dec 30 1761, bapt Feb 7 1762/Jacob Steiner & wf.
Georg Michael Haller, Maria Dorothea/Georg Christoph b Jan 12 1762, bapt Feb 7 1762/Geo. Christoff, Krafft(?) & wf.
Rudolf Rohr, Eva Margaretha/Johan Michael b Feb 15 1762, bapt Feb 21 1762/ Michael Fey & wf.
Johannes Stoll, Catharina/Anna Maria b Jan 25 1762, bapt Feb 28 1762/Adam Schusseler & wf.
Johannes Gomber, Rachel/Peter b Jan 9 1762, bapt Feb 28 1762/Peter Grebell & wf.
Georg Lingefelder, Barbara/Catharina b Nov 29 1761, bapt Mar 14 1762/ Catharina Brunner
Valentiin Schreiner, Elisabeth/Charlotta Amalia b Feb 5 1762, bapt Mar 14 1762/Michael Römer & wf.
Andreas Buschon, Catharina/Son b Dec 17 1761, bapt Apr 25 1762/---
Joh. Peter Engel, Susanna/Samuel b Apr 20 1762, bapt Apr 25 1762/Herman Dullebach, Maria Catharina Engels
Felix Sauter, Susanna/Maria Sophia b May 14 1762, bapt May 20 1762/Peter Scheffer & wf.
Christian Gòtzendanner, Anna/Christian b Aug 18 (1761), bapt May 24 1762/ Christian G8tzendanner & wf.
Johannes Thomas, Catharina/Gabriel b Apr 30 1762, bapt May 30 1762/Gabriel Gotzendanner
Peter Klein, Maria/Peter b Apr 29 1762, bapt Jul 18 1762/Philip Jacob & wf.
Jacob Mayer, Maria Magdalena/Susanna b Jul 1 1762, bapt Jul 18 1762/Mattheus Hirschman & wf.
Jost Maierer & wf./Susanna b Mar 9 1762, bapt Jul 18 1762/---
Jacob Holtz, Catharina/Nicolaus b Jun 11 1762, bapt Aug 1 1762/Nicolaus Rap & wf.
Henrich Heusser, Anna Catharina/Catharina b Jun 14 1762, bapt Aug 1 1762/ Peter Klein & wf.
Conrad Doll, Anna Maria/Anna Maria b Jul 23 1762, bapt Aug 1 1762/---

Jacob Götzendanner, Catharina/Georg Thomas b Aug 6 1762, bapt Sep 19 1762/ Georg Thomas Felty & wf.

Philip Diel, Christina/Anna Margaretha b Sep 7 1762, bapt Oct 3 1762/Jacob Rinzer, Anna Marg. Schmit

Adam Wolff, Catharina/Georg b Aug 23 1762, bapt Oct 17 1762/Georg Doveler & wf.

Peter Kobelenz, Susanna/Johan Adam b May 19 1762, bapt Oct 17 1762/---

Johannes Dorn, Anna Barbara/Anna Maria Oct 29 1762, bapt Nov 12 1762/Anna Maria Weis

Georg Hoffman, Margaretha/Georg b Oct 31 1762, bapt Dec 7 1762/Johannes Hoffman & wf.

Jacob Christ, Catharina/Johan Jacob b Nov 29 1762, bapt Dec 22 1762/Jacob Christ & wf.

Susanna, wid. of Franz Koch/Wilhelm b Nov 13 1762, bapt Dec 24 1762/---

Mattheus Becke, Anna Maria/Johan Georg b Oct 25 1762, bapt Feb 2 1763/Georg Hoffman & wf.

Valentin Wolff, Susanna/Margaretha b Mar 6 1763, bapt Mar 13 1763/Michael Triseler & wf.

Valentin Adam, Margaretha/Magdalena b Jan 14 1763, bapt Feb 13 1763/ Magdalena Adam

Abraham Lingefelder, Anna Barbara/Eva Margaretha b Dec 28 1762, bapt Feb 13 1763/ Georg Lingefelder & wf.

Jacob Steiner, Maria Anna/Jacob b Jan 23 1763, bapt Mar 20 1763/Jacob Sehler & wf.

Henrich Vollweiler, Barbara/Elisabeth b Feb 18 1763, bapt Mar 19 1763/---

Christian Taub, Anna/Johan Georg b Mar 17 1763, bapt May 1 1763/Joh. Georg Fluck & wf.

Georg Remschberger, Maria Elisabetha/Catharina b Dec 21 1762, bapt May 8 1763/Henrich Thomas & wf.

Paul Leschhorn, Anna Dorothea/Johannes b Dec 25 1762, bapt May 22 1763/---

Philip Berger, Christina/Henrich b Feb 15 1763, bapt Apr 2 1763/---

Rudolf Keller, Juliana/Juliana b Mar 14 1763, bapt May 22 1763/Elisabetha Keller

Rudolf Rohr, Eva Gretha/Catharina Elisabetha b Feb 6 1763, bapt May 22 1763/ Joh. Jacob Schell, Maria Elisabeth

John Jacob Schell, Maria Elisabetha/Johan Henrich b Apr -- 1763, bapt May 22 1763/Rudolff Rohre & wf.

Andreas Vogel, Susanna Catharina/Susanna Catharina b Apr 10 1763, bapt May 23 1763/Henrich Hentz & wf.

Gabriel Thomas, Margaretha/Margaretha b Jun 5 1763, bapt Jul 17 1763/ Valentin Thomas & wf.

Bastian Dörr, Elisabetha/Johan Jacob b Dec 20 1762, bapt Jun 29 1763/Jacob Ley

Valentin Kehrt, Anna Maria/Valentin b Jun 3 1763, bapt Aug 21 1763/Valentin Schwartz & wf.

Adam Bens, Catharina/Anna Margaretha b ---, bapt Sep 4 1763/Nicolaus Heuchler & wf.

Wilhelm Kuntz, Anna Maria/Johan Wilhelm b Aug 16 1758, bapt Sep 4 1763/ Johannes Froschauer & wf.

Jacob Eberhard, Elisabeth/Charlotta b Aug 4 1763, bapt Sep 4 1763/Charlotta Keller

Peter De Wit, Sarah/Wilhelm b Mar 17 1763, bapt Jul 27 1763/Wilhelm Krum & wf.
Peter Brunner, Anna Maria/Jacob b Aug 19 1763, bapt Oct 16 1763/Jacob Brunner & wf.
Johannes Adam, Margaretha/Johan Jacob b Oct 4 1762, bapt Nov 9 1763/Johan Jacob Weis
Melchior Heffener, Catharina/Jacob b Nov 1 1763, bapt Nov 4 1763/Jacob Baltzel & wf.
Thomas Schley, Anna Maria/Elisabetha b Nov 14 1763, bapt Jan 1 1764/Jacob Schley & wf.
Ludwig Kämpf & wf./Henrich b Jul 1 1763, bapt Aug 21 1763/---
Jacob Klein, Anna Maria/Maria Margaretha b Jan 27 1764, bapt Feb 9 1764/ Friedrich Haffener & wf.
Adam Eckert, Anna Maria/Peter b Dec 21 1763, bapt Feb 12 1764/Peter Balzel & wf.
Johannes Stoll, Catharina/Jacob b Dec 19 1763, bapt Feb 19 1764/Johannes Täufferly
Peter Engel, Maria Catharina/Susanna b Dec 17 1763, bapt Feb 19 1764/Tobias Reisner & wf.
Bernhard Lingefelder, Barbara/Valentin b Nov 2 1763, bapt Feb 19 1764/ Valentin Lingefelder
Henrich Schober, Anna/Catharina b Dec 6 1763, bapt Mar 8 1764/Elisabeth Wild
Georg Bärr, Magdalena/Georg b Feb 10 1764, bapt Mar 25 1765/Georg Hoffman & wf.
Christopfel Stoll, Philippina/Johan Adam b Oct 10 1763, bapt Mar 25 1764/ Adam Hildebrand & wf.
Franz Jacob, Maria Elisabetha/Juliana b Jan 27 1764, bapt Mar 23 1764/ Juliana Holz
Johan Georg Jans & wf./Eva Catharina b Feb 26 1764, bapt Apr 8 1764/Eva Catharina Hoffman
Georg Hoffman, Margaretha/Valentin b Mar 23 1764, bapt Apr 8 1764/Valentin Adam & wf.
Peter Heny, Margaretha/Peter b Mar 15 1764, bapt Apr 8 1764/Carl Balsel
Felix Sauter, Susanna/Maria Elisabeth b Mar 17 1764, bapt Apr 13 1764/Michel Christ & wf.
Peter Kobelentz, Susanna/Elisabetha b Jan 17 1764, bapt Apr 13 1764/Henrich Scheffer & wf.
Martin Schaub, Maria Sophia/Georg Henrich b Dec 29 1763, bapt Apr 13 1764/ Henrich Scheffer & wf.
Philip Jacob Lehman, Barbara/Jacob b Mar 21 1764, bapt Apr 22 1764/Jacob Froschauer & wf.
Jacob Huber, Christina/Christina b Dec 15 1763, bapt Apr 22 1764/Philip Bleyer & wf.
Adam Remschberger, Catharina/Michael b Dec 15 1763, bapt May 20 1764/---
Philip Jacob, Elisabetha/Maria Catharina b Apr 12 1764, bapt May 27 1764/ Peter Klein & wf.
Daniel Weber, Charlotta/Daniel b Apr 14 1764, bapt May 27 1764/Peter Engel & wf.
Friedrich Jacob Holzman, Anna Clara/Susanna Clara, b Mar 6 1764, bapt May 27 1764/Susanna Morgenstern
Peter Balsel, Catharina/Johannes b Apr 29 1764, bapt Jun 24 1764/Joh. Hoffman & wf.
Johan Werner Schmit, Catharina Margaretha/Joh. Friedrich b Apr 29 1764, bapt Jul 8 1764/Friedrich Riehl & wf.

Jacob Brunner, Barbara/Johan Heinrich b May 1 1764, bapt. Aug 12 1764/ Henrich Schober & wf.

Balsazar Götzendanner, Anna/Maria Catharina b Aug 3 1764, bapt Sep 30 1764/ Catharina Steiner

Adam Gözendanner, Elisabeth/Johannes b Jul 9 1764, bapt Oct 7 1764/---

Peter Doveler, Catharina/Peter b Jul 17 1764, bapt Oct 6 1764/Peter Heny & wf.

Valentin Verdries, Anna Catharina/Johan Henrich b Aug 2 1764, bapt Oct 8 1764/Margaretha Schley, widow

Ulrich Heininger, Susanna/Susanna b Aug 28 1764, bapt Oct 8 1764/---

Henrich Brunner, Magdalena/Jacob b Mar 16 1764, bapt Oct 18 1764/---

Hieronimus Hildebrandt, Margaretha/Eva Margaretha b Nov 4 1764, bapt Nov 18 1764/Leonhard Huber & wf.

Johannes Weber, Elisabetha/Johan Philip b Oct 21 1764, bapt Nov 25 1764/ Philip Bier & wf.

Nicolaus Back, Magdalena/Philip b Sep 1 1764, bapt Dec 9 1764/Philip Färber

Michel Christ, Maria Elisabetha/Anna Barbara b Nov 9 1764, bapt Dec 16 1764/ Anna Barbara Christ

Jacob Schley, Margaretha/Georg b Jan 1 1765, bapt Jan 19 1765/Peter Bier & wf.

Adam Fischer, Margaretha/Adam b Feb 4 1765, bapt Feb 24 1765/Friedrich Arnhold

Christoph Thomas, Susanna/Anna Barbara b Dec 23 1764, bapt Apr 5 1765/Anna Barbara Weis

Valentin Rohre, Margaretha/Anna Maria b Feb 17 1765, bapt Apr 6 1765/Georg Weis & wf.

Wendel Froschauer, Eva/Peter b Dec 7 1764, bapt Apr 6 1765/Jacob Froschauer & wf.

Jacob Froschauer, Anna Maria/Johannes b Feb 21 1761, bapt Apr 6 1765/Wendel Froschauer & wf.

John Jacob Schneider, Anna Gertraut/Johan Peter b Apr 15 1765, bapt Apr 20 1765/Johan Peter Schneider

Georg Remschberger, Maria Elisabeth/Elizabeth b Feb 1 1765, bapt Apr 21 1765/Catharina Thomas

Mattheus Becke, Anna Maria/Maria Apollonia b Jan 1 1765, bapt May 5 1765/ Johan Adam Ox & wf.

Valentin Swarz, Susanna/Susanna b Apr 29 1765, bapt May 8 1765/Susanna Koch

Friedrich Kempf, Regina/David b Oct 25 1764, bapt May 12 1765/---

Johannes Wolff, Anna Margaretha/Anna Margaretha b Apr 6 1765, bapt May 12 1765/---

Jacob Christ, Catharina/Catharina b Jan 22 1765, bapt Feb 24 1765/Georg Zimmerman & wf.

Henrich Kuntz, Dorothea/Henrich b Jan 8 1765, bapt Feb 16 1765/Adam Beckenbach & sister Catharina

Jacob Remschberger, Anna Maria/Catharina b Mar 11 1765, bapt Jun 16 1765/ Catharina Thomas

Ludwig Kämpf & wf./Jacob b Dec 7 1764, bapt Jul 28 1765/---

Christoffel Stoll, Philippina/Catharina b Aug 20 1765, bapt Sep 22 1765/ Henrich Funck & wf.

Philip Berger, Christina/Johannes b Jun 19 1765, bapt Sep 22 1765/---

Johannes Stoll, Catharina/Philippina b Sep 1 1765, bapt Oct 13 1765/ Christoffel Stoll & wf.

(This is the last baptism of Otterbein. The next three baptisms were entered by a good hand, similar to that found before.)

Georg Hoffmann & wf./Georg & Margaretha b Dec 3 1765, bapt Jan 17 1766/Joh. Hoffman, Valentin Adams' wf.

Jacob Huber & wf./Henrich b Mar 19 1766, bapt Apr 13 1766/Henrich Waldter & wf.

Peter Brunner & wf./Son b Jun 5 1766, bapt --/Georg Peter Hoffman

Under the ministry of Carolus Lange, duly called Minister of the Divine Word at Manakess or Frederick town, in the Reformed Church, the following children were baptized (1766-1768):

Georg Oster, Barbara/Maria Elisabeth b Feb 11 1766, bapt Oct 27 1766/ Johannes Brunner, Anna Maria

Christoph Meyer, Anna Margaretha/Maria Catharina b Sep 18 1766, bapt Nov 2 1766/Stephan Römsperger, Maria Catharina

Philip Burger, Barbara/Johannes b Sep 14 1766, bapt Nov 2 1766/Johannes Wendel Froschaurer & Eva

Christoph Thomas, Susanna/Anna Maria b Sep 17 1766, bapt Nov 2 1766/Johan Adam Fischer, Margaretha

Valentin Panz, Susanna/Johann Rudolph b Sep 1 1766, bapt Nov 9 1766/Rudolph Rohr, Eva Margaretha

Valentin Sommer, Juliana/Johannes b Jun 29 1766, bapt Nov 23 1766/Johannes Hummel, Elisabetha Stoll

Georg Beer, Magdalena/Magdalena b Jul 24 1766, bapt Nov 30 1766/Georg Stricker, Catharina

Georg Thomas Schley, Anna Maria/Johannes Henrich b Aug 23 1766, bapt Dec 7 1766/Joh. Jeremias Meyer, Maria Barbara

Philip Caspar, Elisabeth/Christina b Oct 20 1766, bapt Dec 19 1766/Johan Georg Fux, Christina

Heinrich Walther, Rosina/Anna Rosina b Oct 15 1766, bapt Dec 20 1766/ Heinrich Schober, Anna

Georg Schneider, Cath. Margaretha/Magdalena b Oct 20 1766, bapt Dec 28 1766/ Margaretha Zürch, grandmother

Daniel Michel, Maria/Maria Catharina b Nov 28 1766, Jan 1 1767/Georg Peter Schober, Maria

Adam Schäfer, Susanna/Johan Peter b Dec 8 1766, bapt Jan 11 1767/Peter Brunner, Anna Maria

Michael Christ, Maria Elisabetha/Charlotta b Dec 14 1766, bapt Jan 11 1767/ Jacob Römsperger, Charlotta Sturm

David Lebby, Maria Barbara/Johann Jacob b Oct 28 1766, bapt Feb 1 1767/ Johann Jacob Schell, Maria Elisabetha

Jacob Schley, Margaretha/Johannes b Jan 2 1767, bapt Feb 8 1767/Jeremias Meyer, Barbara

Christian Steiner, Luth. Hannah Barbara/Johann Jacob b Jan 19 1767, bapt Feb 12 1767/Johan Jacob Beni, Anna Juliana

Christian Miller, Anna Maria, dec./Maria Margaretha b Feb 11 1767, bapt Feb 13 1767/Eva Barbara Uselman

Johannes Eby, Anna Maria/Johann Rudolf, Oct 25 1765, bapt Feb 23 1765/Rudolf Rohr, Eva Margaretha

Johannes Wittmer, Maria Elisabetha/Johann Michel b Wed before Easter, 1760, bapt Easter 1760 by Rev. Thomas Bacon, recorded Feb 23 1767/Jacob Zinnet, Susanna Margaretha

Baptisms of the Evangelical Reformed Church in Frederick, Maryland

Georg Michael Schneider, Judith/Johan Michael b Jan 19 1767, bapt Mar 3 1767/Johan Michael Wittmayer, Magdalena Schellman

Christian Deubel, Magdalena/Johannes b Dec 30 1766, bapt Mar 15 1767/ Johannes Hoffman, Catharina Barbara

Jacob Walther, Eva Catharina/Catharina Elisabetha b Feb 21 1767, bapt Mar 22 1767/Christoph Domas (Thomas), Susanna Margaretha

Johan Adam Fischer, Margaretha/Anna Maria b Feb 6 1767, bapt Mar 22 1767/Eva Barbara Uselman

Friederich Arnold, Martha/Margaretha b Mar 16 1767, bapt Mar 22 1767/Lorentz Brengel, Margaretha Uselman

same parents/Maria Barbara b Mar 16 1767, bapt Mar 22 1767/Johannes Haas, Maria Barbara

Johann Niclaus Kuentz, Anna Maria/Johann Adam b Dec 11 1766, bapt Mar 25 1767/Johann Adam Kuenz, Magdalena

Johan Adam Kuenz, Magdalena/Johan Nicklaus b Nov 20 1766, bapt Mar 25 1767/ Johan Nicklaus Kuenz, Anna Maria

Peter Wagner, Catharina/Eva Catharina b Feb 28 1767, bapt Apr 12 1767/ Heinrich Wöller, Eva Catharina Weymer

---/Jonas Dyppois, adult, bapt Apr 14 1767/in presence of Mr. Hofman, deacon

Jacob Crist, Catharina/Maria Barbara b Feb 24 1767, bapt Apr 5 by Rev. Swerdfeger, Luth. pastor/Heinrich Gernhard (?) & da. Maria Barbara

Valentin Doman(s), Margaretha/Elisabeth Barbara b Mar 11 1767, bapt Apr 17 1767/Anna Barbara Domas

Philip Heinrich Doman, Catharina/Catharina b Nov 19 1766, bapt Apr 17 1767/ Catharina Domas

Jacob Brunner, Barbara/Maria Louisa b Feb 5 1767, bapt Apr 19 1767/Dr. Friedrich Schollas, Maria Louisa

Michael Hellmedal, Catharina/Johann Jacob b Feb 19 1767, bapt Apr 19 1767/ Johann Jacob Crist, Catharina

Johannes Adam, Margaretha/Johannes b Nov 6 1765, bapt Apr 20 1767/Johann Georg Lingenfelder & Eva Magdal.

same parents/Thomas b Jun 14 1766, bapt Apr 20 1767/Valentin Adam, Eva Margaretha

Philip Crist, Dorothea/Johannes b Mar 9 1767, bapt Apr 26 1767/Johannes Krieger, Barbara Crist

Gottlieb Laver, Charlotta/Michael b Oct 6 1766, bapt Apr 26 1767/Michael Laver, Maria

Friedrich Draxel, Apollonia/Michael b Apr 1 1767, bapt Apr 20 1767, at the Glade/Jacob Herrman, Margaretha Draxel

Valentin Verdries, Anna Catharina/Johann Friedrich b Feb 14 1767, bapt May 12 1767/Dorothea Verdries

Georg Cast, Catharina/Maria Catharina b Jan 6 1767, bapt May 17 1767/Franz Cast, Maria Catharina Williar

Jacob Neuhardt, Susanna Catharina/Catharina b Apr 21 1767/bapt May 31 1767/ Peter Bouquet, Maria Barbara Brengel

Jacob Dellarter, Elisabeth/Anna Maria b Nov 11 1766, bapt Jun 6 1767/ Johannes Brunner, elder, Anna Maria

Michael Hartmann, Susanna/Anna Margaretha b Mar 22 1767, bapt Jun 7 1767/ Gabriel Doman, Anna Margaretha

Jacob Doll, Margaretha/Johannes b Feb 4 1767, bapt Jun 7 1767/Conrad Doll, Anna Maria

Baptisms of the Evangelical Reformed Church in Frederick, Maryland

Bernard Würtenbecher, Eva/Johann Georg b Apr 20 1767, bapt Jun 7 1767, Georg Hofman, elder, Margaretha
Peter Klein, Maria Gertraud/Johan Adam Feb 10 1767, bapt Jun 15 1767/Johann Adam Riss
Wilhelm Miller, Maria Eva/Georg Conrad b May 30 1767, bapt Jul 21 1767/Georg Conrad Rott, Eva Christina
Rudolf Rohr, Eva Margaretha/Anna Margaretha b May 22 1767, bapt Jun 28 1767/ Anna Marg. Schober
Sebastian Deer, Catharina/Maria Susanna b Jun 28 1767, bapt Aug 9 1767/Jacob Brengel, Gertraud
Johann Engels, Anna Barbara/Peter b Jun 6 1767, bapt Aug 9 1767/Peter Engel, Maria Catharina
Weipert Tschudi, Elisabetha/Anna Margaretha b Jul 21 1767, bapt Aug 23 1767/ Anna Margaretha Kuentz
Carl Scot, Elisabetha/Maria Apollonia b Sep 27 1767, bapt Oct 2 1767/Adam Ox, Maria Apollonia
Friedrich Becker, Dorothea/Anna Catharina b Sep 21 1767, bapt Oct 18 1767/ Johann Adam Schober, Catharina Deubelbiss
The following number of children were baptized at various times in different congregations: In Canagetschigg: 8. At Peter Schmidt's: 11.
At the Pipe-creek in the new little church: 7, of which are 4 children of a father named: Mr. Pfister.
At the schoolhouse across the 1st hill: 14; in Scherbsburg: 7.
At the Glade, 29; at William Allbach's 9; of whom 8 were children of Mr. Allbach himself. At the Potomac 13; in Baltimore: 1.
In Taneytown: 2; On two journeys to Virginia, 63, among whom was a woman; a total of 220.

Lucas Fleck, Barbara/Anna Margaretha b Sep 30 1767, bapt Dec 20 1767/Anna Margaretha Uselman
Nicolaus Bucher's relict wid. Eleonora/Margaretha b Oct 8 1767, bapt Jan 3 1768/Valentin Reeb, schoolm., Clara
Christoph Stoll, Philippina/Elisabetha b Oct 27 1767, bapt Jan 10 1768/ Elisabetha Stoll
Peter Haugg, Margaretha/Margaretha b Jan 1 1768, bapt Jan 24 1768/Philip Schappert, Margaretha
Georg Zimmermann, Catharina/Johann Heinrich b Oct 17 1767, bapt Feb 13 1768/ Johann Heinrich Schober, Anna
Adam Wolf, Maria Clara/Ludwig b Oct 24 1767, bapt Mar 6 1768/Lucas Fleck, Barbara
Jacob Winterroth, Barbara/Johann Heinrich b Dec 22 1767, bapt Mar 27 1768/ Johan Heinrich Schober, Anna
Wilhelm Dickenschiet, Catharina/Johan Conrad b Oct 19 1766, bapt Mar 27 1768/Johan Conrad Grosch, Sophia
Michael Domm, Catharina/Anna Margaretha b Jan 4 1768, bapt Mar 31 1768/Maria Magdalena Dietz
Johannes Allbach, Maria Catharina/seven children bapt Apr 1 1768/---
Jacob Schüssler, Anna Maria/Johan Adam b Dec 10 1767, bapt Apr 3 1768/---
Conrad Doll, Anna Maria/Anna Margaretha b Oct 16 1767, bapt Apr 3 1768/Anna Margaretha Schussler
Peter Balzel, Catharina/Maria Elisabetha b Sep 24 1767, bapt Apr 3 1768/ Peter Schäfer, Elisabetha Balzel

Baptisms of the Evangelical Reformed Church in Frederick, Maryland

Georg Stockman, Barbara/Jacob b Jul 14 1767, bapt Apr 3 1768/Jacob Doman, Catharina Zimmerman

Wilhelm Berg, Maria/Maria b Oct 28 1767, bapt Dec 26 1767/Johannes Berg, Martha Crum

Wilhelm Crum, Maria/Maria b Aug 18 1765, bapt Sep -- 1765, by Rev. Otterbein/Johannes Berg, Maria Crum

same parents/Sarah b Oct 17 1767, bapt Dec 26 1767/Juliana Cath. Berg

On my 3rd journey to Virginia 90 children were baptized by me, among whom were two married men and a negro child.

Jacob Krebs, Margaretha/Elisabetha Margaretha b Feb 16 1768, bapt May 29 1768/Maria Elisabetha Sandburg

Jacob Brengel, Gertraudt/Elisabetha b Dec 19 1767, bapt May 29 1768/ Christoph Wolf, Elisabetha

Gabriel Doman, Margaretha/Johann Adam b Feb 10 1768, bapt May 29 1768/Johann Adam Wolf, Maria Clara

Georg Dohler, Catharina/Margaretha b May 1 1768, bapt May 29 1768/Jacob Krebs, Margaretha

Georg Römsperger, Maria Elisabetha/Anna Margaretha b Dec 6 1767, bapt May 29 1768/Anna Marg. Mayer

Johannes Bell, Margaretha/Daniel b Jan 1 1768, bapt May 31 1768/Jacob Weiss

Christian Brengel, Elisabetha/Catharina b Feb 22 1768, bapt Jun 5 1768/ Lorentz Brengel, Barbara Brengel

Jacob Wagger, Elisabetha/Elisabetha b Apr 16 1768, bapt Jun 18 1768/---

Philip Crist, Dorothea/Maria Elisabetha b Mar 31 1768, bapt Jun 19 1768/ Michael Crist, Maria Elisabetha

The following number of children were baptized at different times in the congregations mentioned:

In the schoolhouse over the 1st mountain, 8; at Danetown, 7; at the Glade: 13. Total: 147.

Baptisms by an unknown hand, Feb-Oct 1769.

Valentin Bantz, Margaretha/Valentin b Jan 6 1769, bapt Feb 8 1769/Valentin Reb, Clara

Peter Bohren & wf./Johannes b Jan 2 1769, bapt Feb 8 1769/Joh. Schenckmayer, Elisabetha

Jacob Rapp, Barbara/Eva & Margaret b Mar 29 1769, bapt Apr 23 1769/Lorentz Brengel, Margaretha Rapp

Philip Jacob, Elisabetha/Johann Adam b Oct 5 1768, bapt Apr 23 1769/Adam Riess

Peter Brunner, Maria Elisabeth/Joseph b Apr 29 1769, bapt Jul 12 1769/Joseph Doll, Charlotta

Valentin Schwartz & wf./Magdalena b Apr 24 1769, bapt Jul 12 1769/---

Johannes Engel, Anna Barbara/Elisabetha b ---, bapt Jul 12 1769/Elisabetha Stähelin

Conrad Geduldig, Margaretha/Johannes b Apr 5 1769, bapt Jul 12 1769/Georg Kortz & wf.

Barthel Schmitt, Catharina/Georg Henrich b Apr 23 1769, bapt Jul 12 1769/ Henrich Bruder, Eleonora

Joseph Doll, Charlotta/Joseph b Sep 1 1769, bapt Oct 29 1769/Conrad Doll, Anna Maria

Baptisms of the Evangelical Reformed Church in Frederick, Maryland

Baptisms by the Rev. Frederick Lewis Henop, 1770-1784.

Jacob Christ, Catharina/Johann Peter b Jun 23 1770, bapt Jun 27 1770/Peter Schmeltzer, Barbara

Henrich Bruder, Eleonora/Henrich b May 25 1770, bapt Jun 3 1770/Henrich Schober, Anna

Joh. Weichel, Anna Christina/Susanna b Jun -- 1769, bapt Jun 3 1770/Maria Elisabetha Merckel

Georg Adam Clarsnagel, Catharina/Johan Peter b Oct 7 (1769), bapt Jun 3 1770/Peter Gebhard, Barbara Thomas

Georg Stockman, Barbara/Johan Georg b Dec 12 1769, bapt Jul 8 1770/Lorentz Heim, Barbara Thomas

Michael Weber, Maria Catharina/Georg Michael b Jun 14 1770, bapt Jul 8 1770/ Parents

Daniel Jeremias, Anna Barbara/Johannes b May 7 1770, bapt Jul 8 1770/Johan Jentes & the mother

Johan Bernhard Ott, Anna/Johannes b Mar 17 1770, bapt Jun 15 1770/Johannes Henis, Maria Elisabetha

Georg Remsperger, Maria/Georg Peter b Mar 16 1770, bapt Jun 22 1770/Peter Beckenbach, Barbara

Philip Christ, Dorothea/Johan Philip b Jun 26 1770, bapt Jun 22 1770/Jacob Huber, Christina

Jacob Hoffman, Barbara/Anna Maria Catharina b May 18 1770, bapt Sep 2 1770/ Henrich Thomas, Catharina

Jacob Remsperger, Anna Elisabetha/Elisabetha b Aug 13 1770, bapt Sep 9 1770/ Michael Christ, Maria Elisabeth

Lucas Fleck, Maria Barbara/Maria Barbara b Jul 15 1770, bapt Oct 14 1770/ Adam Wolf, Maria

Gabriel Götzendanner, Magdalena/Jacob b Jul 25 1770, bapt Oct 14 1770/Jacob Götzendanner, Catharina

Bernhard Lingenfelder, Anna Barbara/Magdalena b Aug 29 1770, bapt Oct 24 1770/Jacob Götzendanner, Catharina

Jacob Schüssler, Anna Maria/Anna Maria b Aug 4 1770, bapt Oct 28 1770/Conrad Doll, Anna Maria

Georg Schaub, Catharina/Catharina b Jun 21 1770, bapt Oct 28 1770/Hieronimus Hildebrand

Hieronimus Hildebrand, Eva Margaretha/Johann Adam b Jun 19 1770, bapt Jul 29 1770/Leonhard Huber, Eva Margaretha

---/Jacob b Nov 12 1770, bapt Nov 18 1770/Jacob Zimmerman & wf.

Salomon Klatfelder, Maria Eva/Johan Adam b Sep 11 1770, bapt Dec 16 1770/ Isaac Jauler, Anna

Jacob Rab, Barbara/Catharina b Oct 21 1770, bapt Dec -- 1770/Jacob Holtz, Catharina

Friedrich Arnold, Martha/Johan Ludwig b Aug 1 1770, bapt Dec -- 1770/Ludwig Ritter, Barbara

Johan Adam, Margaretha/Eva Margaretha b Jun 18 1768, bapt -- 1768/Valentin Adam, Eva Margaretha

Stephan Brunner, Magdalena/Johannes b Aug 9 1770, bapt Jan 1 1771/Johannes Schellman, Margaretha

Caspar Keller, Anna Margaretha/Christian b Nov 16 1770, bapt Jan 1 1771/Adam Keller, Catharina

Johannes Balsell, Anna Maria/Johann Jacob b Oct 31 1770, bapt Jan 1 1771/ Jacob Rau

Baptisms of the Evangelical Reformed Church in Frederick, Maryland

Henrich Kuntz, Dorothea/Anna Maria b Aug 10 1770, bapt Jan 1 1771/Jacob Beyer, Anna Maria

Peter Hoffman, Maria Dorothea/Georg b Nov 28 1770, bapt Jan 6 1771/Philip Bier, Eva Catharina

Jacob Schley, Margaretha/Margaretha b Oct 18 1770, bapt Jan 6 1771/Thomas Schley, Margaret

Adam Böhm, Catharina/Margaret Elisabetha b Dec 31 1770, bapt Jan 6 1771, Johan Stein, Margaret

Georg Conrad, Eva/Johan Georg b Nov 6 1770, bapt Jan 1771/Georg Hoffmann, Margaret

Georg Brenckel, Catharina/Anna Maria b Dec 24 1770, bapt Jan 27 1771/Anna Maria Beckenbach

Thomas Bolhaus, Catharina/Georg Friedrich b Jan 17 1771, bapt Jan 27 1771/ Valentin Schwartz, Susanna

Valentin Schreiner, Elisabetha/Johann Georg b Jan 9 1771, bapt Jan 27 1771/ Georg Dertzenbach, Magdalena

Joseph Burckstahler, Anna Magdalena/Daughter b Feb 2 1771, bapt Feb 10 1771/ Jacob Frey & wf.

Adam Fischer, Margaret/Johan Adam b Jan 4 1771, bapt Feb 10 1771/John Haas

Georg Schneider, Elisabetha/Elisabetha b Nov 24 1770, bapt Jan 12 1771/The mother

--- Lewis, Barbara/Sarah b Dec 17 1770, bapt Feb 24 1771/Jacob Zimmerman, Leah

Conrad Dewis, Maria Eva/Susanna b Jan 30 1771, bapt Feb 24 1771/Valentin Breitenbach & Susanna

Johannes Adam, Margaretha/Georg b Dec 18 1770, bapt Mar 3 1771/Georg Peter Hoffman, Maria

Peter Bucke, Anna Maria/Georg b Feb 28 1771, bapt Mar 11 1771/Georg Hoffman, Margaretha

Daniel Schultz, Anna Catharina/Eva Margaretha b ---, bapt Mar 14 1771/ Rudolph Ruff, Eva Margaret

Johannes Stoll, Catharina/Catharina b Jan 7 1771, bapt Mar 20 1771/Catharina Teubelbiss

Caspar Darst, Anna/Anna Maria b ---, bapt May 19 1771/Juliana Koster

Peter Gross, Sophia/Maria Christina b Dec -- 1770, bapt May 19 1771/Juliana Koster, Maria Geduldig

Peter Gross, Sophia/Maria Elisabeth b Jan 25 1769, bapt May 19 1771/Juliana Koster

Michael Schmidt, Magdalena/Maria Eva b Dec 18 1770, bapt May 20 1771/Lorentz Brenckel, Eva Margaret

Jacob Däntz, Catharina/Maria b Apr 20 1771, bapt Jun 10 1771/Adam Stackel, Maria

Balthasar Götzendanner, Anna/Jacob b Jan 21 1771, bapt Jun 10 1771/Jacob Götzendanner, Catharina

Peter Liebig, Susanna/Johan Georg b Apr 30 1771, bapt Jun 10 1771/Nicolaus Johan(?), Catharina

David Lefebre, Maria/Johannes b Dec 2 1770, bapt Jun 20 1771/Parents

Peter Bohrer, Magdalena/Elisabetha b Dec 31 1770, bapt Jan 23 1771/Johannes Schenckmayer & Elisabetha, grandparents

Christoff Meyer, Anna Margaret/Elisabetha b Nov 19 1770, bapt Jul 7 1771/ Cath. Elisabeth Steiner

Baptisms of the Evangelical Reformed Church in Frederick, Maryland

Henrich Thomas, Catharina/Maria Elisabetha b Jan 26 1771, bapt Jul 7 1771/ Maria Elisabetha Remsperger
Johan Engel, Susanna Barbara/Susanna Barbara b Apr 5 1771, bapt Jul 14 1771 /---
Jacob Berton, Anna Margaret/Johannes b Jan 21 1771, bapt Jul 14 1771/ Bernhard Ott, Anna Elisabetha
Anton Boley, Anna Margaretha/Anna Margaretha b Jul 2 1771, bapt Jul 28 1771/ Christoph Meyer, Anna Margaretha
Valentin Bantz, Susanna/Jacob b Jul 12 1771, bapt Jul 28 1771/Joh. Zimmerman
Andreas Flick, Magdalena, Henrich b 8 d. before Shrove Tuesd., bapt Jul 28 1771/Parents
Philip Klaninger, Maria/Johan Philip b Apr 24 1771, bapt Aug 4 1771/Michael Hoffman, Dorothea
Stephan Müller & wf./Johan Georg b Jun 19 1771, bapt Aug 4 1771/Parents
Jacob Weiss, Maria/Jacob b May 25 1771, bapt Aug 11 1771/Peter Gebhard, Eva Margaretha
Andreas Hein, Maria/Maria Barbara b Oct 15 1771, bapt Sep 10 1771/Georg Stockman, Barbara
Christian Teubelbiss, Magdalena, Catharina b Aug 12 1771, bapt Sep 22 1771/ Valentin Reb, Clara
Georg Nicol, Margaretha/Johannes b Mar 27 1771, bapt Sep 22 1771/Johan Thomas, Catharina
Ludwig Kempf, Barbara/Johannes b Feb 28 1771, bapt Sep 29 1771/Parents
Daniel Zwickart, Maria/Eva b May 1 1771, bapt Sep 29 1771/David Heim, Maria
Johan Huff, Catharina/Henrich b Mar 7 1771, bapt Sep 29 1771/Conrad Doll, Maria
Daniel Hauer, Catharina/Nicolaus b Sep 16 1771, bapt Oct 3 1771/Nicolaus Hauer, Catharina
Weinberg Tschudi, Elisabetha/Elisabetha b Sep 26 1771, bapt Oct 20 1771/ Henrich Kuntz, Dorothea Kuntz
Simon Gebhardt, Catharina/Jacob b Sep 6 1771, bapt Oct 27 1771/Valentin Reb, Clara
Melchior Heffner, Anna Catharina/Dorothea b Sep 9 1771, bapt Oct 27 1771/ Martin Witerich, Dorothea
(Joseph) Doll, Charlotta/Daughter b Oct 1 1771, bapt Oct 27 1771/Michael Christ, Maria Elisabeth
Peter Hauck, Margaretha/Michael b Aug 14 1771, bapt Oct 10 1771/Michael Balsell
Jacob Segeser, Anna Maria/Anna Maria b Sep 10 1771, bapt Oct 11 1771/ Friedrich Willheit, Anna Maria
Peter Doffler, Margaretha/Peter Oct 15 1771, bapt Nov 19 1771/Peter Hoffman, Maria
Jacob Kast, Anna Maria/Valentin b Oct 16 1771, bapt Nov 24 1771/Valentin Reb, Clara
Johan Jentes, Maria/Maria Sibylla b Oct 17 1771, bapt Dec 1 1771/Daniel Jentes, Sibylla
Adam Wolff, Maria Clara/Elisabetha b Jul 20 1771, bapt Dec 15 1771 /Georg Remsperger, Maria
Jacob Neihard, Susanna/Daughter b Mar 31 1771, bapt Nov 24 1771/Lorentz Brenckel, Eva Margaret
Andreas Frey, Susanna/Jacob b Apr 18 1771, bapt Dec 22 1771/Jacob Frey & wf.

Baptisms of the Evangelical Reformed Church in Frederick, Maryland

Balsell Immann & wf./Elisabeth b Nov 9 1771, bapt Dec 22 1771/Catharina Haehn

Frantz Jacob, Maria Elisabeth/Jacob b Nov 6 1771, bapt Jan 1 1772/Jacob Holtz, Catharina

Georg Wolff, Anna/Johan Georg bapt Oct 22 1771, bapt Jan 1 1772/Georg Dertzenbach, Magdalena

John Kammel, Jane/Mary b Nov 2 1771, bapt Jan 1 1772/Parents

Christoph Messenkopf, Margaretha/Anna Maria Magdalena b Dec 13 1771, bapt Jan 5 1772/Henrich Schober, Margaretha

Jacob Jauler, Barbara/Catharina b Oct 29 1771, bapt Jan 5 1772/Peter Shudy, Catharina

Jacob Christ, Catharina/Heinrich b Nov 26 1771, bapt Jan 8 1772/Jacob Christ, grandfather

Johannes Keller, Margaretha/Daniel b Jan 4 1772, bapt Jan 26 1772/Daniel Hauer, Catharina

Philip Bier, Eva Catharina/Peter b Dec 12 1771, bapt Feb 9 1772/Peter Doffler, Margaretha

Friedrich Guldy, Anna Margaretha/Johan Daniel b Ascension Day, 1771, bapt Feb 8 1772/Philip Römich, Eve Margaret

Valentin Thomas, Margaretha/Johan Valentin b Oct 31 1771, bapt Feb 28 1772/ Valentin Weiss

Conrad Geduldig, Anna Margaretha/Henrich b Feb 11 1772, bapt Mar 8 1772/ Henrich Bruder & wf.

Jacob Winterroth, Barbara/Maria Barbara b Nov 13 1771, bapt Mar 8 1772/ Parents

Philip Christ, Dorothea/Anna Catharina b Jan 14 1772, bapt Mar 22 1772/Jacob Wolff, Anna Catharina

Philip Jacob, Elisabetha/Anna Elisabeth b --, bapt Easter Day, 1772, Apr 19/ Michael Nuss, Anna Elisabeth

Bartholomaeus Schmidt, Catharina/Catharina b Sep 1 1771, bapt May 10 1772/ Parents

Christian Brenckel, Elisabetha/Elisabetha b Oct 31 1771, bapt May 10 1772/ Johan Steiner & wf.

Friedrich Becker, Dorothea/Maria Elisabetha b Feb -- 1772, bapt May 10 1772/ Ludwig Weltner, Anna Maria

Johan Steiner, Catharina/Christian b Feb 22 1772, bapt May 10 1772/Christian Weber, Catharina

Benedict Steiner, Maria Sibylla/Benedict b --, bapt May 10 1772/Balthasar Götzendanner, Anna

Jacob Liess, Maria Dorothea/Philip b Apr 2 1772, bapt May 10 1772/Wilhelm Liess, Catharina

Johan Study, Margaret/Catharina b --, bapt May 17 1772/Peter Study, Catharina

Isaac Jauler, Anna Eva/1. Adam, 2. Peter, twins b Apr 20 1772, bapt May 17 1772/Salomon Glatfelder & wf., Peter Study

Michael Feist, Salome/Philip b Dec -- 1771, bapt May 17 1772/Philip Borger, Barbara

Philip Borger, Barbara/Catharina b Apr 20 1772, bapt May 17 1772/Catharina Schell

Frantz Kast, Catharina/Johan Jacob b Mar 6 1771, bapt May 24 1772/Jacob Hofman & wf.

Baptisms of the Evangelical Reformed Church in Frederick, Maryland

Jacob Martin, Christiana/Maria Barbara b Sep 30 1771, bapt May 24 1772/Georg Hoffman, Barbara

Nicolaus Paul, Elisabeth/Elisabetha b Mar 27 1772, bapt Jun 7 1772/Eva Eberhardt

Lorentz Brenckel, Eva/Johannes b Feb 18 1772, bapt Jun 7 1772/Johannes Compert, Rachel

Valentin Schwartz & wf./Valentin b May 25 1772, bapt Jun 7 1772/Parents

Henrich Koch, Susanna/Mattheus b Dec 1 1771, bapt Jun 7 1772/Mattheus Bucke & wf.

Philip Hähn, Juliana/Johannes b May 2 1772, bapt Jun 14 1772/Johannes Zimmerman

Jacob Steger, Barbara/Johan Jacob b Mar 28 1772, bapt Jun 14 1772/The mother

Henrich Leonhard, Anna Christina/Henrich b May 9 1772, bapt Jul 12 1772/ Peter Kassel, Maria Catharina

Caspar Keller, Anna Margaretha/Maria Magdalena b Jun 6 1772, bapt Jul 26 1772/Magdalena Keller

Peter Schober, Maria Sophia/Maria Sophia b May 17 1772, bapt Jul 26 1772/ Simon Schober, Maria Barbara

Henrich Bruder, Eleonora/Valentin b Apr 2 1772, bapt Jul 26 1772/Valentin Reb, Clara

Johannes Rein, Anna Maria/Rudolff b May 30 1772, bapt Jul 26 1772/Rudolf Benninger, Juliana Elisabeth

Wilhelm Miller, Maria Eva/Barbara b Feb 1 1772, bapt Aug 9 1772/Conrad Roth, Barbara

Jacob Kern, Christina Barbara/Jacob b Jul 22 1772, bapt Aug 15 1772/Parents

Gabriel Götzendanner, Magdalena/Margaretha b May 26 1772, bapt Aug 15 1772/ Magdalena Kämpff

Henrich Steiner, Elisabetha/Elisabetha b Jul 16 1772, bapt Aug 15 1772/ Christian Brenckel, Elisabetha

Philip Roemich, Margaretha/Michael b Aug 10 1772, bapt Aug 23 1772/Johan Dieter & wf.

Henrich Brunner, Catharina/Henrich b Jul 9 1772, bapt Aug 28 1772/Henrich Sinn, Elisabetha

Jacob Derschheimer, Clara/Son b Mar 20 1772, bapt Aug 28 1772/Nicolaus Heuchely, Catharina

Jacob Remsberger, Anna Elisabetha/Susanna b Jul 28 1772, bapt Aug 29 1772/ Martin Wüterich, Dorothea

Peter Hoffmann, Anna Maria/Johannes b Jul 20 1772, bapt Sep 6 1772/Samuel Becker & wf.

Peter Hoffmann, Anna Maria/Son b Mar 20 1768, bapt --- 1772/Jacob Steiner

Peter Hoffmann & wf./Anna Maria b May 25 1769, bapt -- 1772/Jeremias Mayer, Barbara

Conrad Doll, Anna Maria/Johannes b Jun 2 1772, bapt Sep 6 1772/Johannes Huff, Catharina

Albrecht Hillegas, Anna Maria/Maria Elisabetha b Sep 3 1772, bapt Oct 4 1772/Theobald Etschberger, Maria Elisabeth

Daniel Jentes, Barbara/Johan Georg b Sep 9 1772, bapt Oct 18 1772/Parents

Henrich Jäger, Susanna/David b Aug 16 1772, bapt Oct 18 1772/Dieterich Beyer

Wilhelm Cassel, Elisabeth/Catharina b Oct 20 1772, bapt Nov 8 1772/Georg Jäntz & wf.

John Adlum, Margaretha/Catharina b Feb 13 1771, bapt Nov 8 1772/Jacob Michel, Catharina

Baptisms of the Evangelical Reformed Church in Frederick, Maryland

John Adlum, Margaretha/John b Oct 23 1772, bapt Nov 8 1772/Parents
Georg Remsperger, Maria Elisabeth/Charlotta b Jun 20 1772, bapt Nov 8 1772/ Charlotta C-rumrein
David Löb, Maria Barbara/Valentin b Sep 7 1772, bapt Nov 21 1772/Valentin Thomas, Margaretha
Matheis Bucke or Bouquet, Anna Maria/Catharina b Jun 28 1772, bapt Nov 29 1772/Georg Hoffmann, Margaretha
Nicolaus Theis, Barbara/Elisabetha b Oct 9 1772, bapt Dec 12 1772/Christian Brenckel, Elisabetha
Philip Sinn, Elisabetha/Elisabetha b Sep 7 1772, bapt Dec 12 1772/Henrich Brunner, Catharina
Jacob Schley, Margaretha/Catharina b Dec 13 1772, bapt Dec 14 1772/Philip Bier, Eva Catharina
George Brenckel, Catharina/Rosina b Nov 21 1772, bapt Dec 25 1772/Catharina Derr
Stephan Brunner, Magdalena/Michael b Apr 16 1772, bapt Jan 1 1773/Parents
Johannes Weil, Catharina Margaretha/Elisabetha b Nov 30 1772, bapt Jan 3 1773/Elisabetha Schwamli
Alexander MackDonald, Maria Catharina/John b Jan 12 1773, bapt Jan 31 1773/ Valentin Schreiner, Anna Elisabetha
Christoph Meyer, Anna Margaretha/Anna Margaretha b Oct 15 1772, bapt Feb 28 1773/Nicolaus Heuchler, Anna Margaretha
Gottfried Gebhard, Maria Magdalena/Margaretha b Jan 11 1773, bapt Mar 7 1773/Valentin Reb, Clara
Georg Thomas Schley, Catharina/Johann Nicolaus b Dec 25 1772, bapt Mar 21 1773/Thomas Schley, Sr., Margaretha
Friedrich Arnold, Martha buried yesterday/Johannes b Mar 4 1773, bapt Apr 9 1773/Johannes Schaumer, Anna Maria
Jacob Roth, Anna Maria/Anna Maria b Jan 18 1773, bapt Apr 4 1773/Matthes Fuchs
Henrich Hertzog, Anna Maria/Catharina b Oct 22 1772, bapt Apr 4 1773/ Catharina Hertzog
Johannes Stoll, Catharina/Christina b Dec 22 1772, bapt Apr 4 1773/Johannes Blumenschein, Anna Maria
Balthasar Götzendanner, Anna/Johannes b Feb 19 1773, bapt Apr 11 1773/ Johannes Thomas, Catharina
Lucas Fleck, Barbara/Freidrich b Feb 6 1773, bapt Apr 11 1773/Friedrich Dennwolf, Maria
Johannes Nicol, Philippina/Elisabetha b Jan 27 1773, bapt Apr 11 1773/ Charlotta Nicol
Johannes Benningeraud, Maria/Elisabetha b Jul 28 1772, bapt Apr 11 1773/ Johannes Ulrich West, Catharina
Thomas Bolhaus, Elisabetha/Magdalena b Nov 16 1772, bapt Mar 14 1773/Philip Schmidt, Magdalena
Jacob Klein, Anna Maria/Anna Maria b Mar 22 1773, bapt May 2 1773/Georg Peter Hoffmann, Anna Maria
Joseph Doll, Charlotta/Charlotta b Mar 17 1773, bapt May 9 1773/Charlotta Brunner
Salomon Glatfelder, Maria Eva/Anna Maria b Apr 14 1773, bapt May 16 1773/ Isaac Jauler, Hannah
Henrich Bär, Eva Margaret/Margaretha b --, bapt May 23 1773, Conrad Gedultig, Margaretha

Carl Boley, Elisabetha/Daniel b Apr 18 1773, bapt May 30 1773, Daniel Hauwet, Catharina
Frantz Winterroth, Susanna/Elisabetha b May 15 1773, bapt May 30 1773/Jacob Winterroth, Barbara
Jacob Rab, Barbara/Elisabetha b Apr 4 1773, bapt May 30 1773/Elisabeth Dewis
Frantz Kast, Catharina/Maria Barbara b Jan 8 1773, bapt May 30 1773/Peter Gebhard, Eva Margaret
Adam Hahn, Catharina in Canogocheague/Catharina b Mar 5 1773, bapt May 30 1773/Catharina Keller
Peter Bower, Magdalena/Maria Magdalena b May 20 1773, bapt Jun 5 1773/ Johannes Schenckmeyer & Elisabetha
Jacob Kentel, Anna Maria/Johannes b May 6 1773, bapt Jun 13 1773/Nicolaus Heuchler, Anna Margaretha
Johannes Matte, Catharina/Eva b Feb 24 1773, bapt Jun 13 1773/Parents
Abraham Sovain, Lydia/Maria Catharina b Nov 4 1772, bapt Jun 20 1773/Elias Brunner, Maria Catharina
Peter Becher, Maria, at the Gus Creek, in Va./Anna Catharina b Dec 8 1772, bapt Jun 15 1773/Martin Strasman, Agnes
Jacob Kast, Anna Maria/Johann Jacob b May 17 1773, bapt Jun 20 1773/Jacob Thomas, Susanna
Jacob Hoffmann, Barbara/Margaretha b May 11 1773, bapt Jul 11 1773/Valentin Reb. Schulm., Clara
Jacob Stehly, Catharina/Georg Peter b --, bapt Jul 25 1773/Peter Study, Catharina
Adam Wolff, Margaretha/Anna Barbara b Mar 25 1773, bapt Jul 31 1773/Parents
Jacob Berton, Anna Margaretha/Anna Margaretha b Jan 12 1773, bapt Aug 8 1773/Margaretha Klein
Bernhard Lingenfelder, Anna Barbara/Jacob b Jun 20 1773, bapt Aug 15 1773/ Parents
Jacob Stehly, Barbara/Jacob b Jul 17 1773, bapt Aug 29 1773/Peter Schäffer, Rosina
Jacob Spielman, Anna Margaretha/Johannes b Apr 7 1773, bapt Sep 12 1773/ Jacob Berg, single
Michael Dotterer, Elisabetha/Margaretha b Aug 8 1773, bapt Sep 12 1773/ Margaretha Dotterer
Johannes Adam, Margaretha/Catharina b Mar 7 1773, bapt Sep 19 1773/Parents
Johan Bugue, Susanna Barbara/Isaac b Aug 22 1773, bapt Sep 19 1773/Isaac Jauler, Anna
Peter Hauck, Margaret/Johannes b Aug 22 1773, bapt Oct 10 1773/Johannes Hauck, Catharina
Paul Loschhorn, Dorothea/Catharina b Jan 5 1773, bapt Oct 14 1773/Parents
Bartholomaeus Schmidt, Catharina/Michael b Jul 23 1773, bapt Oct 16 1773/ Michael Schmidt, Magdalena
Jacob Schüssler, Anna Maria/Anna Maria b Mar 2 1773, bapt Oct 24 1773/ Parents
Benjamin Stuart, Maria/Eleonora b Sep 1 1773, bapt Oct 24 1773/Parents
Adolph Eyler, Anna Maria/Anna Maria b Feb 20 1773, bapt Nov 5 1773/Johannes Thomas, Catharina
Marcus Oster, Maria Catharina/Johann Adam b Aug 19 1773, bapt Nov 14 1773/ Adam Oster, Anna Maria
Daniel Stauffer, Christina/Valentin b Nov 7 1773, bapt Nov 13 1773, d. Nov 14/Valentin Breitenbach, Susanna

Baptisms of the Evangelical Reformed Church in Frederick, Maryland

Christoph Meissenkopf, Margaretha/Johannes b Oct 19 1773, bapt Nov 21 1773/ The father & Louisa Ballser

Adam Fischer, Margaretha/Johann Adam b Oct 17 1773, bapt Dec 6 1773/Adam Götzendanner, Elisabetha

Carl Dessloch, Catharina/Susanna Catharina b --, bapt Dec 6 1773/Peter Study, Catharina

Simon Gebhard, Catharina/Catharina b Nov 25 1773, bapt Nov 28 1773/Clara Reb

Peter Engels, Anna Maria/Maria Catharina b Sep 27 1773, bapt Dec 12 1773/ Peter Engels, Maria Catharina

Jacob Götzendanner, Catharina/Margaretha b Oct 30 1773, bapt Dec 18 1773/ Margaretha Kast

Christian Teubelbiss, Magdalena/Johann Henrich b Oct 24 1773, bapt Jan 1 1774/Henrich Remsperger

Peter Winterroth, Anna Maria/Johann Peter b Nov 23 1773, bapt Feb 12 1774/ Peter Buquet, Anna Maria

John Campbell & wf./Elisabetha b Dec 6 1773, bapt Mar 20 1774/Parents

Johannes Kraneisen, Anna Maria/Johannes b Feb 27 1774, bapt Mar -- 1774/ Parents

Benjamin Hisquist, Maria/Margaretha b feb 17 1774, bapt Mar -- 1774/Parents

Johannes Steiner, Catharina Elisabetha/Catharina Margaretha b Feb 4 1774, bapt Apr 1 1774/Anna Margaretha Meyer

Georg Zimmerman,Catharina/Elisabetha b Jan 8 1774, bapt Apr 3 1774/Philip Fein, Elisabetha

Jacob Froschauer, Anna Maria/Henrich b Jan 1 1774, bapt Apr 3 1774/Joh. Henrich Gernhard

Philip Hehn, Juliana/Juliana b Jan 3 1774, bapt Apr 3 1774/Conrad Roth, Barbara

George Doffler, Margaretha/Catharina b Jan 24 1774, bapt Apr 1 1774/Philip Bier, Eva Catharina

Michael Weber, Catharina/Georg Peter b Mar 9 1774, bapt Apr 17 1774/Peter Dertzenbach

Philip Christ, Dorothea/Valentin Christ b Nov 14 1773, bapt Apr 17 1774/ Valentin Reb, Clara

Jacob Lies, Maria Dorothea/Elisabetha b Jan 26 1774, bapt Apr 17 1774/Simon Rab, Elisabetha

Friedrich Ludwig Henop, Maria/Friedrich Ludwig b Mar 22 1774, bapt Apr 17 1774/Ludwig Weltner, Anna Maria

Jacob Adam, Christina/Johann Jacob b Feb 26 1774, bapt Apr 17 1774/Parents

Georg Jantz, Catharina/Sibylla b Feb 2 1774, bapt Apr 1 1774/Sibylla Ogle

Frantz Jacob, Elisabetha/Elisabetha b Feb --, bapt May 7 1774/The mother

Peter Gebhart, Eva Margaretha/Johann Georg b Apr 22 1774, bapt May 1 1774/ Georg Hoffman, Margaretha

Henrich (Stein)er, Elisabeth/Johannes b Mar 12 1774, bapt May 6 1774/Sebastian(?) Derr, Catharina

Johannes Huff, Catharina/Valentin b Sep 26 1773, bapt May 8 1774/Parents

Christian Thomas, Susanna/Michael b Mar 15 1774, bapt May 12 1774/Christian Thomas, Barbara

Frantz Hoffmann, Barbara/Elisabetha b Jan 17 1774, bapt May 12 1774/ Elisabetha ---

Heinrich Brunner, Catharina/Johannes b Feb 6 1774, bapt May 15 1774/Johannes Brunner, Jr., Charlotta

Baptisms of the Evangelical Reformed Church in Frederick, Maryland

Valentin Thomas, Margaretha/Maria Magdalena b Feb 28 1774, bapt May 20 1774/ Parents

Lorentz Brenckel, Eva Margaretha/Jacob b Jan 27 1774, bapt May 22 1774/Jacob Brenckel, Margaretha

Johannes Hauck, Catharina/Johannes b Apr 1 1774, bapt May 22 1774/Gabriel Kemp, Maria

Johannes De Later, Sibylla/Johannes b Feb 28 1774, bapt May 22 1774/ Christoph Meyer, Anna Margaretha

Jacob Jauler, Barbara/Jacob Feb 27 1774, bapt May 22 1774/Conrad Gedultig, Margaretha

Bernhard Ott, Anna Elisabetha/Susanna b Feb 16 1774, bapt May 22 1774/Philip Goreis, Susanna

Jacob Neihard, Catharina/Jacob b -- 1773, bapt May 22 1774/Jacob Hoffman, Barbara

Henrich Remsberger, Susanna/Stephan b Feb 28 1774, bapt May 22 1774/Stephan Remsberger, Catharina Steiner

Friedrich Heffner, Susanna/Anna Margaretha b May 13 1774, bapt Jun 12 1774/ Johannes Schweyer, Anna Margaretha

Jacob Kern, Christina/Henrich b Jan 18 1774, bapt Jun 12 1774/Parents

Georg Nicol, Margaretha/Johann Jacob b Nov 14 1773, bapt Jul 3 1774/Michel Nicol

Peter Stockman, Christina/Johann Georg b Nov 22 1773, bapt Jul 10 1774/ Parents

Michael Christ, Maria Elisabeth/Johann Peter b Jun 23 1774, bapt Jul 24 1774/Joseph Doll, Charlotta

Friedrich Holtzman, Margaretha/Georg b Jun 10 1774, bapt Jul 24 1774/The mother

Johann Henrich Klinck, Anna Margaret/Maria Sophia Elisabeth b May 30 1774, bapt Aug 2 1774/Johannes Imfeldt, Maria Sophia Elis.

Johannes Remsberger, Anna Maria/Anna Maria b May -- 1774, bapt Aug 14 1774/ Michael Spoth, Anna Maria

Philip Sinn, Elisabetha/Philip b Jun 20 1774, bapt Aug 14 1774/Andreas Michel, Barbara

Johannes Mick, Magdalena/Jacob b Jul 18 1774, bapt Aug 21 1774/Jacob Remsberger & wf.

Martin Spohn, Magdalena/Maria Catharina b Feb 15 1774, bapt Sep 1 1774/Maria Catharina Spohn, grandmother

Johannes Buckius, Eva/Johannes b Aug 20 1773, bapt Sep 4 1774/Georg Schnertzel, Barbara

Georg Schnertzel, Barbara/Wilhelm b Feb 11 1774, bapt Sep 4 1774/Parents

Philip Preis, Susanna/Johannes b Jul 22 1774, bapt Sep 18 1774/Johannes Preis, Maria Elisabetha

Elias Remsberger, Catharina/Charlotta b Aug 27 1774, bapt Sep 25 1774/ Johannes Brunner, Jr., Charlotta

Wilhelm Berg, Maria/Jacob b Aug 27 1774, bapt Oct 14 1774/Jacob Berg, Elis. Berg

Gabriel Götzendanner, Magdalena/Henrich b Jun 11 1774, bapt Oct 20 1774/ Parents

Georg Thomas Schley, Catharina/Susanna b ---, bapt Oct 23 1774/Thomas Ogle's wf., Sibylla

Johannes Bell, Anna Margaretha/Johann Georg b Feb 12 1774, bapt Oct 29 1774/ Peter Trautman, Anna Maria

Baptisms of the Evangelical Reformed Church in Frederick, Maryland

Peter Schaeffer, Rosina/Peter b Jul 15 1774, bapt Oct 6 1774/Peter Study, Catharina

Henrich Schlegel, Elisabetha/Elisabeth b Sep 10 1774, bapt Oct 6 1774/Johan Schlegel

Johann Beyer, Margaretha/Elisabetha b Apr 17 1774, bapt Oct 6 1774/Parents

Johan Jacob Schley, Anna Maria/Michael b Sep 20 1774, bapt Nov 20 1774/ Philip Bier, Eva Catharina

Conrad Gedultig, Anna Margaretha/Johann Georg b Nov 1 1774, bapt Nov 20 1774/George Kurtz, Catharina

Philip Jacob, Elisabetha/Philippina b Sep 30 1774, bapt Nov 27 1774/Jacob Simens, Maria Elisabetha

Georg Frantz Winterroth, Susanna/Friedrich b Oct 30 1774, bapt Nov 27 1774/ Parents

Peter Buquet, Anna Maria/Magdalena b Aug 15 1774, bapt Nov 27 1774/Magdalena Hoffman

Stephan Miller, Rachel/Daniel b Aug 2 1774, bapt Nov 27 1774/Parents

Friedrich Becker, Dorothea/Friedrich b Nov 14 1774, bapt Dec 4 1774/Peter Krebil, Barbara

Israel Wolff, Maria/Maria b Nov 4 1774, bapt Dec 25 1774/Parents

Conrad Haas, Anna Maria/Johann Georg b Jul 26 1774, bapt Dec 18 1774/Johann Georg & wf.

Conrad Haas, Anna Maria/Wilhelm b Jul 26 1774, bapt Dec 18 1774/Wilhelm Lauffer

Georg Kortz, Catharina/Susanna b Dec 8 1774, bapt Jan 15 1775/Susanna Reich

Peter Brunner, Anna Maria/Adam b Oct 6 1774, bapt Jan 15 1775/Adam Schaeffer, Susanna

Jacob Schley, Margaretha/Maria b Jan 4 1775, bapt Feb 18 1775/Georg Weiss, Maria

Gottfried Gebhard, Maria Magdalena/Anna Maria b Jan 9 1775, bapt Feb 18 1775/Peter Gebhard, Eva Margaretha

Jacob Remsberger, Anna Elisabetha/Johann Georg b Jan 4 1775, bapt Feb 20 1775/Georg Witerich, Catharina

Jacob Thomas & wf./Henrich b Jan 2 1775, bapt Feb 21 1775/Gabriel Thomas, Jr

David Hoffman, Susanna/Johan Jacob b Feb 8 1775, bapt Feb 21 1775/Jacob Klein, Anna Maria

Georg Franklin, Margaretha/Georg b Oct 12 1774, bapt Mar 3 1775/Georg Tuchman

Georg Brenckel, Catharina/Maria Elisabetha b Feb 11 1775, bapt Mar 19 1775/ Christian Brenckel, Maria Elisabetha

Christoph Thomas, Susanna/Christoph b Jan 10 1775, bapt Mar 19 1775/ Christian Thomas, Barbara

Isaac Jauler, Anna/Johan Jacob b Mar 10 1775, bapt Mar 26 1775/Jacob Stehly, Catharina

Friedrich Weiss, Catharina/Anna Margaretha b Mar 10 1775, bapt Apr 8 1775/ Jacob Schnodenberger, Anna Margaretha

Wilhelm Miller, Maria/Jacob b Feb 1 1775, bapt Apr 9 1775/Jacob Schüssler & wf.

Peter Hauck, Margaretha/Georg b Jan 22 1775, bapt Apr 9 1775/Georg Doffler, Maria Catharina

Joseph Doll, Charlotta/Anna Catharina b Mar 1 1775, bapt Apr 9 1775/Johan Huff, Catharina

Henrich Letherman, Margaretha/Juliana b Jan 15 1775, bapt Apr 16 1775/ Juliana Ballsell
Jacob Sprenger, Elisabetha/Maria Elisabetha b Feb 25 1775, bapt Apr 16 1775/ Jacob Eberle, Maria Elisabetha
Johannes Stoll, Catharina/Johannes b Jan 28 1775, bapt Apr 21 1775/Johannes Blumenschein & Anna Maria
Jacob Messer, Lydia/Catharina b Dec 23 1773, bapt Apr 23 1775/Catharina Weber
Jacob Meyer, Lydia/Anna Margaretha b Apr 9 1941, bapt Apr 23 1941/Anna Margaretha Meyer
Jacob Stehly, Anna Barbara/Johan Peter b Jan 5 1775, bapt Apr 23 1775/Johan Peter Study, Catharina
Nicolaus Hauer, Catharina/Johannes b Mar 14 1775, bapt Apr 23 1775/Daniel Hauer, Catharina
Daniel Hauer, Catharina/Magdalena b Feb 28 1775, bapt Apr 23 1775/Maria Hauer
Salomon Glatfelder, Eva/Elisabetha b Apr 2 1775, bapt Apr 16 1775/Parents
Gottlieb Grist, Margaretha/Son b Mar 25 1775, bapt May 23 1775/Peter Study, Catharina
Joseph Stehly, Juliana/Joseph b Mar 30 1775, bapt May 23 1775/Lorentz Heffner, Margaretha
Baltasar Götzendanner, Anna/Adam b Apr 6 1775, bapt May 23 1775/Adam Götzendanner, Elisabetha
Georg Remsberger, Maria Elisabetha/Stephan b Nov 9 1774, bapt May 23 1775/ Stephan Brunner & wf.
William Robinson, Salome/Joseph b Apr 14 1775, bapt May 28 1775/Christoph Stoll, Philippina
Christoph Stoll, Philippina/Magdalena b Mar 6 1775, bapt May 28 1775/Jacob Holtz, Catharina
Matthes Bouquet, Anna Maria/Peter b --, bapt May 30 1775/Peter Hoffmann, Maria Dorothea
Thomas Ogle, Sibylla/Thomas Schley b Apr 27 1775, bapt Jun 4 1775/Thomas Schley, Sr., Margaretha
Christoph Meyer, Anna Margaretha/Johannes b Jan 18 1775, bapt Jun 4 1775/ Johannes Remsberger, Anna Maria
Georg Oster, Anna Barbara/Anna Barbara b Feb 18 1775, bapt Jun 4 1775/Anna Maria Brunner
Georg Stockman, Anna Barbara/Anna Barbara b Dec 3 1774, bapt Jun 4 1775/ Jacob Schäffer, Catharina
Johannes Imfeldt, Maria Elisabetha/Philip b Apr 3 1775, bapt Jun 11 1775/ Philip Angelberger, Susanna
Jacob Klein, Anna Maria/Georg b Jun 3 1775, bapt Jun 17 1775/Parents
Jacob Adams, Christina/Elisabetha b May 7 1775, bapt Jun 25 1775/Georg Krämer, Magdalena
David Löwi, Maria Barbara/Samuel b Dec 25 1774, bapt Jul 16 1775/Samuel Guldy
Ezekiel Belthes, Christine/Susanna b Oct -- 1774, bapt Jul 16 1775/ Elisabetha Weber
Henrich Jäger, Susanna/Antonius b Jan 14 1774, bapt Jul 20 1775/The Mother
Georg Witerich, Catharina/Jacob b Jun 3 1775, bapt Jul 23 1775/Jacob Remsberger, Elisabetha

Johannes Brunner, Jr., Charlotta/Maria Elisabetha b Jun 13 1775, bapt Aug 20 1775/Parents
Jacob Schussler, Anna Maria/Anna Margaretha b Feb 19 1775, bapt Aug 20 1775/ Parents
Conrad Doll & wf./Anna Margaretha b ---, bapt Aug 27 1775/Georg Borckhard, Anna Margaretha
Thomas Bolhaus, Elisabetha/Eva Margaretha b May 21 1775, bapt Aug 20 1775/ Parents
Christoph Meissenkop, Margaretha/Anna Maria Magdalena b Aug 2 1775, bapt Sep 5 1775/Anna Margaretha Schober
Michael Heyler, Margaretha/Wilhelm b Aug 8 1775, bapt Oct 8 1775/Wilhelm Allbach, Magdalena
Lucas Fleck, Barbara/Anna Maria b Sep 14 1775, bapt Dec 10 1775/Friedrich Tannwolf, Anna Maria
Johannes Kaufman, Johanna/Margaretha b Dec 29 1775, bapt Jan 11 1776/ Nicolaus Klein, Margaretha
Jacob Kendel, Anna Maria/Eva Margaretha b Nov 7 1775, bapt Jan 21 1776/ Balthasar Heck, Eva Margaretha
Christoph Thomas, Susanna/Magdalena b Nov 7 1775, bapt Jan 21 1776/Jacob Thomas, Susanna
Jacob Mumah, Anna Margaretha/Anna Catharina b --, bapt Feb 2 1776/Parents
Nicolaus Theis, Barbara/Georg b Jan 18 1776, bapt Mar 3 1776/Georg Weiss, Maria
Stephan Brunner, Magdalena/Jacob b Jul 8 1775/bapt Mar 11 1776/Johan Jacob Schley, Maria
Bernhard Ott, Anna Elisabetha/Maria Elisabetha b Jan 12 1776, bapt Mar 17 1776/Johannes Preis, Maria Elisabeth
Jacob Ballsel, Anna Maria/Johannes b Feb 12 1776, bapt Apr 7 1776/Georg Eckman, Sophia
Johann Schley, Susanna/Anna Maria b Mar -- 1776, bapt Apr 7 1776/Anna Maria Guldy
Georg Eckman, Sophia/Jacob b Feb 26 1776, bapt Apr 7 1776/Jacob Ballsel, Maria
Friedrich Ludwig Henop, Maria/Friedrich b Mar 16 1776, bapt Apr 7 1776/ Ludwig Weltner, Maria, grandparents
Michael Storm, Magdalena/Michael b Feb 28 1776, bapt Apr 7 1776/Michael Christ, Elisabeth
Philip Preis, Susanna/Johann Adam b Dec 24 1776, bapt Apr 7 1776/Johan Adam Keller, Maria Catharina
Jacob Kern, Christina/Rosina b Dec 15 1775, bapt Apr 14 1776/Rosina Baumann
Christian Teubelbis, Magdalena/Susanna b Feb 24 1776, bapt Apr 14 1776/ Valentin Schwartz, Susanna
Peter Bohrer, Magdalena/Abraham b Dec 2 1775, bapt Jan 4 1776/Johannes Schenckmeyer, Elisabetha
Stephan Brunner, Barbara/Johannes b Nov 27 1775, bapt May 16 1776/Johannes Brunner, Charlotta
Bernhard Lingenfelder, Barbara/Elisabetha b Mar 14 1776, bapt May 29 1776/ Parents
Peter Hoffman, Maria Dorothea/Wilhelm b --, bapt Jun 7 1776/Wilhelm Otterbein, V.D.M.
Jacob Kast, Anna Maria/Christian b --, bapt Jun 16 1776/Christian Ostertag & wf.
Philip Schaed, Dorothea/Anna Maria b May 31 1776, bapt Jun 16 1776/Parents

Baptisms of the Evangelical Reformed Church in Frederick, Maryland

Andreas Adam, Maria Catharina/Elisabetha b Mar 13 1776, bapt Jun 23 1776/ Johannes Brunner, Charlotta
Michael Weber, Catharina/Magdalena b Apr 26 1776, bapt Jul 7 1776/Georg Dertzbach, Magdalena
John Bennet, Catharina/Johannes b Apr 19 1776, bapt Jul 7 1776/John Mansfield, Marg. Wilcke
Thomas Walker, Phillis, Sale (Sally) b —, bapt Jul 7 1776/Thomas Hehs (Hayes?)
Johannes Kessler, Catharina/Margaretha b Dec 22 1775, bapt Jul 15 1776/ Margaretha Kessler
Johannes Engel, Susanna Barbara/Johannes b Jul 15 1776, bapt Jul 21 1776/ Johannes Flack, Apollonia
Henrich Fortaine, Anna Elisabeth/Johann b ---, bapt Jul 21 1776/Johan Christian Bord, Susanna Hanstein(?)
Frantz Winterroth, Susanna/Susanna b Apr 23 1776, bapt Jun 5 1776/Jacob Herman, Margaretha
Jacob Martin, Christiana/Johan Georg b May 2 1776, bapt Aug 1 1776/Jacob Hoffman, Barbara
Henrich Brunner, Catharina/Elisabetha b Jan 3 1776, bapt Aug 4 1776/Henrich Sinn, Elisabetha
Philip Sinn, Elisabetha/Henrich b Apr 7 1776, bapt Aug 4 1776/Henrich Brunner, Catharina
Peter Stümmel(?), Eva/Peter b Apr 16 1776, bapt Aug 4 1776/Parents
Matthias Rockwell, Barbara/Elisabetha b ---, bapt Aug 4 1776/John Mansfield, Elisabeth
Johannes Steiner, Catharina/Christian b Mar 22 1776, bapt Sep 1 1776/ Balthasar Götzendanner, Hannah
Adam Hellwich, Barbara/Elisabetha b Jul 7 1776, bapt Sep 1 1776/Daniel Mathes, Catharina
Jacob Hähn, Catharina/Johannes Jacob b —, bapt Sep 7 1776/Jacob Michel, Catharina
Jacob Michel, Catharina/Catharina b Aug 5 1776, bapt Sep 7 1776/Jacob Hähn, Catharina
Georg Nicol, Margaretha/Georg b -- bapt Sep 7 1776/Gabriel Thomas, Margaretha, single
Daniel Schultz, Eva Catharina/Susanna Margaretha b Apr 5 1776, bapt Sep 7 1776/Susanna Margaretha Thomasius
Peter Brunner, Jr., Sophia/Magdalena b Jun 30 1776, bapt Sep 21 1776/ Albertina Brunner, grandmother
Peter Engel, Anna Maria/Elisabetha b Jul 5 1776, bapt Sep 21 1776/Elisabetha Mertz
Michael Ballsell, Barbara/Margaretha b Jun 15 1776, bapt Sep 21 1776/ Johannes Huber & wf.
Georg Jantz, Catharina/Henrich b Jun 30 1776, bapt Sep 21 1776/Henrich Kuntz, Dorothea
Johannes Hauck, Catharina/Margaretha b May 1 1776, bapt Sep 21 1776/Adam Fischer, Margaretha
Johannes Kraneiss, Anna Maria/Maria Eva b Aug 24 1776, bapt Sep 21 1776/Eva Kraneis
Johannes Nicol, Philippina/Johannes b Sep 14 1776, bapt Nov 3 1776/Parents
Jacob Hausman & wf./Eva Catharina b Jun 14 1776, bapt Nov 3 1776/Parents

Baptisms of the Evangelical Reformed Church in Frederick, Maryland

Georg Thomas Schley, Catharina/Wilhelm b Oct 25 1776, bapt Nov 10 1776/Jacob Ballsell, Margaretha

Jacob Hoffman, Barbara/Jacob b Sep 16 1776, bapt Nov 10 1776/Jacob Weiss, Maria Anna

James Nealy, Mary/Elisabetha Nealy b Oct 30 1776, bapt Nov 8 1776/Peter Allbach & wf.

Lorentz Brenckel, Eva Margaretha/Johann Nicol b Oct 4 1776, bapt Dec 1 1776/ Nicolaus Brenckel, single

Jacob Jauler, Barbara/Magdalena b Sep 29 1776, bapt Dec 1 1776/Johannes Linck, Magdalena

Jacob Remsberger, Anna Elisabetha/Susanna b --, bapt Dec 26 1776/Elisabetha Brenckel

Daniel Stauffer, Christina/Daniel b Aug 13 1776, bapt Jan 27 1777/The Mother

Valentin Bantz, Maria Barbara/Susanna b ---, bapt Feb 16 1777/Conrad Schneider, Susanna

Jacob Pfautz, Margaretha/Maria Barbara b ---, bapt Feb 16 1777/Maria Barbara Bentzel

Christian Ostertag, Juliana/Abraham b Feb 1777, bapt Feb 24 1777/Parents

Adam Paul, Elisabetha/Johann Jacob b Oct 8 1775, bapt Feb 24 1777/Jacob Blessing, Anna Magdalena

Adam Paul, Elisabetha/Eva Magdalena b Feb 14 1777, bapt Feb 24 1777/Jacob Blessing & wf.

Peter Dentzenbach, Margaretha/Georg Adam b Feb 7 1777, bapt Mar 2 1777/Georg Adam Dentzenbach & Maria Magd., grandparents

Jacob Schnaudiel, Maria Barbara/Susanna Margaretha b Jul 12 (1776), bapt Mar 9 1777/Valentin Schwartz, Susanna

Henrich Meyer, Eva/Henrich b Aug 15 1776, bapt Mar 16 1777/Johan Witmer

Henrich Remsberger, Susanna/Johannes b Jan 20 1777, bapt Mar 16 1777/ Johannes Steiner & Catharina

Johannes Huber, Christina/Jacob b Feb 11 1777, bapt Mar 30 1777/Jacob Reser, Margaretha

Nicolaus Boos, Elisabeth/Philip b Feb 13 1777, bapt Mar 30 1777/Johan Philip Decker

Gottfried Gebhard, Maria Magdalena/Johannes b Dec 30 1776, bapt Mar 30 1777/ Daniel Mathes, Catharina

Wendel Werner, Catharina/Anna Margaretha b Jan 26 1777, bapt Mar 30 1777/ Margaret Dexer

Henry Hanson, Brigitta/John b Sep 30 1776, bapt Apr 25 1777/Parents

David Levy, Maria Barbara/Elisabeth b Nov 14 1776, bapt Apr 26 1777/Anna Margaretha, Thomas

Adam Bantz, Elisabeth/Catharina b Sep 5 1776, bapt Apr 26 1777/Barbara Hildebrand

Jacob Stehly, Anna Barbara/Charlotta b Jan 11 1777, bapt Apr 26 1777/ Charlotta Ley

Friedrich Kern, Sophia/Wilhelm b Dec 17 1776, bapt May 8 1777/Peter Adam, Maria

Jacob Ballsell, Anna Maria/Anna Maria b Jan 26 1776, bapt May 18 1777/ Catharina Hoffman

Balthasar Götzendanner, Anna/Anna Elisabetha b Mar 25 1777, bapt May 18 1777/Cath. Elisabeth Sheirer

Johan Peter, Christina/Joh. Peter b Aug 23 1776, bapt May 18 1777/Peter Lieblich, Susanna

Caspar Keller, Margaretha/Anna Margaretha b Jan 4 1777, bapt May 27 1777/ Peter Kassel, Maria Catharina
Martin Weber, Elisabeth/Johannes b Mar 20 1777, bapt May 27 1777/Michael Rey
Joseph Schnorr, Maria/Priscilla b Oct 31 1776, bapt May 27 1777/Joh. Kempel
Philip Jacob, Elisabetha/Catharina b Mar 18 1777, bapt May 27 1777/Catharina Ries
Joh. Gern, Margaretha/Catharina b Jun 15 1776, bapt May 27 1777/Parents
Jacob Springer, Elisabetha/Catharina b Oct 30 1776, bapt Jun 8 1777/ Catharina Masseter
Jacob Lies, Maria Dorothea/Henrich b Mar 19 1777/bapt Jun 8 1777/Valentin Breitenbach, Susanna
Jacob Metera, Rahel/Elisabetha b Jan 22 1777, bapt Jun 8 1777/Sibylla Reisner
Daniel Grimm, Christina/Catharina b Last Tuesd. Jan 1777, bapt Jun 8 1777/ Parents
Johann Bauman, Elisabetha/Maria Barbara b Apr 12 1776, bapt Jun 8 1777/Maria Barbara Bentz
Georg Gebhard, Barbara/Johannes b Feb 5 1777, bapt Jun 16 1777/Peter Gebhard, Eva
Daniel Hauert, Catharina/Georg b May 25 1777, cpat Jun 22 1777/Parents
Nicolaus Hauert, Catharina/Henrich b May 7 1777, bapt Jun 22 1777/Henrich Ziegler & wf.
Georg Valentin Adam, Magdalena/Georg b May -- 1777, bapt Jun 22 1777/Parents
Thomas Ogle, Sibylla/Elisabeth b Apr 29 1777, bapt Jun 22 1777/Peter Doffler, Elisabeth
Elias Remsberger, Catharina/Johann Georg b Apr 3 1777, bapt Jul 6 1777/Georg Remsberger, Elisabeth
Georg Remsberger, Maria Elisabeth/Barbara b May 17 1777, bapt Jul 6 1777/ Elias Remsberger, Catharina
Christian Weber, Catharina/Christian b Feb 8 1776, bapt Jul 6 1777/Parents
Henrich Weiss, Catharina/Catharina b Oct 29 1776, bapt Jul 15 1777/Peter Study, Catharina
Friedrich Schönholtz, Margaretha/Catharina b Jun 17 1777, bapt Aug 10 1777/ Catharina Holtz
Jacob Ballsel, Anna Maria/Catharina b Nov 16 1776, bapt Aug 10 1777/Georg Wüterich, Catharina
Georg Wüterich, Catharina/Jacob b Jul 7 1777, bapt Aug 10 1777/Jacob Ballsel, Anna Maria
Johann Jacob Pley, Anna Margaretha/Johan Thomas b Jul 20 1777, bapt Aug 31 1777/Thomas Schley, Sr.
Henrich Weinmueller (?), Magdalena/Johannes b Jul 11 1777, bapt Sep 7 1777/ Johannes Schenckmeyer & wf.
Michael Weber, Catharina/Maria Magdalena b Aug 2 1777, bapt Sep 20 1777/Geo. Adam Dertzenbach, Maria Magdalena
John Campbell, Jane/Andrew Shmit b May 26 1777, bapt Sep 20 1777/--
Joseph Jons (Jones), Maria/Catharina b Jul -- 1777, bapt Sep 20 1777/ Catharina Jantz
Jacob Stehly, Catharina/Johannes b Jul 18 1777, bapt Sep 20 1777/Parents
Jason Fresel, Comfort/Leard(?) Turner b Jul 22 1777, bapt Sep 24 1777/Parents
Jonathan Thomas, Anna/Anna b May 7 1777, bapt Sep 27 1777/Parents
Ezekiel Beatty, Christina/Barbara b Apr --- 1777, bapt Oct 3 1777/Thomas Cartwright, Barbara
Philip Bier, Eva Catharina/Philip b Jul 27 1777, bapt Sep 5 1777/Parents

Henrich Roth, Catharina/Elisabeth b Sep 1 1777, bapt Sep 5 1777/Dorothea Doffler

Georg Doffler, Margaretha/Georg b Oct 10 1777, bapt Nov 16 1777/Parents

Michael Ballsell, Barbara/Jacob b Sep 20 1777, bapt Nov 16 1777/Jacob Kendel, Anna Maria

Michael Nicol, Maria Catharina/Catharina b May 19 1777, bapt Nov 16 1777/Eva Schopper

Henrich Lederman, Margaretha/Margaretha b Oct 4 1777, bapt Nov 23 1777/ Margaretha Schönholtz

Samuel Jonston, Maria/Samuel b ---, bapt Nov 23 1777/Sarah Hegarty

James Wood, Cleofieha (Ceotieta?)/Priscilla b Apr 12 1777, bapt Nov 23 1777/ The Mother

Benedict Steiner, Anna Barbara/Elisabetha b May 7; bapt Oct 1 1777/Elisabeth Steiner, widow

Peter Hoffman, Maria/Jeremias b Sep 7 1777, bapt Nov 30 1777/Parents

Jeremias Meyer, Barbara/Johann Jeremias b Oct 11 1777, bapt Nov 30 1777/The Mother. The father died before the child was born.

Georg Hoffman, Margaretha/Margaretha b Oct 11 1777, bapt Dec 14 1777/ Mattheus Buquet, Anna Maria

Lorentz Bulget, Catharina Elisabeth/Elisabeth b Sep 3 1777, bapt Dec 25 1777/Parents

Wilhelm Walter, Juliana/Catharina b Dec 13 1777, bapt Jan 18 1778/Peter Krebell, Anna Elisabetha

John Adlum, Margaretha/Joseph b Dec -- 1777, bapt Jan 25 1778/Parents

John Adlum, Margaretha/Elisabetha b Dec -- 1777, bapt Jan 25 1778/Parents

Peter Borer, Magdalena/Barbara b Dec -- 1777, bapt Jan 25 1778/Joh. Schenckmeyer, Elisabetha

Adam Fischer, Anna Margaretha/Christina b Dec 14 1777, bapt Feb 15 1778/ Johannes Hauck & wf. Catharina

Christoff Meyer, Anna Margaretha/Anna Margaretha b Mar 5 1777, bapt Feb 15 1778/Adam Fischer, Anna Margaretha

Georg McDonald, Elisabeth/Joseph b ---, bapt Mar 19 1778/Parents

Christian Thomas, Susanna/Catharina b Nov 11 1777, bapt Mar 22 1778/Frantz Hoffman, Barbara

Jacob Rab, Barbara/Jacob b Oct 15 1777, bapt Mar 29 1778/Jacob Lies, Dorothea

Jacob Schüssler, Anna Maria/Jacob b May 1 1777, bapt Apr -- 1778/Parents

Friedrich Ludwig Henop, Maria/Philip Lucas b Apr 8 1778, bapt Apr 22 1778/ Parents

Michael Christ, Maria Elisabetha/Elisabetha b Dec 31 1777, bapt Apr 26 1778/ Philip Sinn, Elisabetha

Philip Sinn, Elisabetha/Elisabetha b Mar 13 1778, bapt Apr 26 1778/Michael Christ, Maria Elisabetha

Peter Adam, Anna Maria/Peter b Mar 3 1778, bapt Apr 26 1778/Parents

Johannes Bucher, Rosina/Johannes b Feb 18 1778, bapt Apr 27 1778/Parents

Johann Lucas Fleck, Barbara/Johann Lucas b Jan 17 1778, bapt May 17 1778/ Parents

Philip Schmid, Dorothea/Catharina b May 12 1778, bapt May 24 1778/Catharina Holtz

Johannes Huff, Maria/Daniel b Jun 18 1777, bapt May 25 1778/Parents

Joseph Doll, Charlotta/Georg b Apr 17 1778, bapt May 25 1778/Georg Schneider, Catharina

Joseph Stehly, Juliana/Johann Jacob b Mar 1778, bapt May 25 1778/Friedrich Kleis
Georg Peter Hergert, Magdalena/Maria Catharina b Sep 6 1777, bapt May 25 1778/Margaretha Thomas
Bernhard Ott, Anna Elisabetha/Johann Philip b Feb 27 1778, bapt May 28 1778/ Philip Preis, Susanna
Johannes Hoffman, Catharina/Johannes b Dec 6 1777, bapt Jun 3 1778/Parents
Michael Storm, Magdalena/Peter b May 5 1778, bapt Jun 7 1778/Peter Kassel, Anna Maria
Jacob Ballsel, Anna Maria/Georg b May 1 1778, bapt Jun 7 1778/Georg Wuterich, Catharina
Jacob Kendel, Anna Maria/Elisabetha b Feb 16 1778, bapt Jun 7 1778/Michael Reutmeyer, Elisabetha
Peter Becker, Anna Maria/Charlotta b Mar 3 1778, bapt Jun 7 1778/Charlotta Nicol
Peter Engels, Anna Maria/Johann Jacob b Feb 18 1778, bapt Jun 7 1778/Johann Jacob Schley, Anna Maria
Henrich Jäger, Susanna/Anna Elisabetha b Mar 16 1778, bapt Jun 7 1778/Anna Krämer
Samuel Gulty, Sarah/Anna Margaretha b Feb -- 1778, bapt Jun 7 1778/Anna Margr. Gulty, grandmother
Peter Schley, Elisabetha d in childbirth/Elisabetha b May 25 1778, bapt Jun 14 1778/Philippina Geisinger
Carl Sigrist, Apollonia/Johannes b Apr 24 1778, bapt Jun 14 1778/Jacob Weis, Maria Anna
Benjamin Stuart, Maria Stuart/Jardin b Aug 10 1777, bapt Jun 15 1778/---
Jacob Kern, Christina/Johannes b Mar 23 1778, bapt Jun 21 1778/Johannes Brunner, Charlotta
Johannes Kraneis, Anna Maria/Susanna b Jun 22 1778, bapt Jun 25 1778/Susanna Kraneis
Jacob Meyer, Lydia/Christoff b Apr 23 1778, bapt Jun 25 1778/Christoff Meyer, Anna Margaret
Frantz Winterroth, Susanna/Maria Magdalena b Jan 4 1778, bapt Jun 25 1778/ Maria Magdalena Lerch
Johannes Gebhard, Elisabeth/Jacob b May 25 1778, bapt Jun 25 1778/Parents
Johannes Delater, Sibylla/David b Jan 4 1778, bapt Jul 12 1778/Christian Weber, Catharina
James Marchal, Eleonora/Maria Anna b --, bapt Jul 17 1778/Kesia Beckwort
Mattheus Schaupp, Maria Barbara/Catharina b May 4 1778, bapt Jul 26 1778/Eva Schaupp
Simon Gebhard, Catharina/Henrich b --, bapt Jul 26 1778/Henrich Bruder, Leonora
Georg Heckman, Sophia/Margaretha b May 26 1778, bapt Aug 21 1778/Margaretha Ballsell, grandmother
Samuel Kubelming(?), Barbara/Joseph b --, bapt Aug 21 1778/Anna Cock
Christian Teubelbis, Maria Magdalena/Margaretha b Jul 18 1778, bapt Aug 30 1778/Margaretha Trisler
Henr. Rab, Sarah/Elisabetha b Mar 15 1778, bapt Sep 2 1778/Maria Barbara Rab
Andreas Kessler, Maria/Georg b Apr 21 1778, bapt Sep 6 1778/Georg Kessler
Stephan Brunner, Magdalena/Margaretha b Jun 28 1778, bapt Sep -- 1778/ Margaretha Schellman
Conrad Doll, Anna Maria/Georg b Aug -- 1778, bapt Sep 20 1778/Georg Käuffer

Baptisms of the Evangelical Reformed Church in Frederick, Maryland

Thomas Johns, Mary Ann/Mary Lis b Jul 27 1778, bapt Sep 20 1778/Parents
Jacob Mumma, Anna Margaretha/David b Aug -- 1778, bapt Sep 22 1778/Conrad Schreiber, Barbara
Caspar Füss, Anna Maria/Elisabetha b --1775, bapt Sep 28, 1778/Elisabetha Lewis
Edward Baeths, a Brit. soldier & Elisabeth/Edward b Sep 6 1778, bapt Sep 28 1778/Joseph Taylor, Molly Taylor
Thomas Fleming, Agnesia/Nancy b Aug 22 1778, bapt Oct 17 1778/Parents
Jacob Hähn, Catharina/Christina b Sep 3 1778, bapt Oct 17 1778/--
Jacob Schneider, Catharina/Maria Catharina b Sep 7 1778, bapt Oct 17 1778/Parents
Josua Wehler, Marily/Susanna b Aug 14 1778, bapt Oct 29 1778/Parents
Carl Delo, Catharina/Henrich Jacob b Aug 22 1778, bapt Nov 5 1778/Henrich Fuchs, Anna Eva
Michael Kern, Christina/Johannes b Feb 10 1778, bapt Nov 7 1778/Johannes Bauman, Rosina Bauman, his sister
Thomas Ballhaus, Elisabeth/Adam b Sep 25 1778, bapt Nov 27 1778/Georg Dertzbach, Magdalena, grandparents
Jacob Steiner, Maria/Daniel b Nov -- 1778, bapt Dec 13 1778/Philip Bier, Eva Catharina
Lorentz Brenckel, Eva/Catharina b Nov 29 1778, bapt Dec 27 1778/Conrad Roth, Barbara
Michael Nicol, Maria Catharina/Johann Henrich b Oct 8 1778, bapt Dec 30 1778/Parents
Caspar Keller, Anna Margaretha/Johann Daniel b Oct 27 1778, bapt Jan 1 1779/Daniel Kassel
Johannes Schley, Barbara/Eva Catharina b Sep 7 1778, bapt Jan 17 1779/Eva Catharina Bart
Henrich Kuhn, Christina/Elisabetha b Jan 15 1779, bapt Jan 18 1779/Elisabetha Magdalena Muller
Johannes Huber, Christina/Johannes b Dec 4 1778, bapt Jan 22 1779/Parents
Henrich Mayer, Margaretha/Margaretha b Dec 20 1778, bapt Feb 3 1779/Parents
Christoff Stoll, Philippina/Jacob b Aug 20 1778, bapt Feb 7 1779/Jacob Holtz, Catharina
Jacob Ballsel, Anna Maria/Jacob b Dec 27 1778 bapt Jan 29 1779/Parents
John Edwards, Maria Anna/Delilah b Jun 6 1775, bapt Feb 17 1779/The Mother
Thomas Bolhaus, Elisabeth/Adam b Dec 28 1778, bapt Dec -- 1778/Adam Dertzbach, Magdalena
Gabriel Thomas, Anna Margaretha/Georg Jacob b Aug 4 1778, bapt Feb 20 1779/Georg Jose, Barbara
Leonhard Engels, Catharina/Maria Catharina b Jan 22 1779, bapt Mar 7 1779/Peter Engels, Maria Catharina, grandparents
Peter Mantz, Catharina/Esra b Jan 10 1779, bapt Mar 14 1779/---
Lorentz Bulcher, Catharina/Daniel Dec 28 1778, bapt Mar 14 1779/Christoff Wölffly, Susanna
Johannes Hauck, Catharina/Anna Barbara b Sep 10 1778, bapt Mar 14 1779/Stephan Brunner, Barbara
Andreas Wolff, Elisabetha/Jacob b Nov 1 1778, bapt Mar 21 1779/Parents
Henrich Stehly, Catharina/Henrich Sep 6 1778, bapt Mar 21 1779/Parents
Johannes Zimmerman, Leonora/Catharina b Nov 12 1778, bapt Mar 21 1779/Catharina Brunner, widow

Johannes Zimmerman, Leonora/Elisabeth b Nov 12 1778, bapt Mar 21 1779/ Elisabeth Sinn
Jacob Maderi, Rahel/Johannes b Nov 3 1778, bapt Mar 21 1779/Johannes Brunner, Margaretha
Johannes Wittmer, Catharina/Jacob b Jan 15 1779, bapt Mar 21 1779/Jacob Holtz, Anna Barbara
Christian Thomas, Susanna/Wilhelm b Dec 19 1778, bapt Apr 4 1779/Gabriel Thomas, Jr., Anna Maria
Andreas Lars, Anna Maria/Jacob b Mar 13 1779, bapt Apr 4 1779/Jacob Weis, Maria
Philip Christ, Dorothea/Johannes b Oct 30 1778, bapt Apr 4 1779/Johannes Huber, Christina
John Trautman, Jr., Elisabeth Gral/Loth. (Lott?) b Nov 28 1778, bapt Apr 10 1779/Mary Gral
Jacob Jauler, Barbara/Elisabeth Margaretha b Mar -- 1779, bapt Apr 11 1779/ Friedrich Schönholtz, Margaretha
Friedrich Schönholtz, Margaretha/Philip Jacob b Mar 4 1779, bapt Apr 11 1779/Philip Jacob Scheed, Dorothea
Johannes Brunner, Charlotta/Anna Maria b Jan 1 1779, bapt Apr 11 1779/Anna Maria Thomas
Jacob Stehly, Anna Barbara/Anna Maria b Jan 17 1779, bapt Apr 11 1779/Peter Brunner, Anna Maria
Daniel Grimm, Christina/Daniel b Dec 3 1779, bapt May 6 1779/Parents
Gottfried Gebhard, Maria Magdalena/Georg b Apr 10 1779, bapt May 9 1779/Joh. Georg Hoffman, Margaretha
Jacob Remsberger, Anna Elisabetha/Johannes b Feb 16 1779, bapt May 9 1779/ Johannes Remsberg & wf.
Valentin Bantz & wf./Susanna b ---, bapt May 23 1779/Jacob Beringer, Barbara
Nicolaus Theis, Barbara/Anna Maria b Mar 21 1779, bapt May 23 1779/Maria Weiss
Devis Hauert, Maria/William b Feb 5 1779, bapt May 23 1779/Parents
Benedict Steiner, Anna Barbara/Magdalena b Feb 22 1779, bapt May 30 1779/ Anna Maria Thomas
Georg Fulcker, Catharina/Susanna b Mar 8 1779, bapt May 30 1779/Bernhard Ott, Anna Elisabetha
Balthasar Götzendanner, Anna/Balthasar b Apr 3 1779, bapt Jun 6 1779/ Benedict Steiner, Barbara
Bernhard Lingenfelder, Anna Barbara/Georg b Jan 12 1779, bapt Jun 6 1779/ Johannes Brunner, Anna Barbara
Robert Wood, Catharina/Catharina b Dec 11 1778, bapt Jun 7 1779/Parents
Friedrich Dern, Sophia/Esther b Mar 15 1779, bapt Jun 14 1779/Parents
Georg Gebhard, Barbara/Margaretha b Apr 8 1779, bapt Jun 17 1779/Georg Hoffman, Margaretha
Georg Gebhard, Barbara/Susanna b Apr 8 1778, bapt Jun 17 1779/Susanna Lieblich
Georg Wüterich, Catharina/Catharina b Feb 3 1779, bapt Jun 20 1779/Catharina Remsberger
Christian Weber, Catharina/Jacob b Jan 19 1778, bapt Jun 20 1779/Parents
Georg Allbach, Maria/Elisabetha b May 9 1779, bapt Jun -- 1779/Michael Obringer, Anna Margaretha
Thomas Gral, Elisabetha/Absalom b May 20 1779, bapt Jul 8 1779/Parents

Baptisms of the Evangelical Reformed Church in Frederick, Maryland

Elias Remsberger, Catharina/Johann Jacob b Mar 21 1779, bapt Jul 18 1779/ Jacob Schaeffer, Jr.

Joh. Henrich Weinmüller, Magdalena/Johann Henrich b Jun 7 1779, bapt Jul 18 1779/Philip Henrich Sinn, Elisabetha

Henry McClany, Martha/Margaretha b Mar -- 1779, bapt Jul 18 1779/Parents

Wilhelm Müller, Maria Eva/Maria Eva b Apr 16 1779, bapt Jul 18 1779/Conrad Roth, Maria Barbara

Johannes Peffer, Christina Magdalena/David b Feb 18 1779, bapt Aug 1 1779/ David Preuss, Sophia

Henrich Leonhard, Anna Christina/Daniel b Mar 13 1779, bapt Aug 1 1779/ Daniel Kassel, Jr.

Peter Dertzbach, Margaretha/Elisabetha b Jun 7 1779, bapt Aug 15 1779/ Elisabetha Bolhaus

Jacob Schley, Margaretha/Elisabetha b Jul 11, bapt Aug 15 1779/Maria Barbara Meyer

Friedrich Schidenhelm, Barbara/Elisabetha b Jun 30 1779, bapt Aug 22 1779/ Elisabetha Derr(?)

Daniel Stauffer, Christina/Catharina b Jun -- 1779, bapt Aug 22 1779/ Catharina Rohr

Valentin Schwartz, Susanna/Johan Georg b Jul 9 1779, bapt Aug 22 1779/ Johannes Schenckmeyer, Elisabetha

Peter Ehly, Elisabeth/Johannes b May 7 1779, bapt Sep 5 1779/Johannes Häffner

Johannes Buquet, Elisabeth/Georg b --, bapt Oct 3 1779/Johann Georg Buquet

Samuel Linton(?), Margery/Maria b Jan 18 1779, bapt Oct 3 1779/Parents

Thomas Ogle, Sibylla/Johannes Joseph b Jul -- 1779, bapt Oct 3 1779/Thomas Schley, Sr. & the mother

Jeremiah Stuart, Priscilla/John b Sep 1 1779, bapt Oct 10 1779/Parents

Jacob Thomas, Susanna/Magdalena b Aug -- 1779, bapt Oct 11 1779/Parents

Henrich Roth, Anna Catharina/Henrich b Jul 3 1779, bapt Oct 17 1779/Henrich Ziegler, Magdalena Maria

Jeremiah Holtz(?), Elisa/Rael b Apr 11 1779, bapt Nov 2 1779/Parents

Johan Georg Winterroth, Susanna/Johan Georg b Aug 4 1779, bapt Nov 7 1779/ Anna Maria Lerick

Michael Weber, Catharina/Philip b Sep 18 1779, bapt Nov 14 1779/Philip Schmidt, Magdalena

Philip Preis, Susanna/Philip b Oct 16 1779, bapt Nov 17 1779/Johannes Preis, Maria Elisabeth

Daniel Hauert, Catharina/Elisabeth b —, bapt Dec 4 1779/Nicolaus Hauert, Catharina

Balthasar Dotterer, Elisabetha/Maria Barbara b Nov 23 1779, bapt Dec 25 1779/Carl Keltero, Catharina

Johann Jacob Schley, Anna Maria/Maria Margaretha b Nov 9 1779, bapt Jan 1 1780/Johannes Schellman, Maria Margaretha

Johann Hoffman, Marina/Maria b Nov 10 1779, bapt Jan 1 1780/Abraham Gibs, Maria

Caspar Missel, Elisabeth/Maria b Dec 1 1779, bapt Jan 17 1780/Elisabeth Geblinger

Jacob Hauser, Anna Margaretha/Maria Barbara b Jan 12 1780, bapt Feb 20 1780/ Maria Barbara Bentz

Jacob Kern, Christina/Charlotta b Aug 26 1779, bapt Mar 5 1780/Parents

Samuel Fleming, Barbara/Elly b Feb 23 1780, bapt Mar 12 1780/Samuel Fleming, Sr.
Benjamin Stuart, Maria/Mary b Dec 9 1779, bapt Mar 22, 1780/Parents
same Parents/Sarah b Mar 22 1780, bapt Mar 22 1780/Parents
Jacob Thomas, Susanna/Elisabetha b Jan 23 1780, bapt Mar 25 1780/Christian Caspar, Elisabetha
Peter Bergman, Catharina/Elisabeth b Jan 13 1780, bapt Mar 25 1780/Elisabeth Sigrist
Edward Salmon, Elisabeth/Friedrich b Nov 20 1779, bapt Mar 25 1780/Friedrich Becker, Dorothea
Jacob Leis, Maria/Maria b Oct 11 1779, bapt Mar 25 1780/Jacob Weiss, Maria
Caspar Gultig, Juliana/Susanna b Dec 5 1779, bapt Mar 25 1780/Elisabeth Sommer
Joseph Doll, Charlotta/Jacob b Feb 12 1780, bapt Apr 2 1780/Peter Brunner, Anna Maria
Peter Gebhard, Eva Margaret/Rosina Barbara b Feb 15 1780, bapt Apr 2 1780/ Jacob Weiss, Maria
Peter Bohrer, Maria Magdalena/Peter b Mar 9 1780, bapt May 14 1780/Johannes Schenckmeyer, Elisabetha
Charles King, Mary/Sarah b Feb 16 1780, bapt May 14 1780/Henry Brother, Elisabeth
Henrich Jaeger, Susanna. The father d. Oct 7 1779/Henrich b Feb 10 1780, bapt May 14 1780/The Mother
Peter Hans Freund, Margaretha/Johann Jacob b Aug -- 1779, bapt May 14 1780/ Jacob Ballsel, Anna Maria
David Delater, Catharina/Susanna b Feb 13 1780, bapt May 14 1780/Susanna Brunner
illegible, Catharina/Sarah b Jan 19 1780, bapt May 20 1780/illegible
Michael Christ, Maria Elisabetha/Catharina b Feb -- 1780, bapt Jun 4 1780/ Valentin Krieger, Christina
Peter Jons (Johns), Catharine/Johann Georg b Dec 22 1779, bapt Jun 5 1780/ Joh. Georg Rheiner, Apollonia
Peter Stümmel, Eva/Eva b Dec 2 1779, bapt Jun 5 1780/Parents
Jacob Jauler, Barbara/Eleonora b Apr 20 1780, bapt Jun 11 1780/Leonora Bucher
Peter Matthes, Philippina/Catharina b Apr 23 1780, bapt Jun 11 1780/ Margaretha Mathes
Simon Rapp, Sarah/Maria Anna b Jan 17 1780, bapt Jun 11 1780/Maria Anna Keller
Martin Weisshard, Catharine/Barbara b May — 1780, bapt Jun 11 1780/Jacob Christ, Catharina
Jacob Schneider, Maria Catharina/Elisabetha b May 5 1780, bapt Jun 11 1780/ Anna Margaretha Schneider, grandmother
Philip Jacob Schaed, Dorothea/Elisabetha b May 27 1780, bapt Jun 12 1780/ Anna Maria Gibs
Michael Ballsel, Barbara/Michael b Mar 15 1780, bapt Jun 24 1780/Parents
Johannes Kraneis, Anna Maria/Catharina b Jun 9 1780, bapt Jul 9 1780/ Catharina Fey
Stephan Brunner, Barbara/Catharina b Nov 27 1779, bapt Jul 23 1780/Johann Hauck, Catharina
Christoff Meyer, Anna Margaretha/Georg Friedrich b Jul 16 1780, bapt Aug 5 1780/Friedr. L. Henop & Maria, wf.

Baptisms of the Evangelical Reformed Church in Frederick, Maryland

Wilhelm Wood, Maria Barbara/Wilhelm b Oct 15 1779, bapt Aug 5 1780/Anna Margaretha Meyer

Wilhelm Rich, Susanna Haas/Wilhelm b Nov -- 1779, bapt Aug 17 1780/--

Henrich Kempf, Anna Maria Magdalena. She was buried today. Friedrich b Aug 7 1780, bapt Aug 19 1780/Friedrich Kempf, Jr.

Adam Fischer, Margaretha/Maria Barbara b Dec 15 1779, bapt Aug 19 1780/L Ludwig Ritter, Maria Barbara

Andreas Low, Anna Maria/Anna Maria b Aug 15 1780, bapt Sep 10 1780/Georg Brenckel, Catharina

Charles Siegrist, Elisabeth/Jacob b Aug 15 1780, bapt Sep 17 1780/Jacob Bentz, Elisabetha

Michael Nicol, Catharina/Anna Maria b Jul 1 1780, bapt Sep 17 1780/Anna Maria Schopper

Christian Schopper, Margaretha/Johannes b Jul 15 1780, bapt Sep 17 1780/Joh. Levor

Georg Krieger, Catharina/Catharina b Jul 12 1780, bapt Sep 17 1780/Johannes Brunner, Barbara

Theobald Miller, Catharina/Anna Maria b Aug -- 1780, bapt Sep -- 1780/Jacob Klein, Anna Maria

Johannes Brunner, Jr., Susanna/Jacob b Jul 12 1780, bapt Oct 10 1780/Jacob Kast, Anna Maria

Henrich Remsberger, Susanna/Henrich b Aug 2 1780, bapt Oct 15 1780/Henrich Bruder, Leonora

Henrich Schober, Jr., Rosina/Maria b Aug 25 1780, bapt Oct 12 1780/Anna Maria Schober

Georg Wüterich, Catharina/Johannes b May 11 1780, bapt Nov 29 1780/Johannes Remsberger, Junior

Stephan Brunner, Magdalena/Maria Magdalena b Sep 20 1780, bapt Dec 4 1780/ Albertina Brunner, grandmother

Friedrich Ludwig Henop, Maria/Ludwig Weltner b Oct 6 1780, bapt Dec 4 1780/ Parents

Jacob Kendel, Anna Maria/Maria Esther b Aug 1 1780, bapt Dec 17 1780/ Johannes Gompere, Maria Esther

Casper Krämer, Rosina/Catharina b Nov 7 1780, bapt Dec 20 1780/Samuel Krämer, Catharina, grandparents

Peter Mans, Catharina/Maria b Oct 18 1780, bapt Dec 24 1780/The Mother & the grandparents

Georg Hoffman, Margaretha/Johannes b Sep 8 1780, bapt Dec 24 1780/The Mother & Valentin Rebschuld

Peter Bugne, Maria/Georg b May 9 1780, bapt Dec 25 1780/Geo. Valentin Adam, Maria

Christian Weber, Catharina/Johannes b Sep 10 1780, bapt Jan 7 1781/Parents

Jacob Mayer, Lydia/Anna Maria b Oct 5 1780, bapt Jan 7 1781/Parents

Jacob Klein, Anna Maria/Maria Elisabetha b Nov 13 1780, bapt Jan 7 1781/ Maria Apollonia Haffner

Friedrich Schonholtz, Margaretha/Georg Peter b Dec 13 1780, bapt Jan 13 1781/Conrad Foltz, Margaretha

Jacob Madery, Rahel/Anna Magdalena b Oct 1, bapt Jan 21 1781/Anna Maria Schober

William Warrant, Eleonora, British prisoners/Simon b Jan 1 1781, bapt Jan 21 1781/Jacob Hauser, Margaretha

Baptisms of the Evangelical Reformed Church in Frederick, Maryland

Leonhard Lantz, Barbara/Christian b Dec 23 1780, bapt Feb 11 1781/Peter Engel, Maria Catharina
Johannes Gebhard, Elisabetha/Elisabetha b Nov 14 1780, bapt Feb 11 1781/ Parents
Michael Meyer, Eva Margaretha/Michael b Dec 11 1780, bapt Feb 16 1781/ Christian Weber, Catharina
Jacob Christian, Catharina/Johann Jacob b Jul 16 1780, bapt Feb 18 1781, bapt Jacob Rohr, Catharina
Jacob Rohr, Catharina/Rosina b Dec 26 1780, bapt Feb 18 1781/Matheus Buguet, Anna Maria
Jacob Schüssler, Anna Maria/Catharina b Aug 12 1780, bapt Mar 4 1781/Parents
Peter Spery, Elisabetha/Leonora b Mar 9 1781, bapt Mar 31 1781/Parents
Johannes Gompere, Esther/Margaretha b Jan 7 1781, bapt Apr 1 1781/Parents
---/Maria Nellie Zinn bapt Apr 1 1781, aged 17 years/--
Conrad Lonker(?), Magdalena/Conrad b Feb 14 1781, bapt Apr 14 1781/Conrad Foltz, Margaretha
Abraham Herget, Maria/Catharina b --, bapt Apr -- 1781/Peter Herget, Magdalena
Caspar Keller, Anna Margaretha/Samuel b Feb 5 1781, bapt Apr 15 1781/Daniel Ohl, Magdalena
Georg Reinhard, Salome/Georg Martin b Mar 18 1781, bapt Apr 18 1781/Georg Martin Eberhard & Susanna Foltz
Thomas Ogle, Sibylla/Joseph b Feb 7 1781, bapt Apr 22 1781/Parents
Christian Thomas, Susanna/Elisabeth b Oct 23 1780, bapt Apr 22 1781/Henrich Bär, Elisabetha
Johannes Zimmerman, Leonora/Johannes b Jan 30 1781, bapt May 3 1781/Jacob Holtz, Catharina, grandparents
Peter Doffler, Margaretha/Elisabeth b Feb 27 1781, bapt May 3 1781/Michael Christ, Elisabetha
Elias Brunner, Maria Elisabetha/Anna Maria b Apr 8 1781, bapt May 27 1781/ Johannes Brunner, Charlotta
Jacob Hähn, Catharina/Jacob b Mar 9 1781, bapt May 27 1781/Parents
Henrich Leonhard, Christina/Adam b Dec 13 1780, bapt Jun 3 1781/Rosina Morgenstern
Georg Jacob Oster, Elisabetha/Eva Catharina b May 18 1781, bapt Jun 3 1781/ Georg Weisshaar, Maria Apollonia
Henrich Lederman, Margaretha/Anna Maria b Apr 5 1781, bapt Jun 3 1781/Maria Anna Balsel, grandmother
Lucas Fleck, Barbara/Adam b Dec 5 1780, bapt Jun -- 1781/Adam Wolff
Jacob Kast, Anna Maria/Catharina b Apr 12 1781, bapt Jun -- 1781/Jacob Götzedanner, Catharina
Jacob Behringer, Barbara/Catharina b May 17 1781, bapt Jun -- 1781/Catharina Remsberger
Jacob Crepile, Martha/Elisabetha b Feb 19 1781, bapt Jun -- 1781/Parents
Johannes Barkley, Susanna/Johan Philip b Oct 1 1780, bapt Jun 24 1781/Philip Klingenstein, Dorothea
Johannes Wittmer, Catharina/Johannes b Jun 8 1781, bapt Aug 5 1781/Joh. Kauffman & wf.
Georg Gebhard, Barbara/Elisabeth b Jul 11 1781, bapt Aug 5 1781/Susanna Lieblich
Jacob Traut, Elisabetha/Jacob b Jun 17 1781, bapt Jun 26 1781/Jacob Klein, Anna Maria

Baptisms of the Evangelical Reformed Church in Frederick, Maryland

Peter Adam, Anna Maria/Eva Margaretha b Jul 23 1781, bapt Aug 19 1781/ Valentin Adam, Eva Margaretha

Conrad Jung, Margaretha/Charlotta b Jul 23 1781, bapt Sep 2 1781/Henrich Beydeman, Charlotta

Thomas Flemming, Agnes/Eleonora b May 27 1781, bapt Sep 2 1781/Parents

Jacob Stehly, Barbara/Barbara b Jan 21 1781, bapt Sep 8 1781/Joseph Doll, Charlotta

Benedict Steiner, Anna Barbara/Henrich b Dec 10 1780, bapt Sep 12 1781/ Parents

James Clark, Jane/William b Aug 22 1780, bapt Sep 16 1781/---

Andreas Wolff, Elisabetha/Catharina b Aug 3 1780, bapt Sep 17 1781/Johannes Huber, Christina

Johann Georg Naeff, Maria Elisabetha/Elisabetha Margaretha b Jul 5 1781, bapt Sep 18 1781/Elisabetha Fischer

The father had been condemned to death for treason, but the sentence was commuted. Tomorrow he will be taken aboard a French battle ship.

Peter Schaub, Rebecca/Christian b Mar 26 1781, bapt Sep 25 1781/Christian Weber, Catharina

Elias Schumacher, Sophia/Anna Maria b Aug 21 1781, bapt Sep 23 1781/Anna Maria Ballsel

Henry Busy, Anna Maria/Benjamin Thoman b Jan 30 1781, bapt Sep 23 1781/ Parents

Georg Frantz Winterroth, Susanna/Henrich b Mar 10 1781, bapt Sep 23 1781/ Parents

Jacob Roths, Anna/Hezekiah b Jan 6 1781, bapt Sep 23 1781/Parents

Georg Thomas Schley, Catharina/Anna b --- bapt Oct 14 1781/Johann Jacob Schley, Anna Maria

Jacob Ballsel, Anna Maria/Thomas b Jan 11 1781, bapt Oct 14 1781/Thomas Schley, Sr., Margaretha

Georg Jantz, Catharina/Elisabetha b Jul 22 1781, bapt Oct 14 1781/Parents

Samuel Coffin, Catharina/Elisabetha b Aug 18 1781, bapt Oct 14 1781/ Elisabetha Grebil

Philip Preis, Susanna/Catharina b Aug 5 1781, bapt Oct 14 1781/Clara Lehmann

Jacob Remsberger, Anna Elisabeth/Henrich b Jul 2 1781, bapt Oct 28 1781/ Henrich Remsberger, Susanna

Georg Götzendanner, Elisabetha/Catharina b Sep 26 1781, bapt Nov 11 1781/ Sebastian Derr, Catharina

Lorentz Brunckel, Eva/Peter b Aug 1 1781, bapt Dec 6 1781/Johannes Compere, Esther

Jacob Jauler, Barbara/Michael b Oct 9 1781, bapt Dec 16 1781/Michael Storm, Magdalena

Philip Rohr, Catharina/Elisabetha b Nov 25 1781, bapt Jan 13 1782/Johannes Kuntz, Catharina

Gotthard Tresel, Catharina/Elisabetha b Nov -- 1781, bapt Feb 3 1782/Henrich Hildebrand, Elisabetha

Johann Jacob Schley, Anna Maria/Anna Maria b Dec 7 1781, bapt Feb 17 1782/ Johannes Schellman, Margaretha

Adam Bantz, Elisabeth/Adam b Oct 25 1781, bapt Feb 17 1782/Adam Fischer, Margaretha

Henrich Kraneis, Barbara/Maria Philippina b Jan 17 1782, bapt Feb 17 1782/ Philip Schmidt, Maria

Andrew Low, Anna Maria/Johannes b Jan 7 1782, bapt Mar 3 1782/Johannes Beltz, Catharina

Henrich Kempff, Anna Margaretha/Johannes b Jan 5 1781, bapt Mar 3 1782/ Johannes Kempff

Michael Weber, Catharina/Johann Valentin b Dec 15 1781, bapt Mar 24 1782/ Valentin Schreiner, Elisabetha

Balthasar Götzendanner, Anna/Gabriel b Dec 27 1781, bapt Mar 26 1782/ Parents

Johannes Kraneis, Anna Maria/Georg b Mar 6 1782, bapt Mar 31 1782/Parents

Valentin Bantz, Susanna/Georg Henrich b Jan 31 1782, bapt Mar 31 1782/ Henrich Lambrecht, Margaretha

Daniel Hauert, Catharina/Christina b Nov 7 1781, bapt Apr 14 1782/Nicolaus Hauert & wf.

Philip Christ, Dorothea/Anna Maria b Jul 22 1781, bapt Apr 14 1782/Jacob Froschauer, Anna Maria

Simon Rapp, Sarah/Catharina b Nov 23 1781, bapt Apr 21 1782/Johannes Wittmer, Catharina

Friedrich Schidenhelm, Barbara/Georg b Jan 10 1782, bapt Apr 21 1782/Georg Brunckel, Catharina

Johannes Steiner, Catharina/Maria Magdalena b Sep 24 1780, bapt Apr 25 1782/ The Mother

Joseph Doll, Charlotta/Catharina b Mar 1 1782, bapt Apr 28 1782/Jacob Michael, Catharina

Caspar Gütig, Juliana/Magdalena b Feb 2 1782, bapt May 18 1782/Peter Study, Catharina

Joh. Peter Price, Catharina/Anna Maria b Apr 18 1782, bapt May 18 1782/Georg Fingrich, Elisabeth

Philip Jacob Schaed, Dorothea/Philip Jacob b Mar 16 1782, bapt May 18 1782/ Jacob Ballsel, Anna Maria

Jacob Schley, Sr., Margaretha/Jacob b Mar 28 1782, bapt Jun 2 1782/Johann Jacob Schley, Maria

Jacob Thomas, Susanna/Georg b Mar 12 1782, bapt Jun 2 1782/Georg Thomas

Michael Stocker, Maria/Georg b --, bapt Jun 2 1782/Georg Bentz

Johannes Huber, Christina/Peter b May 20 1782, bapt Jun 23 1782/Lorentz Brenckel, Eva

Johann Wacker, Charlotta/Johannes b Jan 10 1782, bapt Jun 23/Lorentz Heim, Christina

same parents/Anna Maria b Jan 10 1782, bapt Jun 23 1782/David Heim, Maria Margaretha

Thomas Kenningham, Sarah/Jeanette b Oct 17 1781, bapt Jul 8 1782/Parents
These are people who are moving to Carolina.

Henrich Weinmüller, Magdalena/Anna Maria b Apr 16 1782, bapt Jul 21 1782/ Parents

Georg Mohn, Catharina/Charlotta b May 26 1782, bapt Aug 5 1782/Johannes Brunner, Charlotta

Jacob Schneider, Catharina/Maria Magdalena b Jun 3 1782, bapt Aug 5 1782/ Maria Magd. Schneider

Edward Salmon, Elisabetha/Wilhelm b Jul 30 1782, bapt Aug 18 1782/Balthasar Heck, Eva Margaretha

Nicolaus Theis, Barbara/Henrich b ---, bapt Aug 18 1782/Henrich Berg, Margaretha

Baptisms of the Evangelical Reformed Church in Frederick, Maryland

Johannes Koch, Juliana/Catharina Elisabetha b Jun 18 1782, bapt Aug 29 1782/ Philip Klingenstein, Dorothea Elisabetha
David Eli, Susanna/Elisabetha b Aug -- 1782, bapt Sep 1 1782/Christian Weber, Catharina
Philip Jacob, Elisabetha/Catharina Barbara b Aug 29 1781, bapt Sep 1 1782/ Wilhelm Lies, Catharina
Johannes Compere, Esther/Elisabetha b Jun 3 1782, bapt Sep 8 1782/Elisabetha Compere
Daniel Stauffer, Christina/Johann Jacob b May 25 1781, bapt Jun 2 1782/Jacob Krebs, Margaretha
Elias Brunner, Jr., Maria Elisabetha/Anna Catharina b Aug 5 1782, bapt Sep 27 1782/Parents
Jacob Hohl, Magdalena/Elisabetha b Sep 13 1782, bapt Sep 29 1782/Henrich Baer, Elisabetha
Johannes Reidenauer, Elisabeth/Johann Jacob b Jul 23 1782, bapt Sep 29 1782/ Jacob Holtz, Jr., Barbara
Philip Grünewald, Maria/Catharina b Jul 2 1782, bapt Oct 14 1782/Parents
Johannes Hauck, Catharina/Catharina b Aug 30 1782, bapt Oct 20 1782/ Catharina Thomas
Johannes Bucher, Rosina/Johannes b Sep 14 1782, bapt Oct 27 1782/Jacob Derr
Robert Gerret, Jeane/William b Jan 26 1771; Robert b Aug 4 1779; Third child b Jun 11 1781 - bapt Nov 5 1782/The mother, the father is an Anabaptist.
Peter Mathes, Philippa/Anna Margaretha b Sep 7 1782, bapt Nov 18 1782/John Herman, Catharina
Lorentz Heim, Catharina/Georg b Nov 1 1782, bapt Dec 25 1782/Georg Schnerzel, Barbara
George Noble Weeler, Catharine/Warren b Nov 20 1782, bapt Jan 5 1783/The Mother
Jacob Füster, Anna Maria/Catharina b Dec 26 1782, bapt Jan 26 1783/Parents
Jacob Traut, Elisabetha/Johann Henrich b Jan 14 1783, bapt Jan 27 1783/ Friedrich Heffner, Anna Maria
Andreas Schily, Apollonia/Johann Friedrich b Nov 2 1782, bapt Jan 27 1783/ Friedr. Heffner, Anna Maria
Thomas Bolhaus, Elisabetha/Johannes b Jan 11 1783, bapt Jan 29 1783/Johannes Dertzenbach
Amos Hague, Mary/Mary Ann b Dec 10 1782, bapt Feb 13 1783/The Mother
Leonhard Lantz, Catharina/Margaretha b Nov 15 1782, bapt Mar 2 1783/Parents
Peter Dertzenbach, Margaretha/Lorentz b Nov -- 1782, bapt Mar 17 1783/ Parents
John Wood, Martha/Susanna b Jan 6 1783, bapt Mar 17 1783/Parents
Arnold Hardy, Barbara/Jonathan b Jan 23 1783, bapt Mar 19 1783/Parents
Friedrich Ludwig Henop, Maria/Daniel b Dec 1 1782, bapt --/--
Jacob Klein, Maria/Ludwig b Mar 15 1783, bapt Mar 18 1783/Ludwig Klein & wf.
Stephan Brunner, Magdalena/Elisabetha b Jan 8 1783, bapt Mar 23 1783/Henrich Baer, Elisabetha
Johann Jacob Rohr, Catharina/Johann Jacob b Feb 20 1783, bapt Mar 23 1783/ Rudolph Rohr
Bernhard Lingenfelder, Barbara/Daniel b Nov 19 1782, bapt Apr 1 1783/Parents
Jacob Wüst, Eva Catharina/Jacob b Jan 17 1783, bapt Mar 24 1783/Parents
Michael Nicol, Catharina/Christina b Nov 23 1782, bapt Apr 13 1783/Johannes Huber, Christina

Peter Engel, Anna Margaretha/Peter b Jan 12 1782, bapt Apr 17 1783/Georg Schnertzel, Barbara
Simon Stöckel, Susanna/Anna Maria bapt Apr 17 1783, about 18 years/--
Simon Stöckel, Susanna/Susanna bapt Apr 17 1783, about 16 years/--
Lorentz Fulger, Catharina/Johannes b Jan 19 1783, bapt Apr 20 1783/Parents
George Sigfried, Elisabetha/Carl b Jan 11 1783, bapt Apr 20 1783/Johannes Federkeil, Catharina
Daniel Adam, Christina/Magdalena b Jan 4 1781, bapt Apr 25 1783/Claudina Richard
Johannes Brunner, Charlotta/Catharina b Nov 30 1782, bapt May 18 1783/ Valentin Petter, Catharina
Jeremiah Stewart, Priscilla/Margaret b Apr 5 1783, bapt May 14 1783/--
Friedrich Schönholtz, Margaretha/Margaretha b Apr 12 1783, bapt May 23 1783/ Conrad Becker, Magdalena
Johannes Gebhard, Elisabetha/Margaretha b Dec 9 1782, bapt May 23 1783/ Parents
Jacob Stehly, Barbara/Jacob b Feb 23 1783, bapt May 23 1783/Jacob Schley, Catharina
Michael Storm, Magdalena/Margaretha b Apr 13 1783, bapt Jun 8 1783/ Margaretha Kessler
Michael Schumacher, Jr., Eva Christina/Maria Catharina b May 17 1783, bapt Jun 8 1783/Maria Dorothea Schumacher
Elias Schumacher, Sophia/Friedrich b May 14 1783, bapt Jun 8 1783/Friedrich Schumacher
Johannes Delater, Sibylla/Johann Adam b Oct 2 1782, bapt Jun 8 1783/Adam Keller, Catharina Margaretha
Johannes Delater, Sibylla/Johann Jacob b Oct 2 1782, bapt Jun 8 1783/ Johannes Brunner, Charlotta
James Morris, Mary/Kisia b Jan 28 1780, bapt Jun 8 1783/--
James Morris, Mary/Nancy b Jun 26 1782, bapt Jun 8 1783/--
Michael Bankhoffer, Cecilia/Sarah b ---, bapt Jun 14 1783/Parents
Abraham Dillo, Susanna/Magdalena b May 30 1783, bapt Jun 14 1783/Magdalena Dertzenbach
George Hauer, Elisabeth/Nicolaus b Feb 19 1783, bapt Jun 15 1783/Nicolaus Hauer, Catharina
Jacob Wiand, Catharina/Catharina b Mar 10 1783, bapt Jun 18 1783/Jacob Hohl, Magdalena
Johannes Bugne, Barbara/Jacob b Apr 13 1783, bapt Jun 18 1783/The Mother
Christoff Meyer, Anna Margaretha/Charlotta b Jan 13 1783, bapt Jul 6 1783/ Johannes Kraneis, Anna Maria
Jacob Christ, Catharina/Philip b May 12 1783, bapt Jul 12 1783/Philip Christ, Dorothea
Henrich Müller, Elisabeth/Susanna b Jan 1 1783, bapt Jul 12 1783/Parents
Gottfried Gebhard, Magdalena/Catharina b Jun 12 1783, bapt Jul 14 1783/ Daniel Mathes, Catharina
Georg Reinhard, Salome/Jacob b Jan 5 1783, bapt Jul 20 1783/Jacob Hauck, Sr.
Henrich Stehly, Catharina/Daniel b Feb 3 1783, bapt Jul 20 1783/Christoff Stoll, Philippina
Michael Kirschner, Maria Anna/Catharina b Jun 3 1783, bapt Aug 3 1783/ Susanna Bagelt
Henrich Baer, Elisabeth/Jacob b May 24 1783, bapt Aug 10 1783/Jacob Schellman, Catharina

Baptisms of the Evangelical Reformed Church in Frederick, Maryland

Peter Sinn, Gertraut/Anna Maria b Mar 19 1783, bapt Aug 10 1783/Anna Elisabetha Dexer, grandmother

Georg Wüterich, Catharina/Elisabetha b May 24 1783, bapt Aug 24 1783/Anna Catharina Remsberger

Samuel Coffin, Catharine/John b Jul 9 1783, bapt Aug 24 1783/Parents

Benedict Steiner, Barbara/Anna Barbara b Feb 20 1783, bapt Aug 24 1783/Anna Götzendanner

Jacob Lies, Maria/Johannes b Jun 16 1783, bapt Sep 7 1783/Johannes Krebs

Georg Valentin Adam, Maria/Elisabetha b Aug 14 1783, bapt Sep 7 1783/ Elisabeth Hauert

Peter Gebhard, Eva Margaretha/Johannes b Sep 5 1783, bapt Oct 19 1783/Georg Hoffman, Jr.

Henry McClary, Martha/Sarah b Jan 3 1783, bapt Oct 26 1783/---

Johannes Wittmer, Catharina/Catharina b Sep 10 1783, bapt Oct 26 1783/David Schultz, Eva

Andrew Low, Anna Maria/Catharina b Sep 6 1783, bapt Nov 9 1783/John Beltz, Catharina

Johannes Rohr, Elisabetha/ Johann Jacob b Oct 13 1783, bapt Nov 18 1783/ Jacob Christ & wf. Anna Cath.

Nicolaus Paul, Elisabetha/ Michael b Apr 30, 1783, bapt Nov 23 1783/Michael Nuss, Elisabetha

Wilhelm Baehr, Elisabetha/Georg b ---, bapt Nov 23 1783/Parents

John Ballser, Elisabetha/Elisabetha b Jun 1 1783, bapt Nov 23 1783/Parents

Michael Christ, Maria Elisabetha/Margaretha b Aug 1 1783, bapt Nov 23 1783/ Peter Doffler, Margaretha

Philip Preis, Susanna/Susanna b Aug 17 1783, bapt Nov 23 1783/Bernhard Ott, Elisa

Jacob Kendel, Anna Maria/Catharina b Nov 1 1782, bapt Nov 30 1783/Catharina Bayer

Jacob Remsberger, Anna/Johann Jacob b Jul 31 1783, bapt Dec 11 1783/Jacob Ballsell, Anna Maria

Henrich Kemp, Anna Margaretha/Maria Cathrina b Oct 30 1783, bapt Dec 11 1783/Catharina Meyer

Jacob Martin, Elisabetha/Charlotta b Oct 27 1783, bapt Jan 18 1784/Charlotta Bucher

Johannes Kramer, Anna Maria/Johann Jacob b Jan 12 1784, bapt Feb 15 1784/ Parents

Andreas Kessler, Anna Maria/Maria Barbara b 1783, bapt Feb 19 1784/Maria Barbara, ---

Johannes Schäffer, Elisabetha/Catharina b ---, bapt Feb 20 1784/Rosina Schäffer

Joh. Ludwig Reling, Margaretha/Jacob b --, bapt Feb 29 1784/Jacob Brunner

Jacob Schussler, Anna Maria/Catharina b May 8 1783, bapt Mar 5 1784/Parents

Daniel Hauert, Catharina/Susanna b Dec 16 1783, bapt Mar 7 1784/Nicolaus Hauert, Catharina

Joseph Stehly, Juliana/Georg b Oct 12 1783, bapt Mar 25 1784/Georg Schaeffer

Daniel Oehl, Magdalena/Maria Magdalena b Sep 16 1783, bapt Apr 10 1784/Simon Schnock, Charlotta

Jacob Schäffer, Elisabetha/Anna Maria b Dec 15 1783, bapt Apr 12 1784/ Johannes Bucher, Rosina

Jacob Kast, Anna Maria/Johannes b Nov 17 1783, bapt Apr 17 1784/Johannes Brunner, Barbara

Georg Gebhard, Barbara/Magdalena b Nov 17 1783, bapt Apr 15 1784/Parents
Michael Ballsell, Barbara/Ludwig b Jul 28 1783, bapt Apr 15 1784/Parents
Henrich Lederman, Margaret/Elisabeth b Oct 4 1783, bapt Apr 15 1784/Parents
Balthasar Gö̈tzendanner, Anna/Ludwig b Nov 13 1783, bapt Apr 15 1784/Parents
Friedrich Morris(?), Catharina/Wilhelm b Apr 15 1784, bapt Apr 24 1784/ Wilhelm Kast, Magdalena
David Schultz, Eva/Maria Elisabetha b Mar 11 1784, bapt May 2 1784/Valentin Brunner, Elisabetha
Peter Brill, Margaretha/Susanna b Sep 8 1783, bapt May 2 1784/Susanna Derr
Johannes Zimmerman, Leonora/Johann Georg b Aug 28 1783, bapt May 16 1784/ Georg Zimmerman, Sr., Catharina
Christoff Wölffly, Philippina/Anna Maria b Mar 14 1784, bapt May 19 1784/ Anna Maria Stehly
Andreas Schiely, Maria Apollonia/David b Mar 1 1784, bapt May 22 1784/Jacob Klein, Anna Maria
Michael Weber, Catharina/Maria Catharina b Dec 26 1783, bapt May 23 1784/ Parents
Georg Michael Rein, Eleonora/Georg Michael b Feb 22 1784, bapt May 30 1784/ Parents
Georg Schmidt, Catharina/Michael May 22 1784, bapt May 30 1784/Michael Christ, Elisabetha
Elias Remsberger, Catharina/Johann Jacob b Feb 24 1784, bapt Jun 10 1784/ Jacob Schäffer, Elisabetha
Lorentz Brunckel, Eva Margaretha/Elisabetha b Mar 13 1784, bapt Jun 12 1784/ Elisabeth Compere
Johannes Compere, Esther/Isaac b Feb 18 1784, bapt Jun 12 1784/Parents
Peter Woest, Catharina/Catharina b Jan 18 1784, bapt Jun 19 1784/Peter Elias Brunner, Maria Elisabeth
Elias Brunner, Jr., Maria Elisabeth/Charlotta b Jun 5 1784, bapt Jun 19 1784/Peter Woest, Catharina
Jacob Hepfner, Dorothea/Henrich b --, bapt Jun 19 1784/Henrich Busch
David Brey, Maria Barbara/Jonathan Philip b Dec 14 1783, bapt Jul 11 1784/ Philip Rohr, Catharina
Michael Kirschner, Maria Anna/Maria Anna b Jun 5 1784, bapt Jul 24 1784/ Peter Engel, Maria Catharina
Ezechial Beathy, Christina/Catharina b Dec 6 1783, bapt May 4 1784/Christina Fiege
Philip Christ, Dorothea/Anna Barbara b May 1 1784, bapt Aug 8 1784/Jacob Hoff, Catharina
Jacob Traut, Elisabeth/Johannes b Jul 5 1784, bapt Aug 15 1784/Michael Ried, Anna Maria
Adam Zimmerman, Susanna/Georg b Jul 6 1784, bapt Aug 15 1784/Georg Remsberger, Barbara Kempff
Christian Becker, Maria/Susanna b Jun 14 1784, bapt Jul 11 1784/Conrad Kriegbaum, Anna Maria, grandparents
Christian Thomas, Susanna/Gabriel b Apr 29 1784, bapt Aug 28 1784/Gabriel Thomas, Anna Maria
Johannes Hoffman & wf./Elisabetha b Apr 24 1784, bapt Sep 4 1784/Parents
(This is the last baptism entered by Fred. Lewis Henop.)
Leonhard Lantz, Catharina/Maria b Oct 28 1784, bapt --- 1784/The Father & Catharine Engel

Baptisms of the Evangelical Reformed Church in Frederick, Maryland

Baptisms by the Rev. William Runckel

Edward Salmon, Elisabetha/Elis. Magdalena b Oct 28 1784, bapt Nov 28 1784/ Adam Fischer, Magd.

Johann Jacob Schley, Anna Maria/Johann Georg b Aug 25 1784, bapt Nov 28 1784/Johannes Schellman, Magdalena

Rudolph Heins, Sarah/Maria b Jan 11 1783, bapt Dec 4 1784/The Father

Johannes Dertzenbach, Catharina/Catharina b Nov 3 1784, bapt Dec 12 1784/ Wilhelm Miller, Eva

Jacob Storm, Catharina/Johann Jacob b Nov 14 1784, bapt Dec 24 1784/The Mother

Johann Federkeil, Catharina/Magdalena b Nov 28 1784, bapt Dec 25 1784/Jacob Hohl, Magdalena

Peter Keil, Elisabetha/Elisabetha b Jun 25 1784, bapt Jan 22 1785/Elisabeth Keil, widow

Abraham Titlo, Elisabetha/Adam b Nov 25 1784, bapt Jan 23 1785/Adam Dertzenbach & his mother, Magdalena

Michael Heuchler, Maria/Johannes b Jan 16 1785, bapt Jan 26 1785/Nicolaus Heuchler, Anna Margaretha

Nicolaus Gibs, Anna Maria/Susanna b May 3 1784, bapt Jan 30 1785/Parents

Thomas Ogle, Sibylla/Johannes b Dec 2 1784, bapt Jan 30 1785/Thomas Schley, Sr.

Henrich Vogeler, Maria/Maria Catharina b Jan 23 1785, bapt Feb 6 1785/ Andreas Gödick, Catharina

Henrich Remsberger, Susanna/Christian b Nov 28 1784, bapt Mar 5 1785/ Christian Remsberger & Susanna

Caspar Missler, Elisabetha/Elisabetha b Jan 26 1785, bapt Mar 10 1785/The Father

Andrew Boyd, Mary/Anna b ---, bapt Feb 19 1785/The Father

Christian Luther, Anna/Paul b Nov 30 1784, bapt Mar 19 1785/Parents

Johannes Richter, Catharina/Johan Georg b Dec 7 1784, bapt Mar 20 1785/Joh. Georg Gantzer

Ant. Zürich, Magd./Jacob b --, bapt Mar 25 1785/Adult

Jacob Fister, Anna Maria/Jacob b Oct 2 1784, bapt Mar 25 1785/Parents

Jacob Mottin, Elisabeth/Barbara b Dec 22 1784, bapt Mar 27 1785/Barbara Dabler

John Dewel, Charity/Elisabetha b Jun 24 1784, bapt Apr 10 1785/Parents

Michael Tempel, Margaretha/Peter b Mar 24 1784, bapt Apr 10 1785/Peter Bob

Lorentz Bölcher, Catharina/Abraham b Dec 19 1784, bapt Apr 13 1785/Parents

Jacob Brunner, Margaretha/Anna Maria b Mar 1 1784, bapt Apr 17 1785/Jacob Kast, Anna Maria

Gottfried Gebhard, Magdalena/Thomas b Feb 24 1785, bapt Apr 17 1785/Georg Hoffman

Johannes Gebhard, Elisabeth/Catharina b Aug 11 1784, bapt Apr 17 1785/ Parents

Friedrich Kempff, Jr., Dorothea/Gilbert b Dec 31 1784, bapt May 5 1785/ Parents

Christian Kreiss & wf./Johann Friedrich b Apr 9 1785, bapt May 15 1785/ Henrich Kreiss

Henrich Krass, Catharina/Catharina b Sep 13 1784, bapt May 15 1785/Parents

Michael Witmer, Catharina/Anna Maria b Aug 18 1784, bapt May 15 1785/Anna Maria Steckel, single

Jacob Ketro Klara/Elisabetha b Jan 2 1784, bapt May 15 1785/The Mother

Baptisms of the Evangelical Reformed Church in Frederick, Maryland

Johan Hauck, Catharina/Jacob b Feb 10 1785, bapt May 23 1785/Jacob Hauck
Philip Rohr, Catharina/Johannes b May 17 1785, bapt May 23 1785/Johannes Rohr, Elisabeth
Jacob Doll, Margaretha/Susanna b Feb 13 1779, bapt May 27 1785/Joseph Doll, Charlotta
Jacob Doll, Margaretha/Abraham b May 9 1781, bapt May 27 1785/Conrad Doll, Anna Maria
Jacob Doll, Margaretha/Anna Maria b Jul 15 1783, bapt May 27 1785/Anna Maria Doll, single
Friedr. Jacob Schäfer, Gertrude/Johannes b --, bapt May 29 1785/Jacob Krebs & Margaret Krebs, grandmother
Georg Jacob Schley, Margaretha/Henrich b Jan 22 1783, bapt Jun 5 1785, d. Jan 7 1786/Adam Fischer, Margaretha
Nicolaus Deiss, Barbara/Wilhelm b Apr 10 1785, bapt Jun 5 1785/Wilhelm Baer, Elisabetha
Peter Herget, Magdalena/Elisabetha b Feb 21 1785, bapt Jun 9 1785/Parents
Orman Hammon, Elisabeth/Nathaniel b Dec 26 1784, bapt Jun 16 1785/Parents
John Raitt, Hannah/Nathanial b Oct 21 1784, bapt Jun 16 1785/Parents
John Gard, Sophia/Hannah b Sep 21 1784, bapt Jun 16 1785/Parents
P. Turner & wf./Daniel b Nov 12 1784, bapt Jun 16 1785/Parents
Wm. Harris, blacks, Catharine/Ara b Oct 4 1781, Elisabeth b May 24 1784, bapt Jun 16 1785/W. Stevans & Sarah owners who promised to have the children instructed.
Nathan Maynard, Susanna/Nathan b Mar 6 1783, bapt Aug 1 1785/Jacob Springer, Elisabeth
Abraham Blumer, Mary/John b Jan 11, bapt Aug 1 1785/Jacob Springer, & wf.
Thomas Maynard, Sarah/Susanna b Feb 23 1784, bapt Aug 1 1785/Parents
Andreas Bossert, Anna Maria/David b Apr 2 1785, bapt Aug 1 1785/Parents
Jacob Seemahn, Maria Elisabetha/Peter b Mar 20 1785, bapt Aug 1 1785/Peter Bäger, single
Thomas Price, Mary/Bowen Lee Matilda b Dec 23 1775, bapt Aug 4 1785/Parents
Henrich Kroneis, Barbara/Henrich b Jun 16 1785, bapt Jul 4 1785/Parents
Wm. Davy, Barbara/Elizabeth b Apr 23 1785, bapt Jul 11 1785/Parents
Jacob Madery, Rachel/Susanna b Jun 13 1784, bapt Jul 24 1785/John Brunner, s. of Jacob, Susanna
Herman Knochenhauer, Lydia/Sarah b Jan 30 1784, bapt Aug 7 1785/Christian Eberhardt, Sibylla
Johannes Schäfer, Elisabetha/Elisabetha b May 31 1785, bapt Aug 14 1785/ Catharina Stoll
Johannes Jerky, Sophia/Catharina Elisabetha b Feb 28 1785, bapt Aug 14 1785/ Cath. Elisabetha Becker
Henrich Erter, Magdalena/Johannes b Feb 19 1776, bapt Aug 15 1785/Philip Berger
Henrich Erter, Magdalena/Elisabetha b Feb 7 1777, bapt Aug 15 1785/Carolina Zimmerman
Henrich Erter, Magdalena/Georg b Jul 23 1782, bapt Aug 15 1785
Henrich Erter, Magdalena/Henrich b Mar 15 1785, bapt Aug 15 1785/Parents
Peter Schneider, Maria/Elisabetha b Jul 10 1785, bapt Aug 16 1785/Elis. Schell, widow
Christian Weber, Catharina/Philippina b Jun 4 1784, bapt Sep -- 1785/Parents
James Newport, Katy/James b Aug 9 1783, bapt Aug 16 1785/---
James Newport, Katy/Mary b Jul 7 1784, bapt Aug 16 1785/---

Baptisms of the Evangelical Reformed Church in Frederick, Maryland

Samuel How, Elizabeth/Joshua b Mar 25 1784, bapt Aug 16 1785/Philip Burger, Mary Barbara
Thomas Knox, Mary/Rachel b Aug 9 1785, bapt Aug 16 1785/Parents
Benjamin Simpson, Elizabeth/Wm. Duval b Jun 11 1785, bapt Aug 23 1785/ Priscilla Dewall
Samuel McIntosh, Sarah/Mary b Aug 1 1784, bapt Aug 26 1785/Andrew Bossart, Mary
Stephan Brunner, Magdalena/Henrich b Jan 28 1785, bapt Aug 28 1785/Joh. Jacob Schley, Anna Maria
Johannes Gulden, Eleonore/Wilhelm b Mar 22 1785, bapt Aug 29 1785/Parents
Samuel Lakins, Sarah/Samuel Blumer b May 6 1785, bapt Aug 31 1785/Parents
Christoph Mayer, Anna Margaretha/Anna Maria b Jul 19 1785, bapt Aug 31 1785/ Johannes Remsberger, Anna Maria
Johannes Reiss, Elisabetha/David b Aug 16 1785, bapt Sep 4 1785/Parents
Georg Witterich, Catharina/Anna Maria b Dec 20 1784, bapt Sep 4 1785/Parents
Simon Schnook, Charlotta/Elisabetha b May 21 1785, bapt Sep 4 1785/Parents
Lamuel Coffin, Catharine/Olive b Jul 13 1785, bapt Sep 6 1785/Parents
Benjamin Stuardt, Margareth/Catharine b Sep 20 1784, bapt Sep 7 1785/Parents
Peter Mades (Mathes), Philippina/Magdalena b Jul 26 1785, bapt Sep 8 1785/ Jacob Balzel, Margaretha
Wilhelm Baer, Elisabetha/Johannes b Aug 13 1785, bapt Sep 11 1785/Parents
Jacob Stehly, Barbara/Friedrich b Mar 13 1785, bapt Sep 11 1785/Parents
Charles Busy, Martha/Joshua b Mar 11 1785, bapt Sep 11 1785/Parents
Wm. Fisher, Patiens/Basel b Mar 5 1784, bapt Sep 17 1785/Parents
Abraham Herget, Anna Maria/Susanna b Jun 6 1785, bapt Sep 18 1785/Parents
Georg Kiet, Anna Maria/Henrich b Aug 6 1785, bapt Sep 22 1785/Christophel Wedekin, single
David Schultz, Eva/Maria Elisabeth b Aug 19 1785, bapt Oct 2 1785/Valentin Brunner, Maria Elisabeth
Geo. Noble Wheeler, Charity/Hezekiah b Aug 14 1784, bapt Oct 2 1785/Parents
Adam Simon, Rosina/Anna Maria b Sep 6 1785, bapt Oct 8 1785/Cath. Engelbrecht, single
Philip Schaed, Dorothea/Johannes b Mar 29 1785,bapt Oct 9 1785/Parents
Peter Mantz, Catharina/David b Jun 29 1785, bapt Oct 9 1785/The Mother
Peter Marks, Anna Maria/Michael b Jul 10 1785, bapt Oct 23 1785/Michael Groh/Magdalena
Lenard, Margaret, blacks/Charles b Mar 23 1785, bapt Oct 23 1785/Wm. Mordecai Beall, owner, engaged to have child instructed
Jacob Krebel, Martha/Maria b Sep -- 1785, bapt Oct 24 1785/Parents
Jacob Reitenauer, Susanna/Elisabetha b Sep 28 1785, bapt Nov 4 1785/ Elisabeth Haas, single
Henrich Baer, Elisabeth/Johannes b Sep 13 1785, bapt Nov 6 1785/Johannes Baer, single
Jacob Scheed, Maria Catharina/Georg Jacob b Oct 30 1785, bapt Nov 6 1785/ Parents
Jacob Rohr, Catharina/Catharina b Oct 22 1785, bapt Nov 13 1785/Rahel Koenig, single
Jacob Getzendanner, Elisabeth/Thomas b Mar 13 1785, bapt Nov 24 1785/Parents
Lorentz Heim, Christina/Johannes b Sep 23 1785, bapt Nov 24 1785/Joh. Bockius, Eva
Elijah Sergeant, Margaret/Rebecca b Dec 31 1785/John Frazier
Elijah Sergeant, Margaret/Ara b Sep 5 1785, bapt Oct 26 1785/Amelia Frazier

Wilhelm Berg, Margaretha/Anna Maria b Nov 21 1785, bapt Dec 2 1785/Parents
Jacob Balsle, Anna Maria/Maria Dorothea b Nov 2 1784, bapt Dec 5 1785/ Magdalena Storm, widow
Jacob Jauler, Barbara/Johan Georg b Jul 14 1785, bapt Dec 6 1785/Nicolaus Schäfer
Dewald Miller, Catharina/Catharina b Jul 16 1785, bapt Dec 6 1785/Matheus Bocky, Anna Maria
Andreas Loh, Anna Maria/Elisabetha b Aug 27 1785, bapt Dec 12 1785/Parents
Johannes Kroneiss, Anna Maria/Simon b Dec 1 1785, bapt Dec 25 1785/Simon Fey, Anna Maria
Wilhelm Michael, Barbara/Wilhelm b Dec 16 1785, bapt Jan 23 1786/Johann Eberhardt, Anna Maria
Jacob Remsberger, Elisabeth/Christian b --, bapt Jan 1 1786/Christian Remsberger, Susanna
Philip Schmit, Jr., Elisabeth/Agnes b Aug 31 1785, bapt Jan 12 1786/Wilhelm Schmit, Agnes
Jacob Faubel, Margaret/Magdalena b Sep 6 1785, bapt Jan 15 1786/Thomas Hickson, Maria Magdalena
Daniel Hauer, Catharina/Anna Margaretha b Nov 28 1785, bapt Feb 22 1786/ Nicolaus Hauer, Catharina
Herman Hellman, Magdalena/Maria Magdalena b Jan 14 1786, bapt Mar 8 1786/ Johannes Reiss, Elisabeth
Johann Brotzman, Anna Maria/Jacob b Mar 20 1785, bapt Mar 8 1786/Jacob Christ, Catharina
Johann Hemp, Anna Margaretha/Johan Henrich b Nov 16 1785, bapt Mar 8 1786/ Parents
Mattheus Jung, Anna Barbara/Johannes b Feb 24 1786, bapt Mar 8 1786/Michael Christ, Elisabetha
William, Jane, blacks/Sarah b Oct 11 1785, bapt Mar 8 1786/Michael Christ, owner, Elisabeth
Samuel Miller & wf./Ferdinandt b Mar 16 1786, bapt Mar 16 1786/Parents
Christian Wiesenminder, Maria Schmit, made conf. in Middletown congregation/Susanna b Dec 31 1786, bapt Mar 23 1786/Johann Mähn, Susanna
Thomas Hickson, Maria/Heinrich b Mar 16 1786, bapt Mar 26 1786/The father & Susanna Schrödter, sister of mother
Wilhelm Runckel, V.D.M., Catharina/Johannes b Feb 22 1786, bapt Apr 2 1786/ Joh. Brunner, Barbara
Elias Brunner, Maria Elisabeth/Elias b Feb 3 1786, bapt Apr 9 1786/Nicolaus Holtz, Susanna
Peter Kempff, Maria/Esther b Nov 12 1785, bapt Apr 9 1786/Parents
Johannes Holtz, Blandina/Susanna b Jan 8 1786, bapt Apr 9 1786/Nicolaus Holtz
Anthony Zürich, Magdalena/Catharina Richter b Oct 20 1762, bapt Apr 14 1786/ Adult
Philip Jacob Lott, Catharina/Margaretha b Feb 22 1786, bapt Apr 16 1786/ Henrich Letterman, Margaretha
Conrad Kempff, Anna/Elisabetha b Apr 14 1785, bapt Apr 16 1786/Bernhardt Hirschberger, Elisabeth
Dennis McGowan, Sarah/Jacob b --, bapt Apr 16 1786/Jacob Brunner
Peter Gebhardt, Eva Margaret/Magdalena b Mar 15 1786, bapt Apr 30 1786/ Parents
Joseph Doll, Charlotta/Margaretha b Mar 4 1786, bapt Apr 30 1786/Parents

Jacob Doll, Margaret/Magdalena b Jan 29 1786, bapt Apr 30 1786/Parents
John Bristor, slave, Anna Free blacks/Isaac b Nov 1 1785, bapt Apr 30 1786/ Stephan Remsberger
David Lohr, Spielman, Elisabeth/Johann Jacob b Jan 13 1786, bapt Jun 4 1786/ Conrad Kriegbaum, A. Maria
Philip Preiss, Susanna/Johann Georg b Sep 23 1785, bapt Jun 4 1786/Adam Schnohk, Anna Maria
Adam Knauf, Christina/Anna Maria b Dec 31 1785, bapt Jun 4 1786/Johan Knauf, A. Maria
Michael Witmer, Catharina/Elisabetha b Apr 10 1786, bapt Jun 14 1786/ Margaretha Steckel, single
Samuel Selby, Ann/Roseman Harris b May 30 1786, bapt June 15 1786/Parents
Georg Reinhard, Salome/Magdalena b Mar 30 1786, bapt Jun 18 1786/Conrad Becker, Magdalena
Geo. Michael Rein, Eleonora/Eleonora b Apr 18 1786, bapt Jun 18 1786/Georg Fantz
Johannes Gomber, Esther/Johannes b Dec 17 1785, bapt Jun 25 1786/Parents
Peter Bohrer, Maria Magdalena/Jacob b Feb 1 1782, bapt Jul 2 1786/Valentin Brunner
Peter Bohrer, Maria Magdalena/Georg b Mar 5 1784, bapt Jul 2 1786/Parents
Johan Miller, Barbara/Johannes b Jun 11 1786, bapt Jul 2 1786/The Father
Peter, Eleonora, blacks/Wilhelm & Magdalena b Feb 7 1786, bapt Jul 28 1786/ Martin Waltz, Barbara
Georg Witerich, Catharina/Maria Elisabeth b May 14 1786, bapt Aug 9 1786/ Parents
John Fleming, Rachel/Caleb b Jun 2 1786, bapt Aug 13 1786/Parents
Daniel Thomas, Margaret/Mary b Apr 7 1786, bapt Jul 20 1786/Parents
Isaac Taylor, Elizabeth/Elizabeth b Dec 29 1785, bapt Aug 21 1786/Parents
Benjamin Davison, Polly, blacks of Thos. Jonson/John Davison b Aug 17 1786, bapt Aug 23 1786/The Father
Georg Gebhardt, Barbara/Catharina b Jun 10 1786, bapt Aug 27 1786/Parents
Joh. Lohr, Delater, Barbara/Anna Catharina b Jun 24 1786, bapt Sep 6 1786/ Parents
Johann Seinen, Margaretha/Wilhelm b May 11 1786, bapt Sep 6 1786/Elisabeth Seinen, single
Augustin Barden, Maria/Abraham b --, bapt Sep 6 1786/Joh. Wendel
David Jordan, Margaretha/Johannes b --, bapt Sep 6 1786/Parents
The above four children were bapt. In Millerstown, Va.
Andrew Boyd, Mary/John b Sep 13 1786, bapt Sep 18 1786/George Hoffman, Marg.
Andreas Götick, Catharina/Anna Maria b Aug 27 1786, bapt Oct 15 1786/Andreas Dörner, Anna Maria
Jacob Hindan, Rosina/Anna Elisabeth b Aug 27 1786, bapt Oct 30 1786/The Father
Christoph Bergman, Anna Maria/Johann Henrich b Sep 22 1786, bapt Nov 5 1786/ Henrich Bantz, single
Johan Schmahl, Philippina/Joseph b Aug 5 1786, bapt Nov 5 1786/The Father
Georg Luther, Elisabeth/Georg b Sep 3 1786, bapt Nov 13 1786/The Father
Michael Drew, Elisabeth/Asahel b Jun 26 1786, bapt Nov 13 1786/Parents
Joseph Tovery, Anna/Elizabeth b Apr 30 1786, bapt Nov 13 1786/Conrad Becker, Christina
Ninian Beall, Mary/Mary Ann b Aug 16 1786, bapt Dec 1 1786/Catharina Stricker

Henrich Vogler, Margaret/Jacob b Oct 24 1786, bapt Dec 3 1786/Jacob Bornhaus, single
Jacob Wüst, Eva/Philip b Dec 10 1786, bapt Dec 15 1786/Parents
Henrich Kempff, Anna Margaret/Elisabeth b Oct 25 1786, bapt Dec 31 1786/ Peter Schnook, Julianna
Friedrich Kempff, Dorothea/Abraham b Oct 10 1786, bapt Jan 1 1787/Parents
Paul Dorst, Catharina/Barbara b -- bapt Jan 5 1787/Parents
Joseph Stehly, Maria Juliana/Salomon b Aug 4 1786, bapt Jan 7 1787/Parents
Mattheus Schmidt, Anna Maria/Susanna b Jan 5 1787, bapt Jan 11 1787/Philip Preiss, Susanna
Peter Lauer, Margaret/Anna Margaretha b May 26 1786, bapt Jan 16 1787/ Elisabeth Sinn, widow
Johannes Brunner, s. of Jacob & Susanna/Johannes b Nov 7 1786, bapt Jan 21 1787/Joh. Brunner, miller
Gabriel Thomas, s. of Val., A. Marg./Elisabeth Barbara b Oct 26 1786, bapt Jan 25 1787/Elisabeth Barbara Thomas, single
Jacob Hoffman, Mary/David & Catharina b Jan 4 1787, bapt Jan 29 1787/Michael Heuchler, Elisabeth Pfeifer
Jacob Thomas, Susanna/Anna Barbara b Dec 22 1786, bapt Feb 7 1787/Frantz Hoffman, Barbara
Philip Rohr, Catharina/David b Jan 18 1787, bapt Feb 15 1787/David Kuhns, single
Georg Schäfer, Catharina/Anna Maria b Oct 29 1786, bapt Feb 27 1787/ Elisabeth Stehly, single
Daniel Ehl, Magdalena/Elisabeth b Dec 15 1786, bapt Feb 28 1787/Parents
James Morris, Dec., Mary/Maria b Dec 21 1786, bapt Mar 1 1787/Geo. Schnertzel, Barbara
Johann Faubel, Anna Marg./Caspar b Dec 28 1786, bapt Mar 4 1787/Parents
Johannes Rohr, Elisabeth/Johannes b Feb 17 1787, bapt Mar 4 1787/Philip Rohr, Catharina
Jacob Brunner, Margaretha/Maria Elisabetha b Jan 25 1787, bapt Mar 4 1787/ Valentin Brunner, Maria Elisabetha
Jacob Schley, Anna Maria/Wilhelm b Dec 10 1786, bapt Mar 11 1787/Jacob Christ
Nicolaus Herman, Christina/Johannes b Sep 28 1786, bapt Mar 21 1787/Johannes Solzer, single
Johann Schäfer, Elisabeth/Jacob b Nov 10 1786, bapt Mar 21 1787/Nicolaus Schafer, Anna Maria
Frantz Kleinert, Maria Salome/Johan Friedrich b Feb 12 1787, bapt Mar 23 1787/Maria Magd. Welsheimer
John Scot, Catharina/Jacob b Feb 7 1787, bapt Apr 1 1787/Jacob Hohl, Magdalena
Henrich Richter, Catharina/Catharina b Oct 30 1786, bapt Apr 1 1787/Parents
Simon Gebhardt, Susanna/Magdalena b Feb 6 1787, bapt Apr 2 1787/Parents
Jost Stimmel, Magdalena/Johan Michael b Oct 11 1786, bapt Apr 9 1787/Michael Stocker, Anna Maria
Anthony Zurich, Magdalena/Johannes b -- bapt Apr 6 1787/Adult---/Susanna & Mary, twins b -- , bapt Apr 6 1787/Parents
Jacob Bellabrega, Maria/Rosina b Feb 20 1787, bapt Apr 11 1787/Susanna Mefford
Henrich Schreiber, Barbara/Anna b Aug 13 1786, bapt Apr 15 1787/Christoph Wölffel, Anna

John James, Martha/Daniel b Feb 5 1787, bapt Apr 28 1787/Parents
Joh. Bier, Julianna/Johannes b Jan 5 1787, bapt Apr 28 1787/Michael Fähr, Maria
Henrich Remsperger, Susanna/Casper b Feb 24 1787, bapt Apr 29 1787/Parents
Jacob Traut, Elisabeth/Matheus b Oct 13 1786, bapt Apr 29 1787/Mat. Buck, Sr., A. Maria
Edward Salmon, Elisabeth/Catharina b Mar 21 1787, bapt Apr 29 1787/Cath. Mants
Johann Bucky, Elisabeth/Henrich b Dec 16 1786, bapt May 2 1787/Henrich Kuhns
Samuel Kinnis, Jemimah/Samuel b Nov 4 1786, bapt May 6 1787/Parents
Posey Stewardt, Prudence/Mary Aug 7 1787 (6?), bapt May 7 1787/Parents
Jeremiah Steward, Priscilla/Jesse b Nov 3 1786, bapt May 18 1787/Parents
Georg Stürmer, Catharina/Christina b May 8 1787, bapt May 27 1787/Parents
Christian Schaup, Elisabeth/Elisabetha b Dec -- 1786, bapt May 27 1787/The Mother
Adam Schnook, Anna Margaret/Johannes b Apr 1 1787, bapt May 28 1787/Parents
Johannes Thomas, s. of Gab., Elisabetha/Anna Margaretha b Apr 5 1787, bapt May 28 1787/Anna Margaretha Remsperger, single
Daniel Jung, Margaret/Maria Elisabetha b Mar 11 1786, bapt Jun 23 1787/ Johann Rohr, Maria Christina
Wilhelm Runckel, V.D.M., Catharina/Catharina b May 16 1787, bapt Jun 30 1787/Parents
Georg Baer, A. Maria/Georg b -- 5--, bapt Jul 1 1787/Peter Kempf, A. Maria
Thomas Ogle, Sibylla/Georg & Maria b Feb 11 1787, bapt Jul 22 1787/Jacob Steiner, Maria Anna
Henrich Stehly, Catharina/Catharina b Sep 11 1786, bapt Aug 6 1787/Parents
Elijah Hut, Nancy, blacks/Elijah b Aug 10 1787, bapt Aug 16 1787/Thomas Price, owner who promised to have them instructed.
Nicolaus Schäfer, Anna Maria/Anna Maria b Aug 7 1787, bapt Aug 24 1787/Peter Schäfer, Rosina
Benedict Steiner, Anna Barbara/Susanna b Nov 25 1785, bapt Aug 25 1787/ Parents
Herman Helleman, Magdalena/Johannes b Aug 8 1787, bapt Sep 16 1787/Parents
Johannes Reiss, Elisabetha/Elisabetha b Jul 13 1787, bapt Sep 16 1787/ Parents
David Schultz, Eva Margaretha/Catharina b Aug 9 1787, bapt Sep 23 1787/ Catharina Mayer, single
Casper Deiwelbiss, Susanna/Sarah b May 20 1787, bapt Sep 23 1787/The Mother
Christian Getzedanner, Maria/Adam b Jun 6 1787, bapt Jul 22 1787/Parents
Wilhelm Baer, Elisabetha/Adam b Aug 7 1787, bapt Sep 30 1787/Parents
Johann Lentz, Magdalena/Christina & Elisabetha b Jul 4 1787, bapt Sep 30 1787/Christina Wagner, Elisabeth Diterlein
Jacob Steiner, Elisabetha/Maria Catharina b Aug 31 1787, bapt Oct 21 1787/ Maria Anna Steiner, single
Jacob Rohr, Catharina/Elisabetha b Sep 15 1787, bapt Oct 21 1787/Johannes Rohr, Elisabetha
Georg Wintz, Catharina/Catharina b Jan 25 1787, bapt Oct 22 1787/Maria Wintz, single
Jacob Stehly, Barbara/Abraham b Sep 20 1787, bapt Oct 26 1787/Parents
Joh. Kroneiss, Anna Maria/Elisabetha b Oct 25 1787, bapt Oct 31 1787, d. Oct 31/Parents

Jacob Schneider, Catharina/Susanna b Oct 23 1787, bapt Nov 4 1787/Elisabetha Schneider, single
Stephan Brunner, Magdalena/Catharina b May 28 1787, bapt Nov 25 1787/Marg. Schellman
Jacob Metzger, Christina/Johannes b Feb 27 1787, bapt Nov 26 1787/Parents
Joseph Doll, Charlotta/Susanna Margaret b Oct 23 1787, bapt Dec 9 1787/ Susanna Marg. Foltz, widow
Henrich Krass, Catharina/Henrich b Sep 23 1787, bapt Dec 7 1787/Parents
Johann Gebhardt, Elisabeth/Susanna & Henrietta b Mar 20 1787, bapt Jan 6 1788/Parents
David Levi, Barbara/Rebecca b Oct 27 1787, bapt Jan 21 1788/The Mother
Chas. Gardrell, Sarah/Patrick b Jan 24 1788, bapt Jan 28 1788/Parents
Linn, Margaret, blacks/Charity b Dec 4 1787, bapt Jan 30 1787/Wm. Mordock Beall, the owner
Lorentz Brengel, Eva/Rahel b Oct 22 1787, bapt Feb 2 1788/Elisabeth Gomber, single
Peter Bell, Margaret/Peter b Jul 13 1787, bapt Feb 1 1788/Parents
Georg Fauk, Elisabeth/Henrich b Aug 8 1787, bapt Feb 10 1788/Parents
Adam Bauman, Elisabeth Balzel/Margaretha b Jan 1 1783, bapt Feb 13 1788/ Jacob Balzel, Charlotta
Jacob Krepell, Martha/Sophia b Dec 19 1787, bapt Feb 18 1788/Parents
Wilhelm Hester, Rahel/Rebecca b Jan 30 1788, bapt Feb 19 1788/Rebecca Bort, single
Georg Bocky, Christina/David b Jan 2 1788, bapt Feb 24 1788/Parents
Abraham Herget, Maria/Johannes b Dec 18 1787, bapt Mar 5 1788/Johann Ott
Elias Brunner, Maria Elisabeth/Daniel b Dec 24 1787, bapt Mar 9 1788/Joh. Brunner
Johan Remsperger, Elisabetha/Elisabetha b Jan 21 1788, bapt Mar 21 1788, d Dec 4 1788/Johann Rohr, Elisabetha
Conrad Löschhorn, Maria/Johannes b Oct 24 1787, bapt Mar 23 1788/Johann Löschhorn
Peter Engel & wf., Anna Maria/Abraham Fah b Jan 12 1784, bapt Mar 23 1788/ Michael Bayer
same Parents/Juliana b Mar 11 1786, bapt Mar 23 1788/Henrich Ziehler, A. Maria
Peter Bayer, Anna Maria/Adam b Mar 3 1788,bapt Mar 24 1788/Hup. Bayer, Susanna Salome
Christian Balzel, Catharina/Johannes b Dec 20 1787, bapt Mar 28 1787/Parents
Henrich Baer, Elisabeth/Wilhelm b Feb 2 1788, bapt Mar 31 1788/Parents
Henrich Hembe, Margaretha/Peter b Dec 30 1787, bapt Apr 6 1788/Adam Wolff, single
Johann Holtz, Blandina/Elisabetha b Dec 9 1787, bapt Apr 6 1788/Ed. Salmon, Elisabetha
Michael Huechler, Maria/Henrich b Oct 23 1787, bapt Apr 7 1788/Elisabetha Hoffman, widow
Philip Pfeiffer, Elisabetha/Philip b Jul 18 1787, bapt Apr 7 1788/Michael Heuchler
Christian Thomas, Susanna/Sophia b Oct 10 1787, bapt Apr 13 1788/Wilhelm Baer, Elisabetha
Georg Engelhardt, Margaretha/Catharina b Dec 15 1787, bapt Apr 13 1788/ Barbara Hirschberger

Johan Paltzer, Elisabeth/Jacob b May 13 1785, bapt Apr 14 1788/Maria Barbara Bentz, Jacob Bentz, single
same Parents/Catharina b Dec 11 1787, bapt Apr 14 1788, same sponsors
Johann Schafer, Elisabetha/Johannes b Apr 3 1788,bapt May 1 1788/Johann Stoll, single
Johan Keplinger, Catharina/Johannes b Mar 20 1788, bapt May 1 1788/Parents
Jacob Schäfer, Elisabetha/Jacob b Nov 6 1787, bapt May 11 1788/Conrad Schäfer
Michael Braun, Rosina/Johannes b Mar 19 1788, bapt May 13 1788/Parents
Andrew Boyd, Mary/Anna b Dec 3 1787, bapt May 16 1788/The Mother
Georg Riehm, Catharina/Johannes b Nov 7 1787, bapt May 18 1788/Parents
Thomas Knox, Mary/Margaret b Oct 20 1787, bapt May 18 1788/Parents
Philip Preiss, Susanna/Jacob b Feb 3 1788, bapt May 19 1788/Jacob Koller, Elisabetha
Jacob Ketro, Clara/Susanna b May 9 1787, bapt May 19 1788/Philip Preiss, Susanna
Johannes Gomber, Jr., Esther/Casper b Sep 22 1787, bapt Apr 26 1788/Parents
Balthasar Wiesinger, Elisabetha/Elisabetha b Feb 4 1788, bapt May 28 1788/ Parents
Andreas Bossert, Anna Maria/Peter b Apr 11 1787, bapt Jun 18 1788/Parents
Jacob Brandenberger, Elisabetha/Johannes b Mar 4 1788, bapt Jun 18 1788/ Henrich Wolff, Margaret
John Wallen, Susana/Henrich b Mar 28 1788, bapt Jun 22 1788/Dorothea Ried wf. of -- Ried
Philip Scheed, Dorothea/Catharina b Aug 25 1787, bapt Jun 22 1788/Parents
Sebastian Scherch, Catharina/Sebastian b Aug 17 1786, bapt Jun 23 1788/ Philip Rohr, Catharina
Jacob Brunner, of John, Anna Maria/Anna Maria b Jun 1 1788, bapt Jun 29 1788/Parents
Henrich Stehly, Catharina/Sophia b Jan 25 1788, bapt Jul 4 1788/The Father
Tobias Hanson, Jane, blacks/Elizabeth b Jun 9 1788, bapt Jul 13 1788/blacks belonging to Baker Johnson
Nicolaus Gips, Maria/Elisabetha b Apr 18 1788, bapt Jul 27 1788/Parents
Lorentz Spielman, Elisabetha/Elisabetha b May 20 1788, bapt Jul 31 1788/ Parents
Henrich Fehling, Elisabetha/Henrich Jacob b Apr 2 1788, bapt Aug 10 1788/ Henr. Jacob Winter
Henrich Hirschberger, Catharina/Georg b Apr 26 1788, bapt Aug 10 1788/Geo. Remsperg
Adam Schreiner, Anna Maria/David b Jan 12 1788, bapt Aug 11 1788/The Mother
Abraham Titlo, Susanna/Thomas b Apr 25 1787, bapt Jul 14 1788/Thomas Hickson, Maria
Jacob Faubel, Margaretha/Margaretha b Dec 13 1787, bapt Jul 21 1788/Parents
Adam Schabacker, Maria Barbara/Adam b Nov 14 1787, bapt Jul 21 1788/Parents
Francis Green, Sophia/Lawrence b Mar 14 1787, Barbara b Jun 20 1788, bapt Jul 23 1788/Parents
Thos. Leaming, Sarah/Samuel b Aug 11 1785, bapt Aug 13 1788/Parents
James Barnes, Sarah/Daniel James b Aug 2 1786, bapt Aug 13 1788/Parents
Thos. Dean, Anna Maria Schmidt/Elisabetha b Jan 30 1787, bapt Aug 20 1788/A. Maria Schmidt, widow
Georg Wiederich, Catharina/Christina b Mar 18 1788, bapt Aug 20 1788/Parents

Peter Engel, Anna Maria/Anna Maria b Jul 15 1788, bapt Aug 29 1788/Susanna Marg. Voltz, widow
Conrad Doll & wf./Elisabetha b Jun 22 1788, bapt Aug 29 1788/Parents
Georg Schmit, Elisabetha/Catharina Philippina b Jul 7 1788, bapt Sep 20 1788/The Mother
Jacob Poley, Elisabetha/Jacob b Sep 9 1788, bapt Sep 21 1788/Johan Keplinger, Catharina
Wm. Cox, Catharina/Elisabetha b Aug 21 1787, bapt Sep 25 1788/The Mother
Henrich Kuhn, Elisabeth/Asenath b Aug 19 1788, bapt Sep 25 1788/Casander Browning
Jacob Traut, Elisabeth/Anna Maria b Jul 1 1788, bapt Sep 28 1788/Margaretha Bucky, single
Peter Wolff, Catharina/Susanna b Apr 23 1788, bapt Sep 28 1788/Nicolaus Holtz, Susanna
Michael Stocker, Anna Maria/Charlotta b Feb 19 1788, bapt Sep 28 1788/Peter Schnook, Juliana
Jost Stimmel, Hannah Magdalena/Hannah Magdalena b Jul 2 1788, bapt Oct 5 1788/Peter Stimmel, Eva
Joseph Richards, Catharina/Benjamin b Oct 10 1786, Daniel b Jan 13 1788, bapt Oct 6 1788/Parents
Wm. Maddin, Mary/Eleonora b Nov 25 1786, bapt Oct 6 1788/Parents
Jacob Mayer, Elisabetha/Elisabetha b Mar 29, bapt Oct 10 1788/The Mother
Jacob Springer, Elisabetha/Anna Magdalena b Aug 29 1788, bapt Oct 13 1788/A. Maria Dengler, widow
Thos. Spurior, Anna/Green b Mar 3 1785, Avis b Feb 12 1787, bapt Oct 13 1788/Parents
Thos. Maynard, Sarah/John Brice b Feb 19 1786, Thomas b Mar 17 1788, bapt Oct 13 1788/Parents
Luke Davis, Mina/Luke b Sep 11 1788, bapt Oct 13 1788/The mother
John James, Martha/Mary b Sep 6 1788, bapt Oct 13 1788/Parents
Henrich Richter, Catharina/Johann Henrich b Aug 28 1788, bapt Oct 19 1788/Parents
Benjamin Jacobs, Elizabeth/Mary b May 23 1788 bapt Oct 25 1788/Parents
Jacob Wiest, Eva Catharina/Jacob b Aug 26 1788, bapt Oct 30 1788/Parents
Samuel Lakin, Sarah/William b Sep 10 1788, bapt Nov 1 1788/Parents
Wm. Atkin, Cavey/Mary Hennis b Jun 7 1788, Rachel b Jun 7 1788, bapt Nov 8 1788/Parents
Jacob Walter, Maria/Jacob b Jul 4 1788, bapt Nov 18 1788/Georg Wintz
John Glister, Elizabeth/Sarah b Oct 24 1786, bapt Nov 12 1788/Michael Naleno, Mary
John Glister, Elizabeth/John b Jul 20 1788, bapt Nov 12 1788/Philip Heintz, Maria
Wm. Doutle, Elizabeth/Mary b Feb 1 86, bapt Oct 12 1788/The Mother
Michael Witmer, Catharina/Michael b Jun 20 1788, bapt Dec 13 1788/Parents
Henrich Kuhns, Margaretha/Maria Elisabeth b Nov 10 1788, bapt Nov 30 1788/Jacob Steiner, Elisabeth
Lock, Amia, blacks/Saul b Oct 26 1788, bapt Jan 10 1789/James Johnson's blacks
Jacob Schneider, Elisabeth/Johannes b Sep 27 1788, bapt Jan 15 1789/Jacob Schneider, Maria
Friedrich Schittenhelm, Maria Barbara/Catharina b Sep 7 1788, bapt Jan 16 1789/Catharina Dorr

Henrich Schreiber, Barbara/Adam b Aug 6 1788, bapt Jan 18 1789, Adam Keller, Catharina

Jacob Hauser, Catharina/Anna Margaretha b Aug 1 1798, bapt Jan 25 1789/A. Margaretha Hauser, widow

Georg Hoffman, Eva Margaretha/Maria b Jan -- 1789, bapt Feb 7 1789/Parents

Jacob Metzger, Christina/Jacob b Jan 1 1789, bapt Feb 12 1789/Parents

Nicolaus Maderi, Susanna/Benjamin b Nov 29 1788, bapt Feb 13 1789/The Father

Philip Schäfer, Anna Maria/Johannes b Dec 28 1788, bapt Feb 14 1789/Nicolaus Gips, Maria

Johan Schultz, Margaret/Margaretha b Nov 5 1788, bapt Feb 16 1789/Philip Borger, Maria Barbara

Leonhardt Lantz, Catharina/Curtis b Jun 25 1787, bapt Feb 17 1789/The Mother

Andreas Göthik, Catharina/Catharina Margaretha b Jan 1 1789, bapt Feb 22 1789/Marg. Hildebrand

David Schultz, Eva Margaretha/Anna Maria b Jan 10 1789, bapt Mar 1 1789/ Parents

Johann Faubel, Margaretha/Elisabetha b Dec 20 1788, bapt Feb 26 1789/Jacob Rohr, Catharina

Georg Gebhardt, Barbara/Charlotta b Jan 24 1789, bapt Mar 11 1789/Susanna Lieblich, grandmother

Johann Nicol, Philippina/Jacob b Oct 20 1788, bapt Mar 11 1789/Valentin Bocky, single

Johannes Bier, Juliana/Johannes Georg b Jan 21 1789, bapt Mar 19 1789/ Parents

Arnold Hardy, Barbara/Casper b Mar 6 1789, bapt Apr 1 1789/Parents

Polly, mother, A Hardy's slave/Eleonor b Sep 16 1787, bapt Apr 1 1789/The owner

Georg Zimmerman, Margaretha/Benjamin b Feb 20 1789, bapt Apr 4 1789/Parents

Johann Brunner, Susanna/Louisa b Oct 20 1788, bapt Apr 4 1789/Johann Remsperger, Catharina

Christian Getzedanner, Catharina/Johannes b Oct 9 1788, bapt Apr 5 1789/ Balthasar Getzedanner & Anna

Andreas Lang, Anna/Maria Magdalena b Oct 12 1789, bapt Apr 5 1789/Nico. Schmit, Magdalena

Michael Hauser, Susanna/Wilhelm b Feb 22 1789, bapt Apr 6 1789/Parents

Peter Immel, Susanna/Maria b Sep 27 1788, bapt Apr 13 1789/Parents & wf. of Joh. Heintz

Henrich Miller, Margaretha/Margaretha b Dec 30 1767, bapt Apr 10 1789/Adult, wf. of Lud. Luckas

Michael Lengefelder, Margaret/Joh. Michael b Mar 20 1789, bapt Apr 24 1789/ Michael Metz, Anna Maria

Herman Hellman, Magdalena/Jacob b Feb 17 1789, bapt Apr 24 1789/Parents

Geb. Bentz, Elisabetha/Margaretha b Feb 3 1789, bapt Apr 26 1789/Margaretha Bentz, widow

Adam Knauff, Christina/Jacob b Oct 15 1788, bapt May 1 1789/Joh. Keplinger, Catharina

Georg Roth, Margaretha/Maria Barbara b Jan 14 1789, bapt May 18 1789/Maria Eva Erhardt

Adam Stoll, Elisabeth/Susanna b Feb 2 1789, bapt May 21 1789/Christian Remsperger, Susanna

Sig. Schauer, Elisabeth/Sigismund b May 5 1789, bapt May 22 1789/Parents
Johannes Löschhorn, Margaretha/David b Mar 31 1789, bapt May 31 1789/The Father & his sister Elisabeth
Thomas Lemon, Sarah/Sarah b Mar 2 1789, bapt Jul 12 1789/Parents
---/Anthony & Jason, black children owned by Thomas Maynard, who promised to have them instructed
Ed. Salmon, Elisabetha/Eduard b Jun 15 1789, bapt Jul 26 1789/Jacob Weiss, Maria Anna
Philip Schmit, Kerehabugh (cf. Job 42:14)/Elisabetha b ---, bapt Jul 30 1789/Elisabetha Schmit, single
Henrich Bantz, Catharina/Wilhelm b May 22 1789, bapt Jul 30 1789/ Philip Schmit
Jacob Baltzel, Charlotta/Anna Maria b Jun 30 1789, bapt Aug 10 1789/Parents
Johannes Keplinger, Catharina/Georg b Jul 14 1789, bapt Aug 12 1789/Parents
Peter Bayer, Anna Maria/Maria Catharina b Aug 13 1789, bapt Aug 13 1789/ Mich. Masseter, Anna Maria
Jacob Aurand, Christina/Daniel b Aug 4 1789, bapt Aug 13 1789/Daniel Heintz, single
Peter Gebhardt, Eva Margaretha/Wilhelm b Jun 5 1789, bapt Aug 16 1789/ Parents
Nicolaus Schäfer, Anna Maria/Elisabetha b Jun 5 1789, bapt Aug 16 1789/Joh. Schäfer, Elisabetha
Henrich Vogler, Margaretha/Henrich b Nov 19 1788, bapt Aug 16 1789/Parents
Joh. Zimmerman, Eleonora/Jacob b Aug 8 1789, bapt Aug 19 1789/Jacob Holtz, Barbara
Mat. Bocky, Christina/Jacob b Jul 4 1789, bapt Sep 5 1789/Parents
Jos. Hildebrand, Magdalena/Joseph b Jul 18 1789, bapt Sep 6 1789/Parents
Michael Braun, Rosina/Georg b Aug 17 1789, bapt Sep 7 1789/Parents
Henrich Schwedner, Elisabeth/David b Feb 8 1789, bapt Sep 9 1789/Philip Heintz, Maria
Joh. Fuhrman, Sarah/David & Sarah/b Jul 4 1789, bapt Sep 10 1789/Parents
Joh. Hoffman, Catharina/Wilhelm b Jan 22 1789, bapt Sep 14 1789/Nicolaus Gipps
Joh. Schneider, Dorothea/Abraham b Feb 14 1787, bapt Sep 15 1789/Philip Borger, Maria Barbara
Joh. Schneider, Dorothea/Magdalena b Aug 1 1789, bapt Sep 15 1789/Anna Maria Borger, single
Wendel Werner, Catharina/Christina b Aug 14 1789, bapt Sep 15 1789/Jacob Aurandt, Christina
Jacob Stehly, Barbara/Johannes b Jun 24 1789, bapt Sep 18 1789/Parents
Joh. Freyberger, Rachel/Henrich b Dec 1 1789(8?), bapt Sep 18 1789/The Father
Henrich Krass, Catharina/Johannes b Jul 4 1789, bapt Sep 18/Parents
Peter Mantz, Catharina/Gideon b Mar 7 1788, bapt Sep 19 1789/The Mother
Jacob Rohr, Catharina/Sophia b Sep 9 1789, bapt Sep 21 1789/Anthony Krumm, Sophia
Joh. Heintz, Gertraut/Wilhelm b Sep 16 1789, bapt Oct 21 1789/Parents
Jacob Schneider, Catharina/Henrich b Sep 20 1789, bapt Oct 11 1789/Henrich Schneider, Margaretha
Peter Bohrer, Magdalena/Benjamin Schenckmayer, b Apr 6 1788, bapt Oct 6 1789/Joh. Schenckmayer, Maria Elisabeth
Robert Mullennecks, Anna/Thomas b Apr 8 1789, bapt Nov 3 1789/Parents

Joh. Leininger, Sophia/Samuel b Dec 30 1788, bapt Nov 4 1789/Friedrich Winter, Catharina
Joh. Gebhardt, Elisabeth/Johannes b Oct 24 1789, bapt Nov 4 1789/Parents
Stephan Brunner, A. Barbara/Anna Barbara b Mar 9 1789, bapt Nov 13 1789/ Parents
Johannes Spohn, Susanna/David b Sep 18 1789, bapt Nov 18 1789/Parents
Jacob Steiner, Elisabeth/Joh. Thomas b May 27 1789, bapt Nov 21 1789/Jacob Steiner, Sr., Maria Anna
Conrad Keller, Margaretha/Johannes b Nov 8 1789, bapt Nov 23 1789/Philip Heintz, A. Maria
Henrich Hemp, Margaretha/Catharina b Mar 28 1789, bapt Nov 25 1789/Parents
Joseph Doll, Charlotta/Joh. Peter b Oct 15 1789, bapt Dec 5 1789/Peter Hardt, single
Joh. Schauer, Elisabeth/Johannes b Oct 29 1789, bapt Dec 6 1789/Parents
Philip Rohr, Catharina/Joh. Peter b --, bapt Dec 6 1789/Peter Hardt, single
Johann Rohr & wf./Elisabetha b --, bapt Dec 6 1789/--
Henrich Hirschberger, Catharina/Joh. Bernhardt b Sep 23 1789, bapt Dec 10 1789/Bern. Hirschberger, Elisabeth
Joh. Remsperger, Catharina/Georg b Oct 6 1789, bapt Dec 10 1789/Georg Remsperger, single
Nicolaus Herman, Christina/Wilhelm b Apr 10 1789, bapt Dec 10 1789/Wilh. Kasman & wf.
Wilhelm Allbach, Catharina/Isaac b Nov 23 1789, bapt Dec 17 1789/Hubertus Bayer, Susanna
Joh. Schäfer, Elisabeth/Anna Maria b Oct 20 1789, bapt Dec 19 1789/Maria Storm, single
Daniel Jung, Anna Margaretha/Daniel b Sep 2 1788, bapt Dec 30 1789/Parents
Joh. Faubel, Margaretha/Philip b Dec 27 1789, bapt Jan 1 1790/Philip Rohr, Catharina
John James, Martha/Sarah b Sep -- 1789, bapt Jan 14 1790/Parents
Christian Hartwig, Juliana/Salomon b Dec 12 1789, bapt Jan 14 1790/Hubertus Bayer, Susanna
Peter Bell, Magdalena/Elisabetha b Jan 10 1790, bapt Jan 26 1790/Elisabeth Stillinger
Christoph Bergman, Anna Maria/Daniel b Jan 1 1790, bapt Jan 31 1790/Mat. Bucky, Christina
Wilhelm Michael, Barbara/Johannes b May 11 1789, bapt Feb -- 1790/Joh. Thomas
Joh. Remsperger, Elisabeth/Johann Adam b Dec 12 1789, bapt Feb 27 1790/Michael Remsperger
Arthur Fleming, Sarah/Arthur b Oct 11 1789, bapt Mar 7 1789/Parents
Jacob Kändel, Maria/Barbara b Apr 12 1785, bapt Mar 8 1790/Parents
Jacob Kändel, Maria/David b Feb 22 1790, bapt Mar 8 1790/Parents
Jacob Hān, Catharina/Wilhelm b Jun 28 1784/bapt Mar 10 1790/Parents
Jacob Hān, Catharina/Catharine b May 8 1786/bapt Mar 10 1790/Parents
Jacob Hān, Catharina/Daniel b Mar 7 1788/bapt Mar 10 1790/Parents
Henrich Christ, Christina/Jacob b Oct 14 1780, bapt Mar 22 1790/Jacob Balzel, Charlotta
Georg Miller, Elisabeth/Maria b Mar 23 1788, bapt Mar 22 1790/The Mother
Michael Christ, Maria Elisabeth/Rosina b Sep 20 1789, bapt Mar 22 1790/ Parents

Will, Jane, blacks/Eleonora b Dec 23 1787, bapt Mar 22 1789/owned by Michael Christ who promised to have them instructed
Elias Lefever & wf./Elias b Jul 20 1770/bapt Apr 2 1790, adult
Elias Lefever & wf./Catharina b Dec 28 1768/bapt Apr 2 1790, adult
--- Miller & wf./Elisabetha b ---, adult, bapt Apr 2 1790/Johan Remsperger's
--- Miller & wf./Anna b ---, adult, bapt Apr 2 1790
Philip Breiss, Susanna/Johann Peter b Nov 30 1789, bapt Apr 4 1790/Mat. Schmit, A. Maria
Jacob Schafer, Elisabetha/Elisabetha b Sep 24 1789, bapt Apr 4 1790/ Margaretha Bucky, single
Adam Schreiner & wf./Valentin b --, bapt Apr 4 1790/Parents
Jacob Levy, Maria/Rebecca b Mar 16 1790, bapt Apr 4 1790/Barbara Levy
Benjamin Dowell, Barbara/Salomon b Apr 13 1789, bapt Apr 25 1790/Elisabeth Springer
Georg Hauer, Elisabeth Margaret/Adam b Apr 21 1790, bapt May 1 1790/ Catharina Hauer, wf. of Nicolaus
Samuel Dorst, Mary Ann/Henrietta b ---, bapt May 2 1790/Henrich Dorst, Maria
Georg Ganzog, Margaretha/Johannes b Nov 8 1789, bapt May 2 1790/Joh. Bode, single
Eckhardt Gills, Catharina/Georg b Apr 10 1790, bapt May 5 1790/Philip Preiss, Susanna
Johann Lentz, Magdalena/Eva Catharina b Oct 10 1789, bapt May 7 1790/Eva Herschberger
Johannes Baer, Anna Maria/Catharina b Oct 19 1789, bapt May 8 1790/Georg Baer, Jr., Catharina
Conrad Leschhorn, Maria/Anna Maria b Sep 12 1789, bapt May 13 1790/Parents
Jacob Traut, Elisabetha/Michael b Mar 22 1790, bapt May 23 1790/Michael Wachter, single
Frantz Gemmer, A. Maria/Eva Margaretha b Jan 5 1790, bapt May 23 1790/Eva Marg. Bucky, single
David Jordan, Margaretha/David b Feb 4 1790, bapt May 24 1790/Valentin Brunner, Elisabetha
Christian Thomas, Susanna/Henrich b Feb 5 1790, bapt May 27 1790/Parents
Henrich Fahling, Elisabetha/Joh. Henrich b Apr 9 1790, bapt May 30 1790/ Henrich Richter
Geo. Biehr, Anna Maria/Joh. Georg b Jan 4 1790, bapt May 15 1790/Adam Wolff, single
Joh. Thomas, Elisabetha/Charlotta b Mar 1 1790, bapt May 15 1790/Charlotta Remsperger
Jacob Faubel, Margaretha/Elisabetha b Jan 1 1790, bapt May 31 1790/Elisabeth Doll, single
Samuel Pannebeck, Susanna/Elisabetha b Aug 24 1789, bapt Jun 22 1790/Cat. Mosseter, single
Thomas Mark, Catharina/Elisabetha b May 21 1790, bapt Jun 22 1790/Anna Maria Bossert
Adam Schnook, Margaretha/Susanna b May 7 1790, bapt Jul 5 1790/Parents
Jacob Mayer, Elisabeth/Barbara b Nov 20 1789, bapt Jul 5 1790/Barbara Mayer, single
Johan Jacob Schley, A. Maria/Friedrich August b May 14 1789, bapt Jul 11 1790/Michael Schellman, single
Henrich Baer, Elisabeth/Susanna b May 3 1790, bapt Jul 11 1790/Susanna Schellman, single

Peter Hufnagel, Elisabeth/Joh. Georg b Jul 4 1790, bapt Jul 14 1790/Johan Rohr, Elisabetha
Malachiah Benham, Mary/James Forrest b Jun 23 1790, bapt Jul 15 1790/Parents
Christian Getzendanner, Catharina/Anna Maria b Jul 5 1790, bapt Jul 6 1790/Balt. Getzendanner, Anna
Conrad Keller, Eliza/Friedrich b Jun 17 1790, bapt Jul 18 1790/Edward Salmon, Elisabetha
Christian Hartman, Catharina/Johannes b Jun 6 1790, bapt Jul 18 1790/Jacob Schneider
Johann Wetzel, Martha/Johannes b Jun 11 1790, bapt Jul 25 1790/Adam Lehman, Margaretha
Leonhart Lantz, Catharina/Susanna b Sep 25 1789, bapt Jul 26 1790/Susanna Bug, widow
Georg Weterich, Catharina/Anna Margaretha b Jan 31 1790, bapt Jul 31 1790/ Johan Remsperger, Elisabetha
Christian Getzendanner, Maria/Elisabetha b Jul 1 1790, bapt Aug 1 1790/Elis. Haas, single
Georg Ebrecht, Magdalena/Barbara b May 7 1790, bapt Aug 1 1790/Barbara Derner, wf. of Jacob
Peter Brunner, Catharina/Daniel b Mar 16 1790, bapt Aug 3 1790/Parents
Johannes Gomber, Esther/Josiah b Oct 21 1789, bapt Aug 3 1790/Parents
Georg Schmit, Catharina/Johannes b Jun 20 1790, bapt Aug 17 1790/Jacob Springer
Henrich Würstler, Catharina/Henrich b Aug 11 1789, bapt Aug 17 1790/Jacob Schneider, Margaret
Joh. Getzendanner, Catharina/Elisabetha b May 29 1790, bapt Aug 8 1790/ Elisabetha Hoffman, wf. of Philip
Richard Griffith, Margaretha/Elisabetha b Mar 28 1790, bapt Aug 26 1790/ Elisabetha Deiss, single
Joh. Freyberger, Rachel/Johannes b Apr 19 1790, bapt Sep 2 1790/The Father
Jacob Brandenberger, Elisabetha/Jacob b Mar 19 1790, bapt Sep 7 1790/Jacob Schneider, Margaretha
Jacob Remsperger, Anna Elisabetha/Susanna Catharina b May 6 1790, bapt Sep 8 1790/The mother
Michael Ott, Elisabetha/Thomas b Sep 18 1789, bapt Sep 20 1790/Parents
Johannes Waldeck, Susanna/Catharina b Feb 25 1790, bapt Sep 26 1790/Parents
Joh. Bucher, Rosina/Georg b Sep 11 1790, bapt Sep 27 1790/Parents
Jacob Brunner, Magdalena/Charlotta b Jul 29 1790/bapt Sep 28 1790/Parents
John Holiday, Mary/John b Sep 30 1790, bapt Oct 7 1790/Elisabeth Schmit, widow
Johann Pfeiffer, Catharina/Johanes b Sep 1 1790, bapt Oct 8 1790/Joh. Pfeiffer
Joh. Leschhorn, Rebecca/Johannes b Jun 27 1790, bapt Oct 8 1790/Elisabeth Leschhorn, single
Benjamin Clary, Catharina/Henrietta b Apr 25 1790, bapt Oct 12 1790/Parents
Henrich Kuhns, Margaretha/Catharina Henrietta b Sep 1 1790, bapt Oct 24 1790/Parents
Georg Schafer, Catharina/Susanna b Jul 4 1790, bapt Oct 24 1790/Philippina Stoll, widow
Georg Borckhard, Ann/Georg b Nov 10 1790, bapt Oct 27 1790/Parents
Andrew Boyd, Mary/David b Aug 20 1790, bapt Nov 22 1790/The mother

Jacob Metzger, Christina/Catharina b Nov 16 1790, bapt Nov 23 1790/Cat. Ackerman
Jacob Schneider, Elisabeth/Anna Maria b Oct 15 1790, bapt Nov 24 1790/ Parents
George Hoffman, Eva Margaretha/Elisabetha b Oct 6 1790, bapt Nov 26 1790/ Elisabeth Doll, single
The late Michael Krämer, Magdalena/Maria Magdalena b Nov 5 1790, bapt Dec 23 1790/Charlotta Lauffer
Nicolaus Madery, Susanna/Elisabetha b Oct 9 1790, bapt Dec 24 1790/The mother
Jacob Hoffman, Salome/Jacob Rau b Oct 17 1790, bapt Dec 25 1790/Henrich Ziehler
Peter Engels, Jr., Susanna/Esra b Nov 13 1790, bapt Dec 27 1790/Peter Engels, Sr., Maria Catharina
Georg Garlach, Charlotta/Catharina b Nov 12 1790, bapt Dec 27 1790/Philip Bier, Balt., Catharina Lantz
Johannes Keller, Ursula/Jacob b Dec 26 1790, bapt Dec 28 1790/Parents
Henrich Bantz, Catharina/Catharina b Jun 9 1790, bapt Jan 6 1791/Parents
Henrich Stehly, Catharina/Elias b Mar 2 1790, bapt Jan 5 1791/Parents
Joseph Hildebrand, Magdalena/Anna Maria b Dec 8 1790, bapt Jan 5 1791/Anna Maria Hildebrand
Mattheus Hauck, Susanna/Georg Michael b Nov 14 1790, bapt Jan 12 1791/G. Michael Morgenstern, Catharina
Mattheus Hauck, Susanna/Anna Elisabetha b Nov 14 1790/Jacob Remsperger, Susanna
Henrich Hoffman, Elisabeth/Henrich b Nov 27 1790, bapt Jan 12 1791/Parents
Elias Brunner, Elisabeth/Daniel b Jan 2 1791, bapt Jan 14 1791/Joh. Brunner
Philip Borsch, Barbara/Eva b Dec 15 1790, bapt Jan 14 1791/The mother
Henrich Kreiss, Barbara/Johannes b Sep 25 1790, bapt Jan 18 1791/The father
Abraham Gippes, Dorothea/Elisabetha b Jan 19 1791, bapt Jan 29 1791/Parents
Abraham Schad & wf./Georg b May 11 1790, bapt Jan 30 1791/Georg Jost, Catharina
Daniel Ehl, Magdalena/Daniel b Dec 19 1790, bapt Feb 1 1791/Parents
Michael Tempel, Margaretha/Catharina b Sep 1 1790, bapt Feb 2 1791/The mother
Wilhelm Baer, Elisabetha/Margaretha b Sep 23 1790, bapt Feb 7/Jacob Metzger, Christina
Georg Heckedorn, Maria Elisabeth/Joh. Henrich b Jul 1 1789, bapt Feb 8 1791/ Georg Ostertag
Joh. Koppenheber, Barbara/Elisabetha b Dec 12 1790, bapt Feb 9 1791/Parents
Gideon Gast, Anna Maria/Elisabetha b Jul 10 1790, bapt Feb 10 1791/Parents
Frantz Geissinger, Sarah/David b Dec 28 1790, bapt Feb 25 1791/Barbara Levy, wf. of Valentin
David Schultz, Eva/David b Jan 3 1791, bapt Feb 25 1791/Parents
Andreas Bossert, Anna Maria/Adam b Nov 24 1790, bapt Feb 26 1791/Parents
Johann Kempf, Elisabetha/Salome b Dec 10 1790, bapt Mar 9 1791/Michael Stocker, Maria
Bernhardt Ott, Anna Elisabeth/Georg b Feb 25 1791, bapt Mar 9 1791/Parents
James Stokes, Anna Maria/Elisabetha b Mar 7 1791, bapt Mar 12 1791/Anna Maria Herp
Balthasar Schneider, Maria/Johannes b Dec 29 1790, bapt Mar 20 1791/Joh. Lack, Louisa Propheter, wf. of Conrad

Baptisms of the Evangelical Reformed Church in Frederick, Maryland

Georg Reinhardt, Salome/Salome b Feb 6 1791, bapt Mar 26 1791/Parents
Daniel Ball, Catharina/William b Aug 6 1790, bapt Mar 27 1791/Jacob Kern, Elisabeth
Joseph Schuster, Elisabeth/Anna Maria b Feb 6 1790, bapt Mar 26 1791/Parents
Michael Eberhardt, Eva Margaretha/Eva Elisabetha b Jan 18 1791, bapt Mar 31 1791/Wilhelm Miller, Maria Eva
Adam Stoll, Elisabetha/Georg b Feb 6 1791, bapt Apr 6 1791/Parents
Jacob Springer, Elisabetha/Jacob b Nov 16 1790, bapt Apr 22 1791/Parents
Peter Frantz, Susanna/Johannes b Mar 8 1791, bapt Apr 22 1791/Johan Zimmerman, Eleonora
Johann Thomas, Catharina/Johan Peter b Mar 2 1791, bapt Apr 9 1791/Peter Thomas, single
Georg Nicol, A. Margaretha/Johan Jacob b Dec 25 1790, bapt Apr 9 1791/ Parents
Georg Remsperger, Christina/Catharina b Oct 15 1790, bapt Apr 9 1791/Parents
Ludwig Kempf, Barbara/Maria b Apr 21 1790, bapt Apr 9 1791/Parents
Johann Bier, Juliana/Elisabetha b Nov 10 1790, bapt Apr 15 1791//Marg. Schneider
Michael Däbler, A. Maria/Catharina b Apr 4 1790, bapt Apr 25 1791/Barbara Wip
Alexander M. Kinsey, Sarah/Margaretha b Feb -- 1784, bapt Apr 9 1791/Conrad Leschhorn
Henrich Kempf, Margaretha/Sarah b Feb 28 1791, bapt May 8 1791/Georg Bernhardt, Catharina
Georg Kettero, Elisabeth/Michael b Jan 23 1791, bapt May 8 1791/Michael Christ, Maria Elisabeth
Georg Silber, Nancy/Jacob b Mar 8 1791, bapt May 8 1791/Jacob Mayer
Philip Schafer, Anna Maria/Georg b Dec 18 1790, bapt May 16 1791/The father
Pippin, Catharine, blacks/Dinah b May 10 1791, bapt May 17 1791/prp. of widow Williamson, who engaged to have them educated
Jacob Spanseiler, Christina/Jacob b May 5 1791, bapt May 18 1791/Parents
Henrich Richter, Catharina/Christina b Mar 27 1791, bapt May 22 1791/Parents
Frantz Germayer, Maria Elisabeth/Maria Elisabetha b Apr 1 1791, bapt May 23 1791/Elisabeth Schmit, widow
Henrich Dersch, Maria/Georg b Apr 16 1791, bapt May 28 1791/Parents
James Taylor, Margaret/Philip b Apr 18 1791, bapt May 29 1791/Henrich Fischer, Maria Dorothea
Henrich Schreiber, Barbara/Daniel b Nov 11 1790, bapt Jun 10 1791/Parents
Jacob Aurand, Christina/Adam b Jul 15 1791, bapt Jul 22 1791/Philip Jacob, Elisabetha
Lorentz Brengel, Eva/Lorentz b Jul 14 1791, bapt Jul 23 1791/Parents
John Usher Charlton, Elisabeth/Elisabeth b Jun 20 1791, bapt Jul 25 1791/ Jane Charlton
Joh. Jacob Schley, A. Maria/Georg Schelman b May 14 1791, bapt Jul 31 1791/ Michael Bayer
Andreas Götick, Maria Catharina/Henrich b May 17 1791, bapt Jul 31 1791/ Christoph Bergman, A, Maria
Leonhardt --, Catharina/Salome b Jun 1 1791, bapt Aug 8 1791/Susanna Engels, wf. of Peter
Georg Bentz, Elisabeth/Johannes b Jun 28 1791, bapt Aug 8 1791/Parents
Benjamin Steward, Mary/Cravin b Jan 28 1791, bapt Aug 11 1791/The mother

Gottfried Gebhardt, Maria Magdalena/Catharina b Apr 23 1791, bapt Aug 14 1791/Peter Schnook, Juliana
Georg Eder, Maria/Thomas b Feb 24 1791, bapt Aug 14 1791/David Bayer, Susanna Griffen
Michael Spannseiler, Sarah/Jacob b Oct 10 1789, bapt Aug 16 1791/Jacob Spannseiler, Christina
Jacob Liess, Maria/Maria b May 5 1790, bapt Aug 16 1791/Maria Jacob, single
Martin Waltz, Barbara/Martin b Jul 7 1791, bapt Aug 17 1791/Parents
Johannes Faubel, Margaretha/Johann Jacob b Apr 1 1791, bapt Aug 19 1791/Jacob Rohr, Catharina
Jacob Steiner, Elisabeth/Wilhelm b Jun 1 1791, bapt Aug 27 1791/Henrich Kuhns, Margaretha
Georg Heckedorn, Maria Elisabetha/Peter b Jun 19 1791, bapt Aug 30 1791/Johannes Nicol, Philippina
Jeremiah Stuart & wf./Jane Chism (Chisholm) b May 13 1791, bapt Aug 30 1791/Parents
Stephan Brunner & wf./Stephan b --, bapt Sep 23 1791/Parents
Michael Reiss, Elisabeth/Jacob b Jun 19 1791, bapt Sep 30 1791/Parents
Lorentz Spielman, Elisabeth/Peter b Jul 6 1791, bapt Sep 30 1791/Peter Kriegbaum
Christian Getzendanner, Catharina/Michael b Jun 26 1791, bapt Oct 9 1791/Parents
Joseph Doll, Charlotta/Jacob b Aug 21 1791, bapt Oct 9 1791/Parents
Peter Bell, Magdalena/Catharina b May 5 1791, bapt Oct 9 1791/Parents
Joh. Hoffman, Catharina/Friedrich Wilhelm b Aug 29 1790, bapt Oct 16 1791/The mother
Peter Schäfer, Catharina/Anna Elisabetha b Sep 14 1791, bapt Oct 17 1791/Bernhardt Ott, Anna Elisabetha
Michael Rau, Elisabeth/Johannes b Nov 31 1788, bapt Nov 8 1791/Elisabeth Dadesman wf. of -- Dadesmann
Michael Rau, Elisabeth/Wilhelm b Dec 6 1790, bapt Nov 8 1791/Elisabeth Miller wf. of Nicolaus
Michael Witmer, Catharina/Catharina b Apr 9 1789, bapt Nov 20 1791/Jacob Kitweiler
Lorentz Eberhardt, Anna Maria/Johannes b Aug 30 1791, bapt Nov 23 1791/Jacob Kern, Maria Elisabeth
Henrich Thomas, Anna Maria/Anna Maria b Oct 25 1791(?), bapt Oct 24 1791/Charlotta Remsperger
Jacob Martin, Elisabetha/Catharina b Feb 21 1791, bapt Nov 24 1791/Parents
Daniel Jung, Margaretha/Susanna b Jul 19 1791, bapt Nov 26 1791/Susanna Streber, single
Johannes Stoll, Margaretha/Catharina b Jul 6 1791, bapt Nov 28 1791/Parents
Peter Mantz, Catharina/Catharina b Dec 19 1789, bapt Dec 7 1791/The mother
Peter Mantz, Catharina/Emmanuel b Oct 17 1791, bapt Dec 7 1791/The mother
Georg Barrall, Elisabetha/Georg b Mar 23 1791, bapt Dec 11 1791/Parents
Johannes Spangler, Maria/Rebecca b Sep 2 1791, bapt Dec 20 1791/Parents
Gabriel Thomas, Anna Maria/Anna Margaretha b Nov 16 1791, bapt Dec 22 1791/Henrich Thomas, A. Margaretha
Conradt Propheter, Maria Louisa/Elisabetha b Nov 19 1791, bapt Dec 24 1791/Parents
Benedict Steiner & wf. Anna Barbara/Jacob b Mar 22 1789, bapt Dec 24 1791/Parents

Benedict Steiner & wf. Anna Barbara/David Eschelman b Oct 23 1790, bapt Dec 24 1791/Maria Jacob, single
Benedict Steiner & wf. Anna Barbara/Christina b Oct 23 1790, bapt Dec 24 1791
Jacob Balzell, Charlotta/Catharina b Oct 16 1791, bapt Dec 25 1791/Maria Christ, single
Mattheus Seifert, Elisabeth/Georg b Sep 25 1791, bapt Dec 25 1791/Parents
Michael Braun, Rosina/Margaretha b Aug 10 1791, bapt Nov 4 1791/ Catharina Jantz, widow
Jacob Levy, Magdalena/Elisabetha b Oct 6 1791, bapt Jan 6 1792/Elisabetha Schreiner wf. of Valentin
Jacob Wiest, Eva Catharina/Georg b Jan 3 1792, bapt Jan 7 1792/Parents
Henrich Steiner, Elisabeth/Henrich b Mar 3 1790, bapt Jan 22 1792/The father
Jacob Hän, Catharina/David b Oct 9 1791, bapt Jan 25 1792/Parents
Christian Balzell, Catharina/Wilhelm b --, bapt Feb 2 1792/Jacob Metzger, Christina
Edward Salmon, Elisabeth/Charles b Dec 18 1791, bapt Feb 19 1792/Parents
Harry, Polly, blacks/William b Jan 30 1792, bapt Feb 20 1792/Baker Johnson's slaves, who will care for their souls
Johann Spohn, Susanna/Sarah b Nov 16 1791, bapt Feb 22 1792/Peter Hauck, Margaretha
Herman Hellman, Magdalena/Christina b Nov 29 1791, bapt Feb 22 1792/Parents
Johannes Heins, Gertraut/Friedrich b Dec 7 1791, bapt Mar 12 1792/Jacob Aurand, Christina
Henry Poole, Margaret/Daniel James b Oct 17 1791, bapt Mar 13 1792/Parents
Michael Zimmerman, Eva/Michael b Dec 17 1791, bapt Mar 17 1792/Parents
Michael Zimmerman, Eva/Henrich b Dec 17 1791, bapt Mar 17 1792/Benj. Zimmerman
Peter Brunner, Jr. Catharina/Peter b Nov 2 1791, bapt Apr 8 1792/Johannes Brunner, son of John
Jacob Rohr, Catharina/Margaretha b Feb 22 1792, bapt Apr 2 1792/Margaretha Kesssler, single
Adam Deiwelbiss, Catharina/Wilhelm b Feb 30 1790, bapt Apr 10 1792/Parents
Francis Green, Sophia/Georg b Feb 29 1792, bapt Apr 11 1792/Peter Haller, Christina Magdalena
John McMullen, Nancy/John b Jan 23 1792, bapt Apr 12 1792/The parents
Johannes Thomas, Elisabeth/Peter b Feb 23 1792, bapt Apr 15 1792/Gabriel Thomas, Jr., Anna Maria
Abraham Herget, Anna Maria/Magdalena b Jan 22 1792, bapt Apr 15 1792/ Magdalena Braun, single
Henrich Lambi, A. Maria/Christina b Feb 14 1792, bapt Apr 15 1792/Christina Eberhardt, single
Peter Gebhardt, Eva Margaretha/Margaretha b Jan 1 1792, bapt Apr 23 1792/ Parents
Valentin Hoffman, Elisabeth/Jacob b Mar 30 1792, bapt Apr 23 1792/Parents
Jacob Schäfer, Elisabeth/Johannes b Oct 9 1791, bapt Apr 23 1792/Georg Schäfer, Catharina
Georg Schäfer, Catharina/Elisabetha b Nov 4 1791, bapt Apr 23 1792/Jacob Schäfer, Elisabetha
Jacob Poley, Elisabetha/Elisabetha b Mar 3 1790, bapt Apr 23 1792/--
Jacob Poley, Elisabetha/Maria b Feb 24 1792, bapt Apr 23 1792/--
Johannes Baer, Anna Maria/Michael b Dec 8 1792(1?), bapt Apr 24 1792/Parents

Johann Rempsperger, Elisabeth/Johannes b Dec 3 1791, bapt May 13 1792/ Michael Remsperger, Catharina
Elias Brunner, M. Elisabetha/Georg b Jan 27 1792, bapt May 13 1792/Benjamin Zimmerman
Georg Remsperger, Christina/Peter b Jan 30 1792, bapt May 13 1792/Peter Herget, Magdalena
Joh. Freyberger, Rachel/Peter b Nov 27 1791, bapt May 17 1792/The father
Georg Hoffman, Mary/Daniel b Dec 11 1791, bapt May 21 1792/Catharina Hoffman, wf. of Johannes
Nicolaus Herman, Christina/Anna Maria b Feb 3 1792, bapt Apr 21 1792/Anna Maria Thomas, wf. of Gabriel
Henrich Christ, Christina/Michael b Feb 5 1792, bapt May 24 1792/Parents
Christian Thomas, Susanna/Susanna b Feb 16 1792, bapt May 24 1792/Parents
Henrich Bantz, Catharina/Gideon b Feb 9 1792, bapt May 26 1792/Parents
Jacob Faubel, Margaretha/Johann Georg b May 9 1792, bapt May 27 1792/Joh. Georg Elias
Adam Hauser, Sibylla/Maria b May 2 1792, bapt May 29 1792/Catharina Jantz, widow
Philip Breiss, Susana/Henrich b Dec 30 1791, bapt Jun 10 1792/Johannes Ott, single
Michael Remsperger, Catharina/Ludwig b May 26 1792, bapt Jul 1 1792/Ludwig Wolff, single
Jacob Krepel, Martha/Johann Georg b --, bapt Jul 8 1792/Georg Bucky
Johannes Schäfer, Elisabeth/Georg b Jul 6 1791, bapt Jun 27 1792/Georg Schäfer, Catharina
Joseph Stehly, Julianna/Moses b Feb 11 1792, bapt Jul 1 1792/Parents
Adam Jacob, Elisabetha/Philip b Jun 29 1792, bapt Jul 29 1792/Philip Jacob, Elisabeth
Christian Getzedanner, Maria/Georg b May 10 1792, bapt Jul 31 1792/Georg Baer, Jr., Catharina
Eckhardt Gills, Catharina/Johann Peter b May 27 1792, bapt Aug 5 1792/Peter Sultzer, Christina
Henrich Baer, Elisabeth/Catharina S. b Jun 3 1792, bapt Aug 5 1792/Susanna Schelman, single
Johannes Gebhardt, Elisabeth/Sophia b May 24 1792, bapt Aug 12 1792/Parents
Georg Gebhardt, Barbara/Barbara b Mar 13 1792, bapt Aug 15 1792/Parents
Conrad Leschhorn, Maria/Susanna b Apr 4 1792,bapt Aug 15 1792/Susan Ott, single
Conrad Leschhorn, Maria/Catharina b Apr 4 1792, bapt Aug 15 1792/Cath. Leschhorn, single
Johannes Leschhorn, Rebecca/Anna Margaretha b Jun 11 1792, bapt Aug 15 1792/ Margaretha Taub, single
Johannes Lentz, Magdalena/Maria b Dec 6 1791, bapt Aug 16 1792/Parents
Christian Miller, Elisabeth/Christian b May 19 1792, bapt Aug 16 1792/ Parents
Frantz Geissinger, Sarah/Elisabetha b Jul 6 1792, bapt Aug 18 1792/Parents
Mattheus Schmit, Ann/Elisabetha b Jul 22 1791, bapt Aug 20 1792/Maria Schmit, wf. of Johannes
Peter Springfield, Anna Maria/Elisabetha b Dec 24 1790, bapt Aug 22 1792/The mother
Peter Springfield, Anna Maria/Peter b Apr 28 1788, bapt Aug 22 1792
Henrich Fehling, Elisabetha/Daniel b Jul 15 1792,bapt Aug 26 1792/Parents

Henrich Krass, dec., Catharina/Samuel b Aug 7 1791, bapt Oct 3 1792/The mother
Joseph Hildebrand, Magdalena/Georg b Aug 19 1792, bapt Oct 3 1792/Georg Schafer, Catharina
Jacob Stehly, Barbara/Susanna b Jan 15 1792, bapt Oct 3 1792/Elisabeth Stehly, single
Henrich Kuhns, Margaretha/Johannes & Catharina b Aug 11 1792, bapt Sep 17 1792/Henr. Kuhns, Dorothea/Jacob Steiner, A. Maria
Jacob Metzger, Christina/Elisabetha b Aug 1 1792, bapt Oct 9 1792/Parents
Jacob Hoffman, Sarah/Charlotta b Sep 11 1792, bapt Oct 14 1792/The mother
Richard Griffith, Margaretha/Child b Jun 29 1792, bapt Oct 17 1792/Parents
Joh. Pfeiffer, Catharina/Jacob b Sep 6 1792, bapt Oct 31 1792/Jacob Schafer, Susanna
David Levy, Maria/Jonathan wilhelm b Aug 11 1792, bapt Nov 19 1792/Parents
Richard Hardin, Rachel/Anna b Aug 29 1792, bapt Nov 19 1792/Parents
Abraham Stiel, Anna Maria/Abraham b Sep 7 1792, bapt Nov 21 1792/Johannes Allbach, Maria Catharina
James Roberts, Elisabeth/Mary b Oct 28 1792, bapt Nov 23 1792/Parents
Peter Dabler, Elizabeth/Johannes b Sep 11 1792, bapt Nov 25 1792/The father
Christoph Bergman, Anna Maria/Christoph b Oct 2 1792, bapt Nov 25 1792/Parents
Jacob Brunner, Magdalena/Johannes b Aug 13 1792, bapt Nov 27 1792/Parents
David Schultz, Eva/Catharina b Nov 20 1792, bapt Dec 18 1792/Parents
Wilhelm Baer, Elisabetha/Elisabetha b Nov 3 1792, bapt Dec 28 1792/Parents
Adam Stoll, Elisabeth/Johannes b Oct 5 1792, bapt Dec 30 1792/Georg Schäfer, Catharina
Johannes Niemeyer, Anna Barbara/Johannes b Nov 22 1792, bapt Jan 1 1793/ Jacob Mangold, Margaret Elisabeth
Jacob Getzedanner, Elisabeth/Christian b Dec 12 1791, bapt Jan 9 1793/ Parents
Joh. Delater, Sibylla/Anna Barbara b Aug 16 1790, Johann Adam b Aug 31 1792, bapt Jan 15 1793/Johannes Hauck & wf.
Philip Schaed, Dorothea/Georg Wilhelm b Dec 22 1792, bapt Jan 20 1793/Georg Berg, Susanna
Georg Ganso, Margaretha/Georg b Jul 24 1792, bapt Jan 20 1793
Peter Wolff, Catharina/Peter b Jul 21 1792, bapt Feb 3 1793/Peter Gayer, Margaretha
Hugh Raundles, Alice/Anne b Sep 20 1792, bapt Feb 4 1793/Parents
Peter Schafer, Catharina/Johannes b Dec 17 1792, bapt Feb 6 1793/Johannes Ott, single
Henrich Hemp, Margaretha/Maria Magdalena b Nov 5 1792, bapt Mar 3 1793/ Parents
Andreas Bossert, Anna Maria/Anna b Dec 19 1792, bapt Mar 20 1793/Parents
Allen Hays, Catharina/Johannes b Aug 9 1792, bapt Mar 20 1793/Andreas Bossert, Anna Maria
Johannes Bier, Julianna/Margaretha b Jul 4 1792,bapt Mar 20 1793/Margaretha Schneider, wf. of Jacob
Wm. Cox, Catharina/Johannes b Dec 10 1792, bapt Mar 20 1793/Peter Beck, single
Johannes Schäfer, Elisabeth/Friedrich b Jan 5 1793, bapt Apr 13 1793/Parents
Christian Hartinger, Julianna/Johannes b Dec 7 1792, bapt Mar 17 1793/ Parents

Johann Schön, Rebecca/Johannes b Feb 7 1793, bapt May 4 1793/The father
Daniel Etzler, Magdalena/Maria b Oct 15 1792, bapt May 11 1793/Parents
Jacob Kern, Elisabetha/Elisabetha b Dec 27 1792, bapt May 15 1793/Christoph Wedekin, Catharina
Henrich Hembe, Maria/Henrich b Apr 27 1793, bapt May 19 1793/Parents
Henrich Hoffman, Elisabeth/Catharina b Dec 23 1792, bapt May 19 1793/ Johannes Hauck, Catharina Ohl
Georg Widerich, Catharina Elisabeth/Anna Catharina b Jun 26 1792, bapt May 24 1793/Parents
Philip Rohr, Catharina/Georg b Apr 25 1793, bapt Jun 2 1793/Georg Berg, Anna
Christian Getzedanner, Catharina/Catharina b Feb 23 1793,bapt Jun 9 1793/ Parents
Jacob Kettero, Clara/Anna Maria b Jan 12 1793, bapt Jun 12 1793/Susan Veist, single
Jacob Aurand, Christina/David b May 26 1793, bapt Jun 19 1793/Friedrich Schittenhelm & Barbara
Henrich Dersch, Anna Maria/Anna Maria b Mar -- 1793, bapt Jul 14 1793/ Parents
Jacob Wiest, Eva/Elisabetha b May 9 1793, bapt Jul 16 1793/Parents
Peter Frantz, Susanna/Margaretha b Jun 6 1793, bapt Jul 17 1793/Georg Zimmerman, A. Margartha
Samuel, Esther, blacks/Jeremiah b May 18 1793, bapt Jul 21 1793/Samuel B. Johnson's sl. R. Aud's slave
Johannes Thomas, Elisabeth/Christina b Jul 13 1793, bapt Jul 27 1793/Parents
Joseph Borckhardt, Maria Eva/Susanna b Feb 6 1792, bapt Aug 5 1793/The father
Elias Brunner, Maria Elisabetha/Michael b Jun 28 1793, bapt Aug 13 1793/ Parents
Henrich Thomas, Anna Margaretha/Michael b Jul 2 1793, bapt Aug 14 1793/ Joseph Wedekin, Catharina
Michael Bast, Maria Barbara/Michael b Feb 28 1793, bapt Aug 14 1793/Michael Remsperger, Catharina
Michael Remsperger, Catharina/Henrich b Jul 12 1793, bapt Aug 14 1793/ Michael Bast, Maria Barbara
Jacob Schneider, Catharina/Susanna b Aug 7 1793, bapt Aug 19 1793/Michael Hauser, Susanna
Christian Weber, Catharina/Sophia b Jul 6 1788, Anna Maria b Nov 16 1791, bapt Sep 7 1793/Parents
Valentin Weber, Catharina/Margaretha b May 8 1793, bapt Sep 7 1793/Jacob Weber, father of the mother
Jacob Traut, Elisabetha/Valentin b Sep 23 1793, bapt Sep 27 1793/Valentin Bucky, Charlotta
Georg Bentz, Elisabetha/Catharina b Jun 29 1793, bapt Aug 29 1793/Parents
Henrich Kempf, Anna Margaretha/Susanna b May 28 1793, bapt Sep 1 1793/ Parents
John Mehoney, Henrietta/William b Aug 2, bapt Sep 7 1793/The mother
Michael Weber, Catharina//Magaretha b Aug 28 1793, bapt Oct 4 1793/Parents
Georg Lieblich, Elisabetha/Elisabetha b Sep 9 1793, bapt Oct 10 1793/ Johannes Nicol, Philippina
John Winter, Mary/Rebekah b Oct 2 1793, bapt Oct 11 1793/The father
Johannes Heintz, Gertraut/Abraham b Jul 28 1793, bapt Oct 15 1793/Leonhard Schreyer

Baptisms of the Evangelical Reformed Church in Frederick, Maryland

Jacob Bartel, Elisabetha/Johannes b Aug 7 1793, bapt Oct 20 1793/Philip Rohr, Catharina

Jacob Steiner, Elisabeth/Sophia b Oct 19 1793, bapt Oct 20 1793/Catharina Hauer, wf. of Nicolaus

Nicolaus Madery, Susanna/Charlotta b Nov 30 1792, bapt Nov 6 1793/The mother

Bernhardt Ott, Elisabetha/Christina b Sep 11 1793, bapt Nov 13 1793/ Christina Sultzer, wf. of Peter

Georg Fahly, Magdalena/Susanna b Nov 1 1793, bapt Nov 14 1793/Julianna Wolff wf. of Henry Wolff

Michael Schmit, Cath. Weimer/Anna Catharina b Dec 28 1791, bapt Nov 15 1793/ Henrich Wied & Elis., grandparents

Valentin Hoffman, Elisabeth/Peter b Sep 23 1793, bapt Nov 21 1793/Parents

Henrich Schreiber, Barbara/Susanna b Aug 11 1793, bapt Nov 23 1793/Parents

Joh. Jacob Holtz, Anna Barbara/Anna Maria b --, bapt Nov 28 1793/Mat. Haux, Susanna

Levin Spurry, Eleonor/Lot b Apr 24 1791, William b Apr 25 1793, bapt Nov 2 1793/Parents

Wm. Clary, Rachel/Leah b Dec 12 1792,bapt Nov 2 1793/Parents

Lewis Gardener, Elisabeth/William b Nov 27 1793, bapt Dec 4 1793/Parents

Gabriel Thomas, Ann Maria/Peter b Oct 17 1793, bapt Dec 11 1793/Gorg Remsperger, single

Georg Dadesman, Elisabeth/Georg b Oct 8 1793, bapt Dec 14 1793/Magdalena Hohl, wf. of Jacob

Wm. McLane, Maria/William b Dec 11 1793, bapt Dec 19 1793/Parents

John Schley, Polly/Henry b Mar 18 1793/bapt Dec -- 1793/Parents

Georg Gier, Maria/Georg b Sep 28 1793, bapt Jan 15 1794/Christoph Zancker, single

Samuel Flower, Mary/Samuel b Aug 7 1793, bapt Jan 15 1794/The mother

Joseph Doll,Catharina/Samuel b Nov 5 1793, bapt Feb 1 1794/Charlotta Doll, single

Conrad Miller, Elisabeth/Joh. Wilhelm b Jan 29 1794, bapt Feb 14 1794/The mother

Jost Stimmel, Magdalena/Maria Elisabetha b Nov 8 1793, bapt Feb 12 1794/ Michael Stocker, Anna Maria

Arthur Flemming, Sarah/Joseph b Jul 18 1793, bapt Mar 27 1794/Parents

Johannes Freyberger, Rachel/Georg b Jun 16 1793, bapt Mar 28 1794/Parents

Eckhart Gills, Catharina/Johannes b Mar 5 1794, bapt Mar 31 1794/Johannes Kern

Jacob Grof, Christina/Jacob b Nov 29 1793, bapt Apr 8 1794/David Levy

Jos. Lentz, Magdalena/Anna Maria b Dec 12 1793, bapt Apr 10 1794/Joh. Tobridsch, Maria

Peter Hufnagel, Elisabetha/Elisabetha b Feb 13 1794, bapt Apr 12 1794/ Elisabeth Paltzer

Philip Kiehfober, Anna Maria/Nicolaus b Feb 20 1756, bapt Apr 18 1794/adult

Jacob Schäfer, Elisabetha/Julianna b Oct 24 1793, bapt Apr 20 1794/Parents

David Lowry, Catharina/David b Dec 25 1787, Sophia b Dec 4 1790, Maria b Apr 10 1792, Friedrich b Feb 21 1794, all bapt Apr 22 1794/Friedrich Missele, Anna Maria

Jacob Getzedanner, Elisabetha/Catharina b Jul 1 1793, bapt Apr 26 1794/Cath. Getzedanner, grandmother

Frantz Geissinger, Sarah/Charlotta b Feb 10 1794, bapt Apr 30 1794/Parents

J. S. Schatz, Elisabeth/Johannes b Dec 12 1793, bapt May 4 1794/Joh. Leschhorn & the child's gr. m.
Joh. Leschhorn, Rebekah/Elisabetha b Mar 10 1794, bapt May 4 1794/The father & Elis. Schatz, cousin of child
Peter, Anna, belonging to Mr. Johnson, blacks/Benjamin b Mar 17 1794, bapt May 5 1794/Mr. Graham has promised to have it instructed
Thomas Hixon, Maria/Thomas Valentine b Aug 11 1794, bapt -- 1794/Valentin Spatz, Susanna
Wm. Carver, Mary/Henrietta b Sep 29 1793, bapt Jun 8 1794/Parents
Jos. Lilly, Elisabetha/Joseph b Jan 10 1794, bapt Jun 8 1794/Parents
Robert Johnson & wf. dec./Juliet b May 1 1793, bapt Jun 8 1794/The father
Peter, Minty, blacks/Katy b Feb 28, bapt Jun 9/prp. of Ben. Lenton, who promised to raise it as Christian
Joseph Hildebrand, Magdalena/Adam b Mar 22 1794, bapt Jun 9 1794/Adam Stein, Maria
Joseph Stehly, Julianna/Susanna b Apr 16 1794, bapt Jun 9 1794/Parents
Michael Mossetter, Philippina/Maria b Mar 16 1794, bapt Jun 15 1794/Parents
John Holiday, Mary/Elisabeth b Sep 16 1794(3), bapt Jul 2 1794/Parents
Wm. Eaton, Ann/John b May 12 1794, bapt Jul 17 1794/Ann Dayly, grandmother
David Kuhns, Maria/Maria b Jul 23 1793, bapt Jul 17 1794/Philip Rohr, Catharina
Richard Griffith, Margaret/Maria Barbara b —, bapt Aug 25 1794/Barbara Deiss, wf. of Nicolaus
John Wallen, Susanna/Wilhelm b Sep 12 1793, bapt Sep 20 1794/The mother
Jacob Kiefaber, Anna Maria/Susanna b Mar 31 1793, bapt Sep 21 1794/Nicolaus Kiefaber, Margaret
Henrich Derkiss, Margaretha/David b Apr 28 1793, bapt Oct 5 1794/Georg Jost, Catharina
Hezekiah Medcalf, Clarissa/John b May 18 1794, bapt Oct 8 1794/Parents
Henry Campel, Savery, free black/Robert b Dec 31 1791, bapt Oct 8 1794/The mother
Jacob Rohr, Catharina/Anna Maria b Aug 23 1794, bapt Oct 13 1794/Margaret Zayer, widow
John Mansfield, Mary/James b Oct -- 1793, Oct 24 1794/The father
Nicolaus Zimmerman, Elisabeth/John b May 20 1794, bapt Nov 8 1794/Parents
Wm. Crum, Elisabeth/Maria b Oct 10 1794, bapt Nov 10 1794/Parents
Johannes Schlotz, Catharina/Johannes b Jul 29 1794, bapt Nov 16 1794/The father
Jacob Balzell, Charlotta/Johannes b Oct 12 1794, bapt Nov 22 1794/Parents
Nathan Marshall, Hannah/Samuel b Dec 2 1794, bapt Dec 7 1794/Parents
Johannes Gebhardt, Elisabetha/Charlotta b Jul 11 1794, bapt Dec 14 1794/ Parents
Elias Brunner, Maria Elisabetha/Elisabetha b Dec 1 1794, bapt Dec 21 1794/ Elisabetha Brunner, single
John Graham, Anne/Thomas Johnson b Nov 24 1794, bapt Jan 3 1795/Parents
Christopher Meck, Elisabeth/James b Apr 25 1794, bapt Jan 8 1795/Parents
Joseph Doll, Charlotta/Michael b Dec 6 1794, bapt Jan 11 1795/Parents
Jacob Sauder, Catharina/Maria Catharina b Oct 14 1794, bapt Jan 15 1795/Carl Gross, Catharina Elisabeth
David Levy, Maria/Sarah b Nov 23 1794, bapt Jan 23 1795/Parents
Peter Wip, Elisabetha/Johann Peter b Jun 1 1794, bapt Feb 12 1795/Joh. Nicol, single

Henrich Horn, Elisabetha/Andreas b Sep 13 1794, bapt Feb 12 1795/Joh. Davis, Elisabetha
Job Jenkins, Sarah/Darky b Dec 20 1794, bapt Feb 12 1795/Parents
Ralph Briscoe, Sarah/Freeman b Nov 8 1794, bapt Feb 12 1795/Parents
Morris, Sarah, blacks/Jane b Sep 26 1794, bapt Feb 12 1795/--
William, Ellender, blacks/Darky b Jan 12 1795, bapt Feb 12 1795/--
Edward, Clara, blacks/Edward b Dec 12 1794, bapt Feb 12 1795/--
Henrich Hembe, Margaretha/Elisabetha b Nov 14 1794, bapt Feb 15 1795/ Elisabetha Brunner, single
Jacob Metzger, Christina/Anna Maria b Dec 2 1794, bapt Feb 27 1795/Rachel Grof, widow
Henrich Bantz, Catharina/Elisabetha b Sep 16 1794, bapt Feb 28 1795/Parents
Herman Hellman, Magdalena/Johann Georg b Jul 1 1793, bapt Mar 5 1795/Parents
Wm. Buteler,Delilah/Henry b Dec 7 1794, bapt Mar 25 1795/Parents
Wm. McClean, Maria/Daniel b Oct 25 1794, bapt Mar 29 1795/Parents
Nathaniel Marshall, Mary/Mary b Mar 31 1790, bapt Apr 2 1795/Parents
Johann Heiwely, Anna/Jacob b Feb 18 1795, bapt Apr 19 1795/Wilhelm Miller, Maria Eva
Adam Hauser, Sibylla/Esra b Apr 2 1795, bapt Apr 24 1795/Parents
Henrich Fehling, Elisabeth/Henrich b Feb 28 1795, bapt Apr 26 1795/Joh. Brunner, son of Johannes
Joh. Thomas, Elisabeth/Barbara b Feb 22 1795, bapt May 17 1795/Marg. Thomas, single
Georg Ehbrecht, Maria Magdalena/Catharina b Mar 7 1795, bapt May 24 1795/ Jacob Derner, Catharina
Johannes Schäfer, Elisabetha/Susanna b Aug 16 1794, bapt May 24 1795/ Magdalena Stoll, single
Johannes Remsperger, Anna Maria/Elisabetha b Aug 24 1776,bapt Apr 3 1795/ adult
Jacob Levy, Magdalena/Sophia b Feb 24 1795, bapt May 24 1795/Peter Walter, Sophia
Jacob Kehler, Sarah/Georg b Apr 2 1795, bapt Jun 3 1795/Parents
Johann Remsperger, Elisabetha/Magdalena b Jan 12 1795, bapt Jun 5 1795/ Elisabeth Sinn, single
Jacob Stehly, Elisabetha/Jonathan b Feb 24 1795, bapt Jun 6 1795/Parents
Johannes Ott, Anna Maria/Georg b Mar 4 1795, bapt Jun 25 1795/Georg Jost, Catharina
Johannes Mohr, Sophia/Elisabetha b Jan 24 1795, bapt Jun 25 1795/Bernhardt Ott, Anna Elisabeth
Ludwig Wolff, Charlotta /Catharina b Mar 12 1795, bapt Jun 25 1795/Michael Remsperger, Catharina
Conrad Leschhorn, Mary/David b Jan 27 1795, bapt Jun 25 1795/Parents
John Schley, Polly/George b Aug 21 1795, bapt --/Parents
Johannes Getzedanner, Catharina/Joseph b Nov 9 1794, bapt Jul 10 1795/Jacob Getzedanner, single
Abraham Wingert, M. Magdalena/Maria Elisabeth b Jan 28 1795, bapt Jul 14 1795/Susanna Schenckmeyer, single
Christian Getzedanner, Maria/Salomon b --, bapt Jul 16 1795/Jacob Getzedanner, single
Michael Witmer & wf./Georg b Aug 29 1792, bapt Jul 19 1795/Parents
Michael Witmer & wf./Nicolaus b Mar 15 1795, bapt Jul 19 1795/Nic. Holtz & Susanna

Ephraim Ridge, Catharina/Christina b Dec 20 1794, bapt Jul 19 1795/Corn. Ridge, Elisabeth
Adam Krieger, Susanna/Christian b Jan 1 1795, bapt Jul 19 1795/Geo. Kriger, single
Christoph Schäfer, Maria Elisabeth/Peter b Feb 24 1795, bapt Jul 19 1795/ Peter Schnook, Julianna
Johannes Thomas, Catharina/Joseph b Jun 6 1795, bapt Jul 26 1795/Adolf Enkof, A. Maria
Philip Nic. Mattern, Barbara/Anna Margaretha b Jul 8 1795, bapt Jul 26 1795/ Marg. Thomas, widow
Frantz May, Catharina/Johannes b Jul 10 1795, bapt Jul 26 1795/Parents
John Cary, Elisabeth/Michael b Mar 29 1795, bapt Aug 3 1795/Michael Hauck, single
Georg Barral, Elisabeth/Jacob b Nov 10 1793, bapt Aug 10 1795/Parents
Christian Hartinger, Juliana/Philip b Oct 28 1794, bapt Aug 10 1795/Parents
Adam Deuvelbiss, Catharina/Adam b Dec 3 1794, bapt Aug 10 1795/Philip Heintz
Georg Eder, Maria/Wilhelm b Oct 30 1793, bapt Aug 12 1795/Parents
Jos. Cadeck, Nancy/Joseph b Aug 5 1780, bapt Aug 18 1795/Parents
Benjamin Hull & wf./John b Aug 7 1780, Eleonor b Mar 28 1785, Mary b Mar 23 1790, Naomi b Jul -- 1792 - all bapt Aug 20 1795/Parents
Richard Hardin, Rachel/Elisabetha b Jun 25, bapt Aug 21 1795/Parents
Johannes Bucky, Elisabetha/Catharina b Aug 4 1795, bapt Aug 23 1795/Eva Marg. Zayer, widow
Michael Barthols, Nancy/John b Jan 3 1795, bapt Aug 28 1795/Parents
Conrad Sattler, Sibylla/Jacob b Nov -- 1794, bapt Sep 5 1795/Michael Sattler
Wm. Clary, Rachel/Mitchell b Jan 26 1795, bapt Sep 5 1795/The mother
Andreas Bittel, Christina/Peter b -- 1792, Rahel b Feb 27 1795, bapt Sep 5 1795/Parents
Jacob Bader, M. Elisabeth/Catharina b Oct 20 1794, bapt Sep 5 1795/Elisabeth Heckedorn
Wilhelm Schmit, Catharina/Georg b May 13 1795, bapt Sep 9 1795/Michael Raymer
Johannes Kuhns, Catharina/Catharina b Jun 12 1795, bapt Sep 10 1795/Jacob Rohr, Catharina
Andreas Gedock, Catharina/Elisabetha b Jun 23 1795, bapt Sep 13 1795/ Catharina Schafer, single
Adam Schnook, Margaretha/Jacob b Jul 28 1795, bapt Sep 13 1795/Parents
Henrich Baer, Elisabetha/Michael Schellman b Aug 1 1795, bapt Sep 19 1795/ Joh. Schellman, single
Georg Engel, Catharina/Georg b Aug 20 1795, bapt Oct 10 1795/Georg Jung, A. Maria
Johannes Bantz, Catharina/Georg b Oct 4 1795, bapt Oct 10 1795/The mother
Christian Baer, Barbara/Catharina b Sep 7 1795, bapt Oct 21 1795/Christoph Wedekin, Catharina
Georg Jost, Catharina/Sophia b Jul 27 1795, bapt Oct 21 1795/Anna Marg. Thomas, widow
John Wallen, Susanna/Johannes b Oct 15 1795, bapt Oct 22 1795/The mother
Georg Getzedanner, Elisabeth/Elisabetha b Aug 4 1795, Sophia b Aug 4 1795, bapt Oct 23 1795/Parents
Henrich Hemp, Margaretha/Susanna b Jul 19 1795, bapt Oct 28 1795/Parents
Adam Schawacker, Maria Barbara/Georg b Oct 11 1795, bapt Oct 30 1795/Jacob Schnaudegel, Maria Barbara

Baptisms of the Evangelical Reformed Church in Frederick, Maryland

Jacob Brandenberger, Elisabeth/Jesse b Jul 8 1795, bapt Nov 3 1795/Parents
Jacob Aurand, Christina/Christina b Oct 5 1795, bapt Nov 6 1795/Jacob Spannseiler, Christina
Johannes Schneider, Dorothea/Anna Maria b Aug 9 1795, bapt Nov 6 1795/Anna Waltz, wf. of Samuel
Johannes Krämer, Maria/Johannes b Jul 8 1795, bapt Nov 8 1795/Parents
Adam Keil, Elisabetha/Johann Adam b Oct 2 1795, bapt Nov 11 1795/Parents
Jacob Derry, Catharina/Susanna b Sep 8 1795, bapt Nov 11 1795/Susanna Schmit, wf. of Jacob
Peter Heckman, Regina/Christina b Jul 15 1795, bapt Nov 11 1795/Philip Sauder, Susanna
Wilhelm Kässman, Elisabetha/Maria b Oct 6 1795, bapt Nov 18 1795/Abraham Herget, Maria
Johannes Holtz, A. Maria/Sarah b Nov 9 1795, bapt Dec 6 1795/Parents
Johannes Zimmerman, Eleonora/Susanna b Oct 25 1795, bapt Dec 9 1795/Parents
Valentin Hoffman, Elisabeth/Johann Jacob b Sep 19, bapt Dec 18 1795/Johannes Doll, single
Jacob Keller, Susanna/Johannes b Sep 2 1795, bapt Dec 21 1795/Parents
Nicolaus Zimmerman, Elisabetha/Georg b Oct 12 1795, bapt Dec 25 1795/Parents
Jacob Wiest, Eva Catharina/Catharina b Sep 5 1795, bapt Dec 25 1795/Parents
James Torrance, Drusilla/Anna b Nov 20 1795, bapt Dec 28 1795/Parents
James Allen, Mary/James b Jul 3 1795, bapt Dec 29 1795/--
Collmer Gitings, Mary Ann/Eliza b Jun 4 1795, bapt Dec 29 1795/Parents
George Fahly, Magdalena/Maria Magdalena b Dec 29 1795, bapt Jan 13 1796/ Catharina Wolff, single
Henrich Wolff, Julianna/Jacob b Dec 5 1795, bapt Jan 13 1796/Lorentz Aurand, Barbara
Georg Baer, Elisabetha/Hannah b Aug 18 1795, bapt Jan 31 1796/The mother
Peter Sauer, Elisabeth/Maria b Jan 4 1796, bapt Feb 2 1796/Parents
Jacob Jung, Catharina/Johannes b Dec 21 1795, bapt Feb 3 1796/Johannes Kern, Magdalena
Henrich Miller, Barbara/Elisabetha b Mar 25 1795, bapt Feb 3 1796/Elisabetha Keller, wf. of Jacob
Johann Dorschtheimer, Magdalena/Johann Anthon b Nov 21 1795, bapt Feb 16 1796/Anthon Amend, Magdalena
Jacob Brunner, Magdalena/Elisabetha b Aug 16 1795, bapt Feb 16 1796/Parents
Wm. McClary, Mary/Henry Slegel b Oct 22 1795, bapt Mar 6 1796/Parents
Robertson Eastborn, Sarah/Ed. Lingan Butler b Apr 7 1794, Eliza Ann Delaschmit b Feb 1 1796, bapt Mar 6 1796/The mother
Henrich Kempf, Anna Margaret, Henrich b Feb 12 1796, bapt Mar 7 1796/Parents
Henrich Thomas, Margaret/Stephan b Jan 5 1796, bapt Mar 16 1796/Johann Thomas, son of Gabriel
--/Salomon b --, bapt -- 1796/adult
Wilhelm Liess, Elisabetha/Margaretha b Feb 20 1796, bapt Mar 27 1796/ Margaretha Griffith
Adam Gayer, Margaretha/Johannes b Feb 6 1796, bapt Mar 27 1796/Jacob Gayer, Susanna Moor, widow
Samuel Bager, Catharina/Samuel b Feb 3 1796, bapt Mar 29 1796/Jacob Stimmel, Elisabetha
Heinrich Kohlhaus, Judith/Benjamin b Jan 12 1796, bapt Mar 30 1796/The mother

Jeremiah Linton, Ruth/Rachel b Apr 10 1795, bapt Mar 30 1796/Maria Duvall, Maley (Molly) Fisher
Eckhardt Gills, Catharina/Anna Maria b Feb 24 1796, bapt Apr 3 1796/Anna Maria Sulzer, single
Andreas Miller, Catharina/Susanna b Dec 7 1795, bapt Apr 3 1796/Henrich Hemp, Margaretha
Peter Riess, Anna/Catharina b Feb 24 1796, bapt Apr 3 1796/Mat. Schmit, A. Maria
Henrich Richter, Catharina/Johannes b Apr 3 1796, bapt Apr 4 1796/Parents
Jacob Lehman, Catharina/Susanna b -- 27 1796, bapt May 8 1796/Philip Breiss, Susanna
Thomas Hix, Maria/Susanna b Aug 19 1796, bapt --/Valentin Schaarz, Susanna
Nicolaus Herman, Christina/Friedrich b Oct 27 1795, bapt May 12 1796/Parents
Georg Lieblich, Elisabetha/Maria Barbara b Mar 30 1796, bapt May 16 1796/ Philippina Nicol, single
Peter Frantz, Susanna/Wilhelm b Mar 12 1796, bapt May 22 1796/Parents
Peter Koxrich, Catharina/Georg b Mar 26 1796, bapt May 29 1796/Parents
Adam Schiwell, Catharina/Rebeckah b May 29 1796, bapt Jun 8 1796/Parents
Philip Stuber, Dorothea/Wilhelm b Nov 19 1794, bapt Jun 12 1796/Parents
Frantz Geissinger, Sarah/Henrietta b Mar 31 1796, bapt Jun 29 1796/Parents
Stephan Klein, Margaretha/Johannes b Mar 19 1796, bapt Jun 29 1796/Catharina Schultz, widow
Georg Reissinger, Elisabetha/Johannes b Jul 3 1796, bapt Jul 3 1796/Parents
Johannes Sultzer, Maria Elisabetha/Michael b Mar 12 1796, bapt Jul 3 1796/ Michael Bast, Barbara
Peter Bucky, Christina/Anna Maria b Apr 7 1796, bapt Jul 3 1796/Johannes Letter, A. Maria
Augustin Wasky, Salome/Julianna b Apr 7 1796, bapt 3 1796/Abraham Herget, A. Maria
Georg Borckhardt, Hannah/Eleonora b Dec 15 1795, bapt Jul 17 1796/Parents
Wilhelm Schmit, Catharina/Johann Georg b Jul 24 1796, bapt Jul 24 1796/Jacob Rauzahn, Christina
Gabriel Thomas, Anna Maria/Anna Maria b Jun 8 1796, bapt Jul 31 1796/Nic. Lat, A. Maria
Philip Sauder, Susanna/Michael b May 28 1796, bapt Aug 7 1796/Michael Bogen, Elisabetha
Daniel Ragan, Ruth/Sarah b Sep 11 1795, bapt Aug 7 1796/Parents
Jacob Koller, A. Maria/Johannes b Jun 11 1796, bapt Aug 8 1796/Johannes Koller, single
Zacharias Linton, Mary/Washington b Jan 20 1796, bapt Aug 10 1796/Parents
John Montgomery, Loshan(?)/James b Jan 27 1795, bapt Aug 10 1796/Parents
Hezekiah Metcalf, (Clarissa)/William b Mar 23 1796, bapt Aug 10 1796/Parents
Jos. Brunner, Elisabetha/Peter b Jul 14 1796, bapt Aug 16 1796/Peter Brunner
Justinian Maybury, Maria/Elisabetha b Jul 27 1796, bapt Aug 29 1796/ Elisabetha Reissinger, wf. of Georg
Abraham Lakin, Mary/Benjamin b Oct 26 1795, bapt Sep 10 1796/Parents
David Bayer, Sarah/David b Jul 26 1796, bapt Sep 22 1796/Johannes Krämer, single
Johannes Ott, Maria/Susanna b Aug 4 1796, bapt Sep 25 1796/Susanna Schaefer, widow
Jacob Schuck, Elisabetha/Catharina b Jun 9 1796, bapt Sep 25 1796/Henrich Derckes, Margaretha

Henry Poole, Mary/Henry b Jan 15 1796, bapt Sep 27 1796/Parents
Dennis Poole, Henrietta/Elisabeth Gaither b Apr 22 1796, bapt Sep 27 1796/ Parents
Michael Engelbrecht, Elisabetha/Elisabetha b Jul 4 1796, bapt Oct 8 1796/ Peter Schnook, Juliana
Abraham Titlo, Susanna/Charlotta b Jun 10 1795, bapt Oct 12 1796/Parents
Peter Schaefer, Catharina/Susanna b Sep 9 1796, bapt Oct 19 1796/Susanna Ott
Christoph Howerter,Catharina/Jacob b Oct 21 1796, bapt Nov 2 1796/Jacob Haller
Henrich Fehling, Elisabetha/Henrich b Sep 25 1796, bapt Nov 6 1796/Johannes Brunner, son of Jacob
Jacob Metzger, Christina/Margaretha b Oct 8 1796, bapt Dec 9 1796/Christoph Bernthausel and Cath.
Georg Berg, Nancy/Thomas Willable b Sep 26 1796, bapt Dec 15 1796/Parents
Johannes Thomas son of Gabriel, Elisabetha/Eva b Oct 26 1796,bapt Dec 25 1796/Joh. Thomas, Catharina
A. Downy, Polly/Jane b Nov 11 1796, bapt Jan 17 1797/Parents
Basil, Rachel, blacks/Basil b Jan 4 1796, bapt Jan 17 1797/the property of -
Edward, Eleonor, blacks/Simon b Dec 31 1796, bapt Jan 17 1797/the property of Mr. Briscoe
Morris, Sarah, blacks/Sarah b Sep 22 1796, bapt Jan 17 1797/ditto
Peter De Grange, Barbara/Johannes b Aug 2 1796, bapt Jan 31 1797/Parents
Johann Breiss, Elisabetha/Susanna b Dec 23 1796, bapt Feb 1 1797/Philip Breiss, Susanna
Philip Singstock, Wilhelmina/Carl Philip b Dec 31 1796, bapt Feb 14 1797/ Parents
Wm. McLay, Maria/Maria Catharina b Jan 1 1797, bapt Feb 19 1797/Georg Daub, Catharina
Jacob Gettinger, Barbara Schaefer/Henrietta b Jul 23 1796, bapt Mar 13 1797/ Conrad Schafer, bro of the mother
Adam Krieger, Susanna/Carl b Jun 9 1796, bapt Mar 15 1797/The father
Jacob Schmit, Catharina/Catharina b Dec 29 1796, bapt Mar 15 1797/Mat. Schmit, A. Maria
David Levy, Maria/Maria Anna Barbara b Sep 13 1796, bapt Mar 17 1797/Parents
Georg Schmit, Anna Maria/Elisabetha b Dec 22 1796, Catharina b Dec 22 1796, bapt Mar 19 1797/Henrich Derckes, Margaretha
Philip Imschweiler, Susanna/Peter b Nov 26 1796, bapt Mar 19 1797/Joseph Dillinger, single
Robert Macky, Sarah/Nancy b Mar 18 1797, bapt Mar 22 1797/The father
Peter Hardt, Charlotta/Johann Peter b Feb 26 1797, bapt Apr 2 1797/Parents
Henrich Christ, Christina/Elisabetha b Feb 10 1797, bapt Apr 16 1797/ Elisabeth Christ, widow
Valentin Steckel, Catharina/Elisabetha b Sep 28 1796, bapt Apr 19 1797/ Elisabetha Remsperger, single
Johannes Schaefer, Elisabetha/Michael b Apr 1 1796, bapt Apr 30 1797/Parents
Jacob Hoffman, Sarah/Esra b Feb 28 1797, bapt Apr 30 1797/The mother
Friederich Miesel, Rosina/Johannes b Feb 5 1797, bapt May 7 1797/The father
Abraham Wingert, Maria Magdalena/Johann Peter b Dec 23 1796, bapt May 21 1797/Valentin Brunner
Georg Borckhardt, Anna/Margaretha b Feb 11 1797, bapt May 21 1797/Parents
Nicolaus Zimmerman, Elisabetha/Anna Maria b Mar 15 1797, bapt May 25 1797/ Parents

Baptisms of the Evangelical Reformed Church in Frederick, Maryland

Adam Becker, Julianna/Julianna b Apr 24 1797, bapt Jun 4 1797/Parents
Peter Heckman, Regina/Philip b Apr 23 1797, bapt Jun 5 1797/Philip Sauder
Michael Sauder, Elisabetha/Magdalena b Apr 25 1797, bapt Jun 5 1797/Widow Mayer
Frantz May, Catharina/Magdalena b Jan 24 1797, bapt Jun 5 1797/Magdalena Gross, single
Johannes Dörr, Catharina/Catharina b Apr 28 1797, bapt Jun 7 1797/Parents
John Schley, Polly/David b Oct 7 1797, bapt -- 1797/Parents
Jacob Balzell, Charlotta/David b May 1 1797, bapt Jul 2 1797/M. Elisabeth Christ, widow
Johannes Niemayer, Barbara/Jacob b Jul 6 1797, bapt Jul 16 1797/Jacob Manigold, Magdalena
Friedrich Hedge, Christina/Sophia b Jun 24 1797, bapt Jul 30 1797/Parents
Adam Stoll, Elisabetha/Anna Elisabetha b Mar 8 1797, bapt Aug 21 1797/Jacob Remsperger, Anna Elisabetha
Henrich Richter, Catharina/Margaretha b Jun 31 1793, bapt Aug 27 1797/The mother
same parents/Johannes b Mar 10 1797, bapt Aug 27 1797/The mother
--/Frederick, a foundling b Jul -- 1797, bapt Sep 10 1797/Wid. Margaret Hauser
Jacob Stehly, Elisabetha/Catharina b May 26 1797, bapt Sep 10 1797/Jacob Stehly, Catharina
Georg Schaefer, Catharina/Catharina b May 21 1797, bapt Sep 10 1797/Anna Maria Stoll, single
Philip Stuber, Dorothea/Salomon b May 16 1797, bapt Sep 24 1797/Henrich Hembe, Margaretha
John Casney, Elisabetha/Johannes b Aug 20 1797, bapt Sep 24 1797/Elisabetha Christ, widow
Ludwig Wolff, Charlotta/Peter b Aug 15 1797, bapt Oct 1 1797/Peter Wolff, single
Stephan Steiner, Barbara/Charlotta b Aug 13 1797, bapt Oct 15 1797/Valentin Bucky, Charlotta
Henrich Kempf, Anna Margaretha/Henrich b Aug 27 1797, bapt Nov 1 1797/The mother
Peter Fein, Gertraut/Peter b Sep 10 1797, bapt Nov 3 1797/Friedr. Schittenhelm, Barbara
Christian Hartinger, Julianna/Jacob b Aug 1 1796, bapt Nov 3 1797/Parents
Gilbert Wheeton, Drusilla/Margaret b Dec 10 1796, bapt Nov 22 1797/Parents
Henrich Derckes, Margaretha/Anna Maria b Aug 6 1797, bapt Dec 3 1797/Parents
Ludwig Cross, Maria/Joh. Ludwig Steckel b Dec 24 1797/Johann Buckius, widow Cath. Steckel
Conrad Leschhorn, Maria/Daniel b Oct 2 1797, bapt Dec 31 1797/Parents
Johannes Holtz, A. Maria/Johann Benedict b Dec 29 1797, bapt Jan 7 1798/ Peter Wolff, Catharina
Michael Holtz, Anna Margaretha/Jacob b Nov 9 1797, bapt Jan 7 1798/Parents
John Briscoe, Jane/Ralph Delaschmit b Aug 23 1797, bapt Jan 16 1798/Eliza Butler
Wm. Walling, Elizabetha/Nelson Delaschmitt b Nov 28 1797, bapt Jan 16 1798/ Eliza Butler
Wm. Hicks, Maria/Sarah b Dec 25 1796, bapt Jan 21 1798/Parents
Johannes Geickerly, Alice/Anne b Jul 8 1797, bapt Jan 30 1798/Parents
Henrich Dersch, A. Maria/Wilhelm b Aug 2 1797, bapt Feb 11 1798/Parents

Jacob Getzedanner, Elisabetha/Henrich b Oct 23 1797, bapt Feb 11 1798/ Parents
Johann Getzedanner, Catharina/Catharina b Jun 13 1796, bapt Feb 12 1798/ Parents
Anthony Chase, Sarah, blacks/Philippina b Jun 26 1795, Samuel b Jun 20 1797, bapt Feb 12 1798/Joh. Getzedanner as owner
Nicolaus Freidinger, Esther/Ludwig Christian b Jul 17 1797, bapt Feb 18 1798/Ludwig Kempf, Barbara
Andreas Gödeck, Catharina/Elisabetha Margaretha b Oct 29 1797, bapt Mar 4 1798/Parents
Johannes Faubel, Margaretha/Georg b Oct 29 1797, bapt Mar 11 1798/Philip Roth, Catharina
Adam Schnook, Margaretha/Philippina b Nov 19 1797, bapt Mar 14 1798/Parents
Jacob Kern, Margaretha/Johannes b Feb 11 1797, bapt Mar 14 1798/Joh. Kern, Magdalena
Aaron Ankrim, Mary; Sereena b Oct 23 1797, bapt Mar 19 1798/Parents
Michael Witmer, Catharina/Barbara Susanna b Nov 9 1797, bapt Mar 19 1798/ Joh. Kopenhewer, Barbara
Michael Eberhardt, Margaretha/Johannes b May 31 1797, bapt Mar 22 1798/Joh. Koppenhewer, Susanna
Johannes Nussbaum, Margaretha/Elisabetha b Jan 26 --, bapt Apr 6 1798/adult
Mattheus Seiffert, Elisabetha/Wilhelm b Jan 24 1798, bapt Apr 9 1798/Michael Haller, Catharina
Robert Macky, Sarah/Sarah b Mar 24 1798, bapt Apr 13 1798/Ruth Rakin
Conrad Specht, Elisabetha/Barbara b Feb 8 1798, bapt Apr 15 1798/Barbara Schaefer, single
Georg Johs, Catharina/Anna Maria b Nov 16 1797, bapt Apr 15 1798/Margaretha Thomas
Johannes Ott, Anna Maria/Bernhardt b Feb 4 1798, bapt Apr 15 1798/Bernhardt Ott, Elisabetha
David Levy, Maria/Johann Leonhardt b Jan 28 1798, bapt Apr 15 1798/Leon. Storm
Jacob Levy, Maria Magdalena/David Jacob b Mar 24 1798, bapt Apr 15 1798/ Barbara Levy
Jacob Brunner, Magdalena/Johann Valentin b Aug 28 1797, bapt Apr 16 1798/ Valentin Brunner
Wm. Crum, Elisabetha/Abraham b May 31 1796, Wilhelm b Apr 17 1798, bapt Apr 17 1798/Parents
Frantz Geissinger, Sarah/Sarah b Mar 21 1798, bapt Apr 17 1798/Parents
Michael Hauck, Magdalena/Margaretha b Mar 3 1798, bapt May 13 1798/Peter Hauck, Margaretha
Georg Ebrecht, Magdalena/Johann Georg b Mar 22 1798, bapt May 27 1798/ Parents
Johannes Brunner, Susanna/Benjamin b Feb 10 1798, bapt May 27 1798/Johannes Thomas, Catharina
Benjamin Hopkins, Anna/James Makle Briscoe b Mar 16 1798, bapt May 27 1798/ Johannes Brunner, Susanna
Zephaniah Hill, Barbara/George b Apr 6 1798, bapt May 27 1798/Georg Deschner
Philip Sauder, Susanna/Elisabetha b Feb 28 1798, bapt May 28 1798/Carl Gross, Elisabetha
Wm. Oliver, Elisabetha/Esther b May 1 1790, bapt May 31 1798/Valentin Bucky, Charlotta

Adam Jacob, Elisabetha/David b May 27 1798, bapt Jun 7 1798/Parents
Daniel Bergesser, Sarah/Johannes b Jan 7 1798, bapt Jun 10 1798/Parents
Joseph Doll, Catharina/Sophia b Mar 23 1798, bapt Jun 10 1798/Parents
Henrich Hemp, Margaretha/Anna Margaretha b Jan 22 1798, bapt Jun 22 1798/ Parents
Peter Christ, Margaretha/Anna b Feb 23 1798, bapt Jul 8 1798/Jacob Balzell, Charlotta
Wm. Harrington, Elisabetha/Johannes b Mar 9 1797, bapt Jul 10 1798/Parents
Wm. Hammond, Sarah/William b May 1 1796, bapt Jul 12 1798/Parents
Johannes Schaefer, Elisabetha/Johann Peter b Jan 25 1798, bapt Aug 1 1798/ Peter Schaefer, single
Georg Lieblich, Elisabetha/Maria Magdalena b Jul 24 1798, bapt Aug 4 1798/ The mother
Felix Beck, Anna Maria/Catharina b Feb 5 1798, bapt Aug 4 1798/Henrich Bernhardt, Catharina
Peter Boehm, Esther/Salomon b Jun 11 1798, bapt Aug 12 1798/Parents
Nicolaus Zimmerman, Elisabetha/Catharina b Jun 11 1798, bapt Aug 19 1798/ Parents
Stephan Klein, Margaretha/Susanna Margaretha b Aug 25 1798, bapt Aug 27 1798/Susanna Schultz, single
Peter Wipp, Elisabetha/Magdalena b Apr 1 1798, bapt Sep 2 1798/Georg Nicol, Margaretha
Nicolaus Kortz, Margaretha/Elisabetha b Jul 12 1798, bapt Sep 2 1798/ Elisabetha Zimmerman, single
Gilbert Wheelan, Drusilla/Elisabeth b Aug 27 1798, bapt Sep 3 1798/Parents
Philip Singstock, Wilhelmina/Henrich Wilhelm b Aug 31 1798, bapt Sep 7 1798/ Parents
Jacob Schellman, Catharina/Johannes b Jul 13 1798, bapt Sep 11 1798/Parents
Conradt Bauer, Elisabeth/Anna Maria b Aug 30 1798, bapt Sep 16 1798/Mat. Schmit, A. Maria
Wm. Haff, Mary/Mary Jane b Jul 10 1798, bapt Sep 17 1798/Parents
Johannes Bantz, Elisabeth/Elisabetha b Sep 27 1798, bapt Sep 27 1798/Maria Dorothea Beyerly
Henrich Brunner, Elisabetha/Maria Anna b May 18 1798, bapt Sep 30 1798/Peter Wolff, Catharina
Georg Borckhardt, Hannah/Charles b May 22 1798, bapt Sep 30 1798/Henrich Brunner, Elisabetha
Abraham Herget, Catharina/Jacob b Aug 13 1798, bapt Sep 30 1798/Augustin Wasky, Salome
Johannes Sulzer, Elisabetha/ Johann Peter b Jul 2 1798, bapt Sep 30 1798/ Peter Sulzer, single
Jacob Aurand, Christina/Elisabetha b Sep 22 1798, bapt Oct 9 1798/Philip Heintz, Maria
Georg Ketro, Elisabetha/Catharina b May 15 1798, bapt oct 10 1798/Barbara Wachter, wf. of Michael
Gabriel Thomas, A. Maria/Elias b Sep 17 1798, bapt Oct 14 1798/Johannes Brunner, son of Jacob
Johannes Getzedanner, Catharina/Jonathan b Mar 19 1798, bapt Oct 20 1798/ Parents
Adam Strickstrock, Maria Ottilia/Adam b Oct 8 1798, bapt Oct 23 1798/Parents
Peter Schaefer, Catharina/Peter b Aug 11 1798, bapt Oct 24 1798/Peter Wolff, single

Michael Sauder, Elisabetha/Maria Margaretha b Aug 16 1798, bapt Oct 25 1798/ Grandparents
Joseph Hildebrand, Magdalena/Johannes b Jul 19 1798, bapt Oct 28 1798/ Johannes Gleiss, single
Peter Degrange,Barbara/Anna Maria b Sep 5 1798, bapt Oct 29 1798/Joh. Rewer, Maria Catharina
Peter Stehly, Elisabetha/Peter b Aug 23 1798, bapt Nov 8 1798/Parents
Peter Frantz, Susanna/Peter b Sep 1 1798, bapt Nov 11 1798/Parents
Jacob Lehman, Catharina/Child b Oct 2 1798, bapt Nov 14 1798/Jacob Froschauer
Johannes Fessler, Barbara/Rosina b Aug 4 1798, bapt Nov 20 1798/Parents
Jacob Mamgold, Anna Margaretha/Johan Jacob b Oct 19 1798, bapt Nov 25 1798/ Joh. Niemayer, Barbara
Wm. Weeks, Maria/Johannes b Oct 10 1798, bapt Dec 10 1798/Christopher Heckman, Elisabetha
Johannes Breiss, Elisabetha/Christian b Oct 30 1798, bapt Dec 12 1798/Jacob Lehman, Catharina
Friedrich Becker, Susanna/Sophia b Oct 21 1798, bapt Dec 21 1798/Parents
David Ihly, Catharina/Sophia b Sep 4 1798, bapt Jan 13 1799/Michael Mayer
Henrich Cox, dec., Margaretha/Henrietta b Oct 18 1798, bapt Jan 13 1799/ David Ihly
Georg Gag, Elisabetha/Maria b Dec 14 1798, bapt Jan 16 1799/Parents
Michael Lehr, Maria/Johan Friedrich b Sep 10 1798, bapt Jan 20 1799/Friedr. Peter Lehr, Catharina
Johannes Gebhardt, Elisabetha/Friedrich b Jul 7 1798, bapt Feb 6 1799/ Parents
Johannes Nussbaum, Margaretha/Salomon b May 8 1771, Abraham b Nov 10 1775, Johannes b Jun 3 1782, Jacob b Jul 28 1773, Maria b Apr 10 1780, Catharina b --, all bapt Mar 22 1799/adults
John Crum, Elisabetha/Ephraim b Dec 22 1771, bapt Mar 22 1799, adult
Benjamin Riddle, Margaret/Anna b Nov 19 1781, bapt Mar 22 1799, adult
Joseph Fibius, Elisabetha/Joseph b Dec 28 1798, bapt Mar 24 1799/Conradt Fibius, Christina Schlicher
Jacob Rohr, Catharina/Daniel b Mar 12 1799, bapt Mar 28 1799/Parents
Hugh Rannels, Alice/Matilda b Apr 15 1798, bapt Apr 3 1799/Parents
John, Polly, blacks/Frederick b Nov -- 1797, bapt Apr 3 1799/The owner, Mr. Rannels
Thos. P. Wilson, Rebekah/Wm. Mordecai Beall b Apr 7 1799, bapt Apr 8 1799/ Mr. M. Beall
Georg Nickol, Elisabetha/Maria b Feb 2, bapt Apr 14 1799/Parents
Henrich Gärtner, Elisabetha/Georg b Apr 19 1799, bapt May 5 1799/Georg Riehl, Elisabetha
Georg Engel, A. Maria/Elisabetha b Jan 10 1799, bapt May 12 1799/Parents
Friedrich Blochberger, Mary Ann/Christian Benjamin b Mar 17 1799, bapt May 12 1799/Christian Benj. Blochberger
Adam Stoll, Elisabetha/Philippina b Jan 16 1799, bapt May 12 1799/A. Maria Stoll
Jesse Maybury, Maria/Maria b Dec 10 1798, bapt May 17 1799/The mother
Geo. Remsperger, Elisabetha/Susanna b Jan 4 1799, bapt Apr 25 1799/Susanna Steiner, wf. of Johann Steiner
Jacob Metzger, Christina/Christina b Mar 25 1799, bapt May 17 1799/Parents
Henrich Schmit, Maria/Henrietta b Jan 18 1799, bapt May 17 1799/Parents

Johannes Schatz, Elizabetha/Margaretha b Oct 20 1799, bapt May 19 1799/ Parents
Johannes Keplinger, Catharina/Elisabetha b Jul 15 1798, bapt May 17 1799/ Parents
James Torrance, Drusilla/James b Jan 20 1799, bapt May 20 1799/Parents
Georg Dofler, Catharina/Rebekah b Apr 26 1799, bapt May 20 1799/Parents
Michael Ott, Elisabeth/Johannes b Jan 26 1799, bapt Jun 12 1799/Parents
Johannes Hauck, Elisabetha/ Henrich b May 4 1799, bapt Jun 12 1799/Parents
Henrich Otto, Margaretha/Elisabetha b Mar 16 1799, bapt Jun 16 1799/ Elisabeth Hefner, single
Benjamin Zimmerman, Catharina/Henrich b Feb 1 1799, bapt Jun 16 1799/Henrich Christman, single
Henrich Hirschberger, Catharina/Ferdinand b Feb 22 1799, bapt Jun 23 1799/ Parents
Johannes Fuchs, Catharina/Georg b May 31 1799, bapt Jul 21 1799/Parents
Andreas Mill, Catharina/Daniel b Mar 22 1799, bapt Jul 21 1799/Christina Stoffel, wf. of Henrich
Philip Gutmann, Elisabetha/Elisabetha b Apr 15 1799, bapt Jul 24 1799/The mother
Jacob Getzedanner, Elisabetha/Joseph b Dec 6 1799, bapt Jul 24 1799/Parents
Adam Becker, Julianna/Charlotta b May 20 1799, bapt Jul 27 1799/Charlotta Lehmann, single
Johannes Holtz, A. Maria/Johan Jacob b Jul 24 1799, bapt Aug 7 1799/Parents
Johannes Fieck, Margaretha/Henrich b Jan 9 1799, bapt Aug 11 1799/Parents
Henrich Lamm, Maria Elisabetha/Melchior b May 22 1799, bapt Aug 24 1799/ Parents
Johannes Hinckel, Maria/Georg b Oct 20 1799, bapt Aug 24 1799/Henrich Hemp, Margaretha
Johannes Schley, Polly/William b Oct 31 1799, bapt -- 1799/Parents
Stephan Steiner, Barbara/Georg b -- bapt Sep 8 1799/Philip Rohr, Catharina
Wilhelm Liess, Elisabeth/Wilhelm b Aug 23 1799, bapt Sep 11 1799/The mother
Salomon Steckel, Charlotta/Samuel b Aug 22 1799, bapt Sep 12 1799/Parents
Jacob Drill, Eva/Eva Anna b Mar 5 1799, bapt Sep 23 1799/Parents
Philip Körb, Catharina/Jacob b May 1 1799, Friedrich b May 1 1799, bapt Sep 23 1799/Jacob Drill, Eva
Adam Schreiner, Maria/Wilhelm b Jun 18 1799, bapt Sep 25 1799/The mother
Henrich Kauffman, Elisabeth/Maria b Jan 25 1799, bapt Sep 25 1799/Parents
Joh. Rickert, Margaretha/Henrich b --, bapt Oct 6 1799/Henrich Hembe
Johannes Leder, A. Maria/Susanna b Dec 19 1798, bapt Oct 6 1799/Georg Widerich, Catharina
Philip Schatz, Catharina/Jacob b Jun 10 1799, bapt Oct 6 1799/Parents
Christian Getzedanner, Catharina/Elisabetha b Sep 4 1799, bapt Oct 7 1799/ Georg Widerich, Sr., Catharina
David Schreyer, Catharina/Maria Magdalena b Sep 12 1799, bapt Oct 13 1799/ Parents
Friedrich Nuss, Catharina/Friedrich Esra b Sep 17 1799, bapt Oct 15 1799/ Parents
Daniel Emerich, Eunice/Anna Martha b Oct 4 1799, bapt Nov 4 1799/Anna Martha Emerich
Wilhelm Umbach, Catharina/Magdalena b Mar 21 1799, bapt Nov 4 1799/Magdalena Gross, single
Michael Holtz, A. Maria/Michael b Oct 17 1799, bapt Nov 10 1799/Parents

Baptisms of the Evangelical Reformed Church in Frederick, Maryland

Christopher Höwarter, Catharina/Georg Michael b Sep 5 1799, bapt Nov 19 1799/Jacob Haller
Jacob Hoffman, Salome/Salome b Sep 19 1799, bapt Nov 20 1799/The mother
Johannes Bohrer, Elisabetha/Susanna b Feb 19 1799, bapt Nov 24 1799/Jacob Wiest, Susanna
Henrich Hoffman, Elisabetha/Jacob b Jul 15 1799, bapt Nov 24 1799/Henrich Kempf
Jacob Baltzell, Charlotta/Margaretha b Oct 28 1799, bapt Dec 16 1799/Parents
Johannes Redig, Barbara/Elisabetha b Oct 25 1799, bapt Dec 18 1799/Hubertus Bayer
Johannes Waltz, Elisabetha/Michael b Oct 18 1799, bapt Dec 18 1799/Adam Waltz
Johannes Zimmerman, Eleonora/Johann Jacob b Oct 10 1799, bapt Dec 22 1799/ Benj. Zimmerman, Catharina
Peter Christ, Margaretha/David b Sep 28 1799, bapt Dec 25 1799/Parents
Georg Doll, Catharina/Anna Maria b Nov 27 1799, bapt Jan 22 1800/Mat. Schmit, Anna Maria
Johannes Faubel, Margaretha/Maria b Jan 27 1800, bapt Feb 17 1800/Parents
Johannes Dodero, Maria/Maria b Oct 28 1799, bapt Feb 23 1800/The mother
Jacob Brunner, Maria Magdalena/Sophia b Sep 25 1799, bapt Feb 26 1800/ Parents
Christoph Branthausel, Catharina/Jacob b Sep 26 1799, bapt Feb 26 1800/Jacob Metzger, Christina
Andreas Hedges, Christina/Enos b Jan 27 1800, bapt Mar 11 1800/The father & Magdalena Braun, widow
Georg Schaefer, Catharina/Philippina b Aug 4 1799, bapt Mar 30 1800/Parents
Michael Engelbrecht, Elisabetha/Maria b Mar 2 1800, bapt Apr 2 1800/Parents
Johannes Remsperger, Anna Maria/Stephan b Feb 24 1781, bapt Apr 11 1800/ adult
Johannes Ott, Maria/Anna Maria b Feb 2 1800, bapt Apr 27 1800/Susanna Schaefer, single
Conrad Specht, Elisabetha/Catharina b Feb 24 1800, bapt Apr 27 1800/Peter Schaefer, Catharina
Georg Jos, Catharina/Catharina b Oct 29 1799, bapt Apr 27 1800/Catharina Herget, single
Wilhelm Käseman, Elisabetha/Anna Catharina b Dec 19 1799, bapt Apr 27 1800/ Catharina Herget, single
Georg Gier, Anna Maria/Anna Margaretha b Dec 18 1799, bapt Apr 27 1800/ Christoph Wedegin, Catharina
Jacob Thomas, Rosina/Catharina b Feb 25 1800, bapt Apr 27 1800/Catharina Thomas, single
Michael Mostetter, Philippina, Christian b Feb 17 1800, bapt Apr 30 1800/ Parents
Georg Barrol, Elisabetha/Adam b May 30 1796, bapt Apr 30 1800/Parents
Georg Barrol, Elisabetha/Salomon b Mar 10 1799, bapt Apr 30 1800/Parents
Jacob Stehly, Elisabeth/Samuel b Oct 6 1799, bapt May 8 1800/Parents
Jacob Martin, Elisabetha/Wilhelm b Feb 29 1799, bapt May 18 1800/Parents
Jacob Kern, Magdalena/Gabriel b Dec 31 1799, bapt May 18 1800/Georg Thomas, single
Thomas Johnson, Elisabeth/Frances Russel b Nov 11 1799, bapt May 18 1800/ Parents
Wm. Crum, Elisabeth/David b May 12 1800, bapt May 23 1800/Parents

Baptisms of the Evangelical Reformed Church in Frederick, Maryland

Anthony, Sarah, blacks/Eleonora b Feb 15 1800, bapt May 25 1800/Property of John Getzedanner
Nicolaus Zimmerman, Elisabeth/Margaretha b Jan 31 1800, bapt Jun 2 1800/ Parents
Jacob Jung, Catharina/Friedrich b Apr 11 1800, bapt Jun 2 1800/Andreas Gödeck, Catharina
Joseph Doll, Catharina/Esra b May 12 1800, bapt Jun 5 1800/Parents
Peter Thomas, Barbara/Margretha b Apr 20 1800, bapt Jun 18 1800/Parents
Peter Bayer, Maria/Elisabetha b Jan 29 1800, bapt Jun 20 1800/Parents
Johannes Dorr, Catharina/Johannes b Nov 28 1798, bapt Jun 20 1800/Parents
Johannes Bantz, Elisabeth/Esra b May 20 1800, bapt Jun 21 1800/Geo. Beyerly, Susanna
Michael Hauck, Magdalena/Maria b Jan 21 1800, bapt Jun 22 1800/Jacob Kohler, Maria
John Karny, Elisabeth/Maria b Dec 20 1799, bapt Jun 22 1800/Peter Christ, Margaretha
Michael Häffner, Elisabetha/Jacob b Jun 14 1800, bapt Jun 22 1800/Parents
Philip Sinn, Elisabetha/Catharina b Mar 12 1800, bapt Jun 23 1800/Parents
Abraham Titlo, Susanna/Elisabetha b Oct 3 1799, bapt Jun 29 1800/Johannes Weber
Leonhart Thomas, Barbara/Anna Maria b Dec 2 1799, bapt Jun 29 1800/ Margaretha Thomas
Jacob Getzedanner, Elisabetha/Maria b Dec 4 1799, bapt Jul 20 1800/Parents
Valentin Thomas, Elisabetha/Georg b Jun 15 1800, bapt Jul 27 1800/Georg Thomas, single
Abraham Herget, Anna Maria/Georg b May 23 1800, Anna Margaretha b May 23 1800, bapt Jul 27 1800/Georg Jost, Catharina, Georg Nickol, Margaretha
Joseph Hildebrand, Magdalena/Daniel b Jun 16 1800, bapt Jul 29 1800/Jacob Stehly, single
John Mace, Ann/John b Apr 12 1800, bapt Aug 9 1800/Parents
Henrich Kempf, Margaretha/Georg b Jul 8 1800, bapt Aug 13 1800/The mother
Georg Engel, Susanna/Jacob b Jul 30 1800, bapt Sep 2 1800/Parents
John Dorsey, Rachel/Absalom b Jun 19 1800/bapt Sep 9 1800/Parents
Jacob Wiest, Susanna/Maria Margaretha b Aug 27 1800, bapt Sep 28 1800/ Valentin Brunner, Elisabeth
Peter Brunner, Catharina/Henrich b Jun 11 1800, bapt Oct 6 1800/Henrich Sinn, single
Friedrich Steiner, Margaretha/Maria b Aug 22 1800, bapt Oct 6 1800/Peter Brunner, Catharina
Adam Jacob, Elisabeth/Daniel b Aug 25 1800, bapt Oct 12 1800/Parents
Thos. Wheeler, Eleonore/Elisabeth b Dec 20 1799, bapt Oct 13 1800/Parents
Peter Storm, Susanna/Sophia Elisabetha b May 11 1799, bapt Oct 16 1800/ Michael Kolb, Maria Sophia
David Fortny, Elisabeth/Elisabetha b Aug 25, bapt Oct 26 1800/Elisabeth Breyer
Conrad Leschhorn, Maria/Johannes b Sep 29 1800, bapt Oct 26 1800/Parents
Nicolaus Kortz, Margaretha/Daniel b Sep 12 1800, bapt Oct 26 1800/Parents
Georg Remsperger, Catharina/Elisabetha b Aug 23 1800, bapt Oct 26 1800/ Elisabeth Thomas, widow
Johannes Schatz, Elisabetha/Christian b Jun 16 1800, bapt Oct 26 1800/ Parents

Baptisms of the Evangelical Reformed Church in Frederick, Maryland

Balthasar Schmit, Catharina/Margaretha b Oct 23 1800, bapt Nov 20 1800/Parents

Wm. McLane, Maria/Cyrus b Jun 20 1800, bapt Nov 27 1800/Parents

Frantz Geissinger, Sarah/Johann Jacob b Aug 9 1800, bapt Dec 3 1800/Parents

Johannes Weber, Maria/Catharina b Sep 28 1800, bapt Dec 7 1800/Michael Weber, Catharina

Johannes Doll, Susanna/David b Nov 1 1800, bapt Dec 21 1800/Parents

Jacob Miller, Nancy/Rebecka b Jul 18 1800, bapt Feb 15 1801/Johann Koppenheber, Barbara

Michael Eckman, Maria/Jacob b Dec 4 1800, bapt Mar 1 1801/Adam Jacob, Elisabetha

Joseph Stehly, Maria Julianna/Maria Julianna b Dec 20 1800, bapt Mar 11 1801/The mother

Peter Stehly, Elisabetha/Conradt b Oct 25 1800, bapt Mar 11 1801/Conrad Schaefer, Single

Georg Ebrecht, Magdalena/Elisabetha b Dec 14 1800, bapt Mar 14 1801/Elisabetha Schaefer, single

Peter Degrange, Barbara/Jacob b Dec 11 1800, bapt Apr 5 1801/Jacob Reber, Anna Maria

Stephan Klein, Margaretha/Catharina b Sep 27 1800, bapt Apr 5 1801/Catharina Schultz, widow

Friedrich Wilbahn, Catharina/Margaretha b Oct 4 1800, bapt Apr 16 1801/Christian Weber, Catharina

Adam Stoll, Elisabetha/Friedrich b Dec 16 1800, bapt May 14 1801/Geo. Remsperger

Georg Remsperger, Elisabetha/Anna Elisabetha b Oct 4 1800, bapt May 14 1801/Anna Elisabetha Remsperger

Christian Hertinger, Maria Julianna/Christian b Apr 1 1800, bapt May 24 1801/Parents

Andreas --, Catharina/Johannes b Oct 26 1800, bapt May 24 1801/Johannes Schaefer, Anna Maria

Carl Gross, Elisabetha/Georg b Feb 19 1783, bapt May 23 1801/adult

Abraham Wingert, Maria/Catharina Elisabeth b May 27 1800, bapt May 26 1801/Elisabeth Brunner

Henrich Schmit, Maria/Daniel b Nov 8 1800, bapt Jun 13 1801/Parents

Henrich Dorsch, Maria/Rebecca b Mar 14 1800, bapt Jun 21 1801/Parents

Jacob Schleich, Hannah/Child b Dec 1 1799, bapt Jun 21 1801/The father

Walter Schuck, Catharina Gross/Elisabetha b Jul 17 1797, bapt Aug 12 1801/The mother

David Schreyer, Catharina/Georg b Jul 17 1781, bapt Sep 20 1801/Parents

Jacob Bohley, Elisabetha/Catharina b -- 1794, Charlotta b May -- 1796, Sarah b Jul -- 1798, bapt Sep 22 1801/Barbara Bell, widow, Elisabeth Hauer, Barbara Bell

Daniel Balzel, Susan/Maria b Dec 3 1800, bapt Aug 4 1803/Parents

Abraham Phoh, Maria/Julianna Maria b Dec 23 1792, Sophia Elisabet b Oct 28 1794, bapt Nov 11 1803/--

Henrich Steiner & wf./Wilhelm b Feb 1 1791, bapt Nov 11 1793/--

Christoph Bergman, Anna Maria/Anna Maria b Mar 7 1795, Christian b Dec 17 1798/Jacob Kast

Nicolaus Paar, Elisabeth/Elisabeth b Jun 25 1795, Margaret b Jan 13 1797, Magdalena b Oct 5 1798, Freidrich b Nov 11 1800, Barbara b Oct 19 1803, all bapt Aug 5 1804

Nicolaus Paar, Elisabeth/Christina b Mar 23 1791, bapt earlier
Nicolaus Paar, Elisabeth/Henrich b Mar 15 1793, bapt before 1804/--

Part II: Records of Marriages

List of the Persons who during the minsistry of John Conrad Steiner were joined in marriage in the Reformed Congregation in Manakesse (Monocacy). He hopes therefore, that through faith they may be participants of the spiritual marriage with Christ and thus share in the eternal marriage of heaven at the last.

1756, Oct 31 Jacob Sinn and Maria Magdalena Biber.
Nov 2 Carl Friedrich Medard and Catharina Gerson.
Dec Thomas Ogle and Sarah Ogle.
Dec 13 Johannes Sturm and Anna Barbara Hoffmann.
Dec 20 Georg Reimesperger and Maria Elisabetha Brunner.
Dec 30 Johannes Weber and Maria Elisabetha Haas.
1757, Jan 22 George Beall and Elisabeth Turner.
Feb 1 Daniel Schumacher and Maria Elisabetha Hofmann.
Feb 7 Joh. Adam Ochs and Maria Apollonia Hofmann.
Mar 1 William Betty and Maria Dorothea Crusch.
Mar 22 Johan Bernhart Würtenbecher & Maria Eva Hein.
Mar 23 Johannes Schönefeld & Maria Catharina Mezier.
Mar 29 Johann Josua Meyerer & Maria Kämpf.
Apr 3 Jacob Giezendanner & Catharina Kast.
Apr 17 Philip Renner & Anna Maria Finck.
Apr 17 Peter Tofler & Anna Maria Sturm.
May 3 Christian Schellenbaum & Margaretha Casselmann.
May 24 Johannes Scheidegger & Eva Maria Many.
Jun 2 David Ulmer & Rosina Margaretha Hirschmann.
Jul 19 Johannes Mittelkauf & Maria Elisabetha Brunner.
Aug 9 Peter Jung & Barbara Bergard.
Aug 9 Jacob Leemann & Anna Maria Jung.
Aug 16 Adam Ekhart & Eva Reiss
Sep 25 Johann Adam Diez & Maria Magdalena Thom.
Nov 20 Johannes Bley & Maria Elisabetha Apfel
Nov 29 George Michael Schneider & Juditha Unseld
Dec 1 Wilhelm Schmidt & Agnes Mey.
Dec 13 Christophel Thomas & Susanna Margaretha Weiss.
Dec 29 Johannes Scherer & Maria Susanna Dentlinger.
1758 Mar 28 Christian Schär & Maria Salome Bargelt.
Apr 19 Johan Wilhelm Geiniz & Johanna Weissmann.
Apr 25 Hans Georg Müller & Magdalena Maderi.
Apr 18 Joh. Valentin Weiss & Catharine Froschauer.
May 8 Leonhardt Schneebeli & Margaretha Weiss.
May 8 Rudolph Hoffmann & Dorothea Weiss.
May 11 Baltsasar Giezendanner & Anna Steiner.
May 15 Daniel Michel & Maria Schober.
May 16 Georg Thomas Schley & Maria Giezendanner.
May 17 Jacob Steiner & Maria Anna Schley.
May 28 Jacob Keller & Elisabeth Leitert.
Aug 6 Joh. Friedrich Becker & Maria Dorothea Düremann.
Aug 8 Wendel Strickler & Susanna Sax.

Oct 24 Wilhelm Hauser & Susanna Freund.
Nov Charles Adkin & Rachel Makeby.
1759 Jan 1 Jacob Bruder & Mrs. Margaret Huber.
Jan 9 Heinrich Weiss & Catherina Brunner.
Jan 10 Andreas Geomi & Anna Elisabeth --.
Feb 20 Nicolaus Heichler & Anna Marg. Meyer.
Mar 27 Baltsasar Dorry & Barbara Henckel.
Apr 1 Jacob Brunner & Maria Barb. Käufer.
Mar 18 Gabriel Leidig & Catherina Delater.
Apr 12 Christophel Leck & Sophia Rosina Urbach
Apr 19 Johannes Klein & Anna Barly
May 6 Peter Coblenz & Susanna Keller.
May 6 -- & Margaret Schweinhart.

Marriages by the Rev. Philip William Otterbein, 1760-1765

1760 Nov 2 Henrich Balzel & Margaretha Alexander.
1761 Feb 10 Georg Bernhard Lingefelder & Barbara Brunner.
Feb 15 Johannes Adam & Margaretha Weiss.
Feb 24 Abraham Muller & Margaretha Hützel.
Feb 22 Johannes Bob & Magdalena Hufleder.
Feb 23 Adam Hildebrand & Anna Maria Schaub.
Mar 2 Jacob Huber & Christina Kern, both 2nd marriage.
Apr 7 Daniel Sturm & Anna Maria Stempel.
Apr 7 Matthias Eberz & Catherina Magdalena Maas.
May 5 Peter Dorry & Catherina Feldmann.
May 5 Franz Jacob & Maria Elisabetha Holtz.
May 28 Johannes Heiner & Margaretha Gebhart.
May 31 Christian Traxel & Catherine Dorr.
Jul 23 Johannes Jacob & Catharina Wenderoth.
Jul 30 Jacob Brengel & Gertraut Bell.
Jul 5 Jacob Brenner & Margaretha Geiffer.
Jul 7 Georg Schaffer & Ursula Arnodt.
Aug 6 Michael Ebert & Maria Clara Kappel.
Aug 18 Johann Henrich Egg & Rosina Schmitt.
Sep 9 Stoffel Braun & Magdalena Mann.
Sept 10 Johannes Darich & Maria Marschand.
Sep 14 Jacob Holtz & Catharina Hätt.
Sep 15 Peter Becker & Anna Maria Nicol
Sep 20 Christoph Stoll & Philippina Sthäl.
Sep 20 Conrad Doll & Anna Maria Schisler.
Oct 20 Philip Schmitt & Christina Sebastian.
Oct 26 Wilhelm Schonfeld & Margaretha Gissinger.
Dec 29 Leonhard Sturm & Catherina Dail.
Nov 30 Andrew Stephan & Elizabeth Kohler.
1762 Jan 30 Peter Weiss & Margaretha Meyer.
Feb 23 Valentin Alexander & Elisabetha Dail.
Feb 21 Georg Henrich & Sophia Hoffman.
Feb 23 Peter Balzel & Catharina Rühel.
Mar 5 Bastian Mersch & Magdalena Burghard.
Mar 8 Jacob Schuti & Catharina Fries.
Mar 16 Stephan Müller & Rachel Bobb.
Mar 16 Wilhelm Krans & Catharina Rieser.

Apr 5 Philip Becker & Elizabeth Bäcker.
Apr 6 Elias Willjahr & Rosina Gemb.
Apr 8 Johannes Remsperger & Anna Maria Brenner.
Apr 12 Adam Traub & Catharina Muselmann.
Aug 3 Christian Schaffer & Anna Maria Muller.
Aug 17 Jacob Hoff & Catharina Faut.
Aug 3 Joseph Fyer & Anna Maria Dommer.
Sep 25 Ludwig Hen & Susanna Muller.
Sep 10 Christophel Reber & Catharina Mack.
Oct 17 Johannes Berg & Elizabetha Gramm.
Oct 19 Isaac Ritsch & Anna Catharina Berg.
1763 Jan 4 Nicolaus Kuntz & Anna Maria Eckhard.
Jan 16 Johannes Bamberger & Elisabetha Ulmann.
Mar 6 Freidrich Schonefeld & Maria Elisabetha Wesselbach.
Mar 25 Georg Kornman & Sarah Harrison.
May 8 Johannes Teufferbach & Margaretha Krämer.
May 8 Georg Krämer & Maria Magdalena Holtz.
Jun 19 Henrich Scheffer & Elisabetha Keller.
Aug 9 Nicolaus Beck & Magdalena Gallmann.
Nov 15 Georg Zimmermann & Catharina Christ.
Nov 23 Georg Zwickel & Elisabetha Ruthenauer.
Dec 29 Michael Christ & Maria Elisabetha Stein.
1764 Jan 3 Michael Duttenhofer & Rachel Wilkens.
Jan 17 Jacob Kuntz & Margaretha Nagel.
Feb 7 Johan Henrich Theis & Elisabetha Jons.
Feb 28 Peter(?) Michael & Dorothea Schmitt.
Jun 5 Friedrich Lederman & Catharina Sailer.
Jun 11 Friedrich Arnholt & Martha Schaner.
Jul 1 Johan Eberhard Darich & Anna Reitenauer.
Jul 1 Georg Richtner & Anna Maria Flenner.
Sep 11 Nicolaus Steel & Elisabetha Hermann.
Sep 18 Johan Nicolaus Kunz & Johanna Navin.
Sep 26 Andreas Adam & Catharina Delater.
Oct 8 Philip Bier & Eva Catharina Schley.
Nov 5 Peter Kobelenz & Elisabetha Steffan.
Nov 6 Philip Sinn & Elisabetha Zimmermann.
Dec 2 Andreas Schneberger & Catharina Gerber.
Dec 2 Martin Bächtly & Veronica Schnebeli.
1765 Feb 19 Johan Adam Grund & Christina Hoffmann.
Apr 1 Georg Genterman & Rachel Milhaus.
Feb 12 Johannes Ebi & Anna Maria Bens.
May 2 John Michael Häger & Hannah Keller.
Jul 2 Johan Peter Stock & Esther Alexander.
Sep 24 Valentin Lingefelder & Maria Elisabetha Daub.
Oct 2 Ludwig Hoff & Catharina Fortune.

Under the Ministry of Carolus Lange, the following persons were joined in Marriage.

1766 Nov 2 Jacob Sinn & Philippina Garner.
Nov 30 Jacob Baltzel & Margaretha Schley, widow.
Dec 9 Philip Seeler & Christina Eberli.
Dec 21 Peter Dofler & Margaretha Schley.

Marriages of the Evangelical Reformed Church in Frederick, Maryland

1767 Jan 6 Georg Peter Hofmann & Maria Dorothea Leu, widow.
Jan 13 Jacob Klein & Anna Maria Seiler.
Jan 22 Georg Schmidt & Catharina Sturm.
Feb 10 Andreas Lyss & Catharina Wolf.
Feb 18 Valentin Eberly & Anna Barbara Schmid, widow.
Mar 30 Georg Rat & Hannah Calcum.
Aug 19 Daniel Jacob & Salome Leder.
Aug 20 Nicolaus Frey & Catharina Schneter.
Aug 22 Abraham Oberhold & Anna Wittmor.
Sep 29 Jacob Hess & Rebecca Margaretha Ohrendorf.

The following persons were married on my second journey to Virginia, namely:
Nov 7 Peter Primon & Magdalena Forsch.
Nov 8 Jacob Hamilton & Maria Gibs.
Nov 10 Daniel Maus & Eva Spieglin (Spiegel).
Nov 16 David Wolff & Anna Maria Miller.
Nov 16 Johann Georg Niclas & Anna Barbara Hofman.
Nov 25 Georg Michael Holzinger & Anna Barbara Schneider.
Nov 25 Johan Jacob Baumann & Elisabetha Keller.
Nov 26 Johannes Hazenbiller & Barbara Schnegt.
Dec 9 Christoph Wagner & Catharina Schneider.
1768 Jan 12 Jacob Weiss & Maria Anna Hofmann.
Jan 19 Jacob Keller & Maria Humbhart.
Jan 27 Heinrich Ziegler & Elisabetha Schumacher.
Jan 31 Peter Borer & Magdalena Schenkmayer.
Feb 9 Simon Schnock & Charlotta Keller.

The following persons were married on my 3rd journey to Virginia.
Apr 4 Nicolaus Klein & Anna Maria Cruger.
Apr 10 Jacob Serber & Catharina Caufeldt.
May 24 Georg Michael Alter & Margaretha Messmor.

Jun 12 Andreas Flick & Magdalena Reichhardt.
Jun 21 Jacob Ragg & Maria Barbara Brenglin (Brengel).
Jun 26 Jacob Hofmann & Barbara Brunner.
Jun 28 Heinrich Beer & Margaretha Winter.

(Marriages by Frederick Ludwig Henop, 1770-1784 Missing)

Marriages by William Runckel, 1784-1800

1784 Dec 14 George Waters & Sarah Austin. Wit: Henrich Neer & James Waters. Both parties from Antietam, Frederick Co.
Dec 20 Christian Degenhart & Anna Maria Miller. Wit: Bro.-in-law of bridegroom. From Middletown, Fred. Co.
1785 Jan 4 John Brightnell & Mary Dodson. Wit: Wm. Plain, Rich. Brighwell.
Jan 2 Benj. Simpson & Elisabeth Dewall. Wit: Mr. Dewall, a relation. of Fred. Co.
Jan 11 Peter Herzog & Catherine Lea, of Fred. Co. Wit: Wilhelm & Joh. Herzog.

Marriages of the Evangelical Reformed Church in Frederick, Maryland

Jan 25 Jacob Stattelmayer & Hedwig Schumacher, of Middletown. Wit: Martin Kuhns, Joh. Alexander, Henry Alexander.
Jan 26 Abraham Rothrock & Elisabeth Roberts, Antietam. Wit: Gesham Roberts, John Anderson, Daniel Rothrock.
Feb 1 James Waters & Leanna Thomas, Anteitam. Wit: Josiah Harper, Wm. Waler.
Feb 15 Humphrey Collins & Sarah Bell, Hunting Creek. Wit: Mat. Collins & Math. Bell.
Feb 17 Zaddock Griffith & Sarah Hantel, on rd to Georgetown. Wit: David Boyer, Geo. Simmons
Feb 22 Abraham Eder & Catharina Reich.
Mar 20 Leonhard Thomas & Barbara Johs.
Mar 20 Karl Bernhard Miller & Margretha Groff.
Mar 20 Johannes Geyer & Elisabeth Scheffy. Wit: Daniel Lehr, Jacob Schneyder.
Mar 3 George McMinn & Sarah Campbell.
Mar 27 Sam. Constable & Rebecca Dobston. Wit: Nicholas Tice, Mich. Crowenhinton, James Wilson.
Mar 27 Walter Hanson Stone & Ann Muncaster. Wit: James Muncaster, Jeremiah Gray.
Mar 29 Andreas Amman & Barbara Luther.
Apr 5 Jacob Schmitt & Anna Maria Benter.
Apr 5 Henrich Weyand & Elisabeth Fein.
Apr 12 Isaac McKardill & Sarah De Coin. Wit: Wm. Koch, Peter Hard.
Apr 18 Robert McComsy & Catherine Warner. Wit: Lorentz Brenckel.
May 5 Hugh McMillan & Mary Hicks.
Apr 26 Daniel Lettig & Margaretha Dickson.
May 15 Benj. Jefferys & Elisabeth Schmit.
May 15 Benj. Rhodes Hackney & Eliz. Warner Philpot. Wit: The father of bridegroom and others.
May 15 Thomas Hickson & Mary Swartz. Wit: Wil. Koch, Peter Hardt.
May 16 Christian Wiesenmilder & Elis. Schneider. Wit: Henrich Krass, Christian Kreiss.
May 24 Adam Kern & Rosina Willjahr. Wit: The father of the bride.
Jun 7 Solomon Longsworth & Lucretia McElfish. Wit: Rachel Nelson.
Jun 14 Daniel Fergusson & Charity Auson.
June 19 Friedrich Rehkop & Susanna Schafer. Wit: Sam. Nixdorf, Peter Hard.
Jun 19 Nicolaus Holtz & Susanna Zimmerman. Wit: Geo. Schafer, Con. Schafer, Joh. Zimmerman.
Jun 19 Henry Ramsower & Mary Smith. Wit: Michael Rein, Thos. Mark.
Jun 24 Wm. Thomas & Sarah Perkins.
Jul 12 Jacob Warn & Henrietta Gasseway. Wit: Sam. Gasseway.
Jul 12 Johannes Schaup & Barbara Mayer.
Jul 19 Johannes Steiner & Elisabeth Planck. Wit: Stephan Remsperg, Joh. Steiner, Sr.
Aug 9 John Stanton & Susanna Murphy.
Aug 7 Carl Bocklop & Catharina Lang.
Aug 9 John Prather & Amelia Philips.
Aug 2 Henrich Bohmer & Anna Maria Albach.
Aug 21 Thomas Barnee & Barbara Neuschwanger.
Aug 23 John Waters & Christina Schön. Wit: Georg Waters.

Aug 28 Middleton Smith & Julianna Keller. Wit: Edward Salman & Isaac Nell.
Sep 5 James Crossly & Deborah Runnel. Wit: John Brown & Moses Harper.
Sep 6 Johannes Getzendanner & Rebecca Faut. Wit: Thomas Getzendanner, Henrich Kempff.
Sep 15 James Cambel & Linny Hyatt.
Sep 18 Bartho. Bucher & Susanna Walter. Wit: B. Bucher.
Sep 20 Thomas Eisenkagel & Susanna Spannseiler. Wit: Joh. Georg Heil.
Oct 11 Aaron Smedly & Rebecca Lear. Wit: Henrich Landes, Peter Shraner.
Oct 11 Wm. Webb & Mary Meredith. Wit: Ab. Moor, Thos. Ellis.
Oct 11 Georg Hineman & Elizabeth Howard. Wit: Peter Bahl, Con. Brug.
Oct 11 Johannes Schmehl & PHilippina Planck. Wit: Michael Bayer.
Oct 30 Herman Henrich Schroder & Susanna Schwartz. Wit: Wilhelm Koch, Peter Hardt.
Nov 1 Andreas Hag & Maria Wolff.
Nov 15 Jacob Stimmel & Elisabeth Bossart. Wit: Jacob Stimmel, Sr. Dan. Bossert.
Nov 15 Thomas Stanley & Catherine Rice. Wit: John Henly, Doct. Rich'd Coates.
Nov 8 David Bayer & Sarah Krum.
Nov 22 Michael Jauzy & Christina Schmidt. Wit: Jacob Schmidt.
Nov 22 Stephen Fluheart & Elizabeth Randel. Wit: Valentin Rein, Joh. Rein.
Nov 27 Matthew Collins & Susanna Bowlass.
Dec 6 Michael Spanseiler & Sarah Price. Wit: Andrew Watt, Michael Zimmerman.
Dec 10 Wm. Scurlock & Charity Norman. Wit: John Watt, Anthony Becker.
Dec 20 Jacob Schmidt & Julianna Jung.
Dec 25 Georg Schaefer & Catharina Stoll. Wit: Conrad Schaefer, Jacob Schaefer.
Dec 25 Adam Schreiner & Maria Geissinger. Valentin Brunner, Valentin Schreiner.

1786

Jan 1 Adam Wirtenbecher & Elisabeth Reeb. Wit: Georg Hofman, Peter Gebhard.
Jan 3 Matthaeus Schmit & Elisabeth Beckenbach. Wit: Jacob Jost, -- Scholl.
Jan 16 Wm. Hope & Bridget Warner. Wit: Thos. Wilks, Wm. Evans.
Jan 24 Johannes Wagner & Margaretha Rupp. Wit: Jacob Riess, Adam Wagner.
Jan 24 Christian Schaup & Elisabeth Fister. Wit: Joh. Mahn, Jacob Runckel.
Jan 29 Georg Baer & Maria Adams. Wit: Adam Keller, Dan. Lahr.
Feb 7 Christian Brandt & Rosina Walter. Wit: Johannes Brunner, — Haller.
Feb 12 Michael Harth & Maria Rau.
Feb 21 Michael Schmit & Susanna Steckel. Wit: Michael Witmer, Philip Lipps.
Feb 21 David Bossert & Catherina Schuck. Wit: Peter Jung, Ludwig Starck.
Mar 9 Thos. Brookover & Mary Thomas. Wit: Richard Jacobs, Posey Steward.
Mar 9 Alexander Naylor & Mary Mills. Wit: G. Salmon.
Mar 21 Georg Keller & Susanna Hedges. Wit: Joh. Kraemer, Robert Wickham.
Mar 26 Michael Braun & Rosina Jantz. Wit: Geo. Hoffman, Christian Balsel.

Apr 2 Christian Götzendanner & Catharina Remsperger. Wit: Bal. Götzendanner, -- Remsperger.
Apr 2 Georg Hoffman & Eva Margaretha Jantz. Wit: Michael Braun, Georg Hoffman, Sr.
Apr 13 John James & Martha Haff. Wit: ---
Apr 16 Nathanael Buckhardt & Margaret Simmons. Wit: ---
Apr 23 Johannes Peter & Catharina Haller. Wit: -- Haller, -- Stern.
Apr 23 Michael Ott & Elisabeth Wertenbacher. Wit: -- Brand, -- Wirtenbacher.
Apr 30 Johannes Thomas & Elisabeth Remsperger. Wit: Gab. Thomas. Geo. Remsperger.
May 1 Henry Baker & Elisabeth Geringer. Wit: Georg Bauerschmit, Thos. Gilbert.
May 2 John Scott & Catharina Levan. Wit: Mis. Boon, Benj. Gahway.
May 2 Peter Fein & Cath. Margaret Bennet. Wit: B. Gahway, Ad. Boon.
May 30 Robert Barnet & Nancy Stallings. Wit: --
Jun 20 Abraham Bayer & Eva Beringer. Wit: Witmer.
Jul 11 Reuben Triplet & Rebecca Comb. Wit: Joh. Brunner.
Jul 27 Moritz Albach & Cath. Boehmer.
Jul 20 Grove Harrison & Hannah Fuller. Wit: Benj. Todd, Jos. West.
Jul 23 Solomon Turner & Casandra Harvey.
Aug 13 Jacob Brunner & Magdalena Schneider. Wit: Jacob Schmid, Jacob Zurrich.
Aug 8 Peter Berg & Catharina Berg.
Aug 15 Johannes Miller & Barbara Schmit. Wit: Conrad Kronenbach, Joh. Schmit.
Aug 22 Michael Scheydecker & Maria Marg. Roth. Wit: Hen. Rauser.
Sep 21 Jacob Steiner & Elisabeth Hauer. Wit: W. Koch, Thos. Schley.
Sep 26 Peter Springer & Jane Fulton. Wit: Edward Springer, Charles Springer.
Oct 10 Alexander Schultz & Mary Price. Wit: Dr. -- Rauen, Anthon Becker.
Oct 12 Adam Cooper & Rebecca Hamilton. Wit: Lewis Browning, Robert Cooper.
Oct 17 Jacob Keller & Susanna Schmidt. Wit: Henrich Berg, Phil. Schmidt, son of Wm.
Oct 23 James Parrish & Priscilla Street. Wit: Wm. Curren.
Oct 24 Johannes Lentz & Maria Magd. Wagner. Wit: Joh. Getzendanner.
Oct 24 Thomas Maxwell & Marg. Steckel. Wit: Michael Witmer, Simon Steckel.
Dec 21 Jeremiah Hillary & Ann Clary. Wit: Jos. Madden & Jas. Murphy
Nov 21 Edward Steward & Susanna Klee. Wit: Andreas Burman, Thos. Grover.
Dec 10 Christopher Watkins & Sarah Grover. Wit: Benj. Hill, Robert Hill.
Nov 28 Jacob Keil & Abigail Gallman. Wit: Jacob Baulus, Nicolaus Keil.
Dec 15 Moses Kannyman & Hannah Barrel. Wit: Benj. Steward & Geo. Cumberledge.
Dec 26 John Thornbury & Sarah Bently. Wit: Jacob Guckerle, -- Thornbury.

1787

Jan 11 Jacob Balsel & Chalotta Christ. Wit: Michael Christ & P. Hauck.
Jan 11 Gerret Ball & Elizabeth Cecil. Married by H. Krug, banns thru me.
Jan 15 Mat. Fluck & Catharina Jung. Wit: -- Dieterly.
Feb 4 Jacob Dörr & Margaret Wintz. Wit: Thos. Schley, Joh. Bockius.
Feb 8 Daniel Leakin & Ann Shekle. Wit: Hen. Herschberger, -- Weiss.

Feb 13 Jacob Brandenburger & Elisabeth Rein. Wit: Casper Rein, F. Egan.
Feb 18 Johannes Martin & Anna Barb. Fünfrock, widow. Wit: Anthon Becker, Marg. Wagner.
Feb 18 John Ritschie & Catherine Beatty. Wit: Wm. Ritschie, James Beatty.
Feb 20 Samuel Bowling & Mary Ann Plumer. Wit: John Mackelfish, Wid. Weis, Marg. Raser.
Feb 22 Georg Miller & Catharina Engelbrecht. Wit: Remsperger, Mrs. Ziegler.
Feb 26 James Nichols & Ann James. Wit: Marg. Wagner, Ellen Stephens
Mar 5 Caleb Evars & Eva Wedel. Wit: -- Faubel, Joh. Brunner
Mar 6 Heinrich Hembe & Ann Marg. Dofler. Wit: Peter Dofler, -- Briede, --Dofler.
Mar 6 Nicholas Dehoff & Susanna Cath. Vogel. Wit: -- Vogel, -- Vogel.
Mar 15 Heinrich Neuschwanger & Catherine Butz. Wit: Bernhardt Schulmeist, -- Wenner.
Mar 29 Wilhelm Schilling & Catherine Gilbert. Elias Miljahr, -- Dunckel.
Apr 15 Samuel Pool & Jemima Norwood. Wit: John Pool, James Norwood.
Apr 17 Henrich Conradt & Maria Lath. Wit: Jacob Kitweiler, Mich. Witmer.
Apr 22 Georg Bocky & Christina Haas. Wit: Joh. Brunner, Val. Bocky.
Apr 24 Johannes Remsperger & Elisabeth Miller. Wit: Geo. & Mich. Remsperger.
Apr 29 Johannes Keplinger & Catherine Poley. Wit: Wilhelm Miller, -- Poley.
May 6 Wilhelm Haffner & Rachel Boot. Wit: Joh. Gebhard, Edward Salmon.
May 10 Hezekiah Owen & Eliz. Dewall. Wit: Thos. Winsor, Jacob Riesser.
May 13 Henrich Hirschberger & Catharina Remsperger. Wit: Geo. Remsperger, -- Hirschberger.
May 20 Jacob Gomber & Susanna Beatty. Wit: Lorentz Brengel, Chs. Beaty.
May 22 Carl Bockley & Christina Puhl. Wit: Eliz. Gardiner, Cath. Magd. --
May 22 Peter Bayer & Anna Maria Mossetter. Wit: -- Bayer, -- Mossetter.
Jun 26 Peter Dehaven & Mary Cellars. Wit: John Brunner & Ann Becker.
Jul 15 Henry Smith & Mary Ramsower. Wit: Francis Hagon, Peter Kempf.
Jul 22 John Noland & Ann Watkins. Wit: Jacob Eichelbrenner & Jos. Hill.
Aug 5 Jos. Burneston & Julianna Grof. Wit: Geo. Baer, -- Barton
Jul -- Joseph Mackdonald & Rachel Showels. Wit: Sam. How, John Stutz.
Aug 12 Edward Springer & Elisabeth Krieger. Wit: Thos. Ogle, Sarah Smith.
Sep 25 Peter Hedges & Elisabeth Bayer. Wit: David Bayer, -- Crum.
Oct 7 Adam Wolff & Margaretha Steinbrenner. Wit: Adam Wolff, Peter Hardt.
Oct 9 Christoph Ambrosius & Cath. Getzendanner. Wit: Bal. & Christian Getzendanner.
Oct 13 Jacob Hauser & Catharina Bader. Wit: Michael & Adam Hausser.
Oct 14 Warner Stockton & Nancy Gladdon. Wit: -- Stockton, Geo. Adams.
Oct 14 Henrich Steiner & Elisabetha Brengel. Wit: Conrad Doll, Edward Salmon.
Oct 14 Thomas Getzendanner & Maria Ann Kuhns. Wit: Jacob Bucher, Johannes Bucky.
Oct 21 Basil Nelson & Sarah Maynard. Wit: -- Maynard.
Nov 4 Benjamin Jacobs & Elis. Gilbert. Wit: Richard Jacobs, John Richards.
Nov 22 John Hambleton & Elizabeth Philips. Wit: Thos. Ogle.

Nov 24 Peter Beltz & Magdalena Moll. Wit: Andreas Beltz, Tho. Moll, London.
Nov 2 Daniel Schreyack & Maria Kassel. Wit: Peter Hardt, — Kassel.
Dec 6 Richard Brightwell & Betsy Howard. Wit: John Williams, Cornelius Howard.
1788
Jan 15 Joseph Rice & Elisabeth Melvin. Wit: John Leakin, Benjamin Rice.
Jan 29 Francis Hagon & Marg. Ramsower. Wit: -- Ramsower, Dolly McNeil.
Jan 29 Masharek Hinton & Elizabeth Joseph. Wit: Shadrach Hinton, Wm. Joseph.
1787
Dec 7 Elijah Barber & Nancy Todd. Wit: -- Barber, Chs. Miles.
Dec 12 Casper Traut & Maria Ament. Wit: Virginia Ament, Joh. Krumbacher.
Dec 24 David Kinney & Betsy Kirk. Wit: Benjamin Kirk, Ed. Ward.
Dec 25 Henrich Kuhns & Margaret Steiner. Wit: Thos. Ogle, Thomas Schley.
Dec 16 Matthias Brandenburger & Barbara Keller. Wil. Brandenburger, Cath. Runckel.
1788
Jan 15 John Rice & Elisabeth Melvin. Wit: John Leakin, Benj. Rice.
Jan 29 James Hoggan & Marg. Ramsower. Wit: -- Ramsower, Dolly McNeil. (These last two entries conflict with above for same date)
Feb 4 Richard Hebb & Anna Thomas. Wit: Geo. Schley, Wil. Koch.
Feb 19 Daniel Harlan & Eliz. Justice.
Feb 21 Samuel Harrison & Elisabeth Schaun. Wit: Ab. Eder, -- Schaun.
Mar 9 Johnson Dorsey & Sarah Hammond. Wit: Dan. Dorsey, Joh. Norris.
Mar 11 James Coale & Mary Carter. Wit: Luke Pool, David Hays.
Apr 6 Georg Bentz & Elisabeth Gomber. Wit: Lorentz Brengel, Jacob Bentz.
Apr 8 Robert Cron & Christina Schmidt. Wit: Jacob Schmidt, bride's father & others.
Apr 1 John Camel & Elizabeth Harlin. Wit: Jos. Wood, -- Harlin.
Apr 13 Georg Baer & Catharina Hauer. Wit: Christ. Thomas, Mich. Hausser.
May 1 Philip Schmit & Kerenhappush Brothers. (See Job. 42:14) Wit: Geo. Stürmer, -- Derren.
Apr 15 Benjamin Dowell & Barbara Springer. Wit: -- Moseter.
May 13 Eckhardt Gills & Catharina Sulzer. Wit: Philip Preiss, -- Preiss.
May 13 Georg Letter & Christina Laufer, by Mr. Krug. Wit: Michael Laufer, Joh. Letter.
May 16 Friedrich Steiner & Clarissa Reb.
Jun 1 Daniel Krieger & Barbara Schmidt. Wit: Adam Schnook, Phil. Preiss.
Jun 14 Philip Hoffman & Elizabeth Getzendanner, widow. Wit: Joh. & Christian Getzendanner.
Jun 14 James McCormick & Nancy Moore. Wit: Thos. Ogle, Geo. Roth.
Jun 22 Lorentz Brengel & Catherina Scheffy. Wit: Lorentz Brengel, E. Salmon.
Jun 29 Peter Wip & Elizabeth Nickol. Wit: -- Nickol.
Aug 5 Johannes Finckbohner & Susanna Brucker. Wit: -- Silber, A. Maria Schmidt.
Aug 9 Henrich Bantz & Catharina Schmidt. Wit: Adam Schissler, Joh. Rohr.
Aug 26 Michael Squire & Judith Merckel. Wit: Gabriel & Adam Merckel.
Aug 31 Joseph Hildebrand & Magd. Eliz. Häffner. Wit: Friedrich Kleiss, Joh. Stein.
Sep 24 Abraham Stiehl & Maria Ailbach. Wit: Joh. Albach, Hub. Bayer.

Sep 28 Henry Roby Hill & Ann Talbert. Wit: Thos. Jones, Benj. Shaw.
Oct 1 Michael Burns & Elizabeth Kemp. Wit: George Close & Susann Warren.
Oct 5 Philip Reblogel & Eleonor McLean. Wit: -- Wolffly, -- Eckhardt.
-- Justice Gerecht & Elizabeth Drenter. Wit: Lohr. Heim, Andr. Helbig.
Nov 4 Elias Thrasher & Sarah Lemar. Wit: Wm. Bishop Lamar, Thos. Thrasher.
Nov 11 Ludwig Ripley & Maria Miller. Wit: Adam Schnook & Ludwig Reply.
Nov 12 John Richards & Aberrella Norris. Wit: Henrich Hertzog, Nico. Dehoof.
Nov 18 Samuel Stevenson & Lucy Dorsey. Wit: Basil Dorsey, Evan. Dorsey.
Dec 14 Henrich Kreiss & Barbara Volck. Wit: -- Volck . Cath. Runckel.
Dec 14 Thomas Smother & Silvia, per permission of Dewall. free negro.
Dec 7 John Carr & Mary Keller. Wit: Robert Short, Eliz. Short.
Dec 16 Wm. Ward Padgist & Mary Grover. Wit: Wm. Burgis, Eva Watkins.
Dec 21 Ruben Harlan & Catharina Richards. Wit: Hen. Hertzog, Nico. Dehof.
Dec 21 Matthias Davis & Rachel Maynard. Wit: Mat. Fuchs, Nico. Dehoof.
Dec 21 Henry Maynard & Eleonore Howard. Wit: Ephraim Howard, -- Krabster.
Dec 25 Robert Briggs & Priscilla Jefferson. Wit: Henry Jefferson, John Howard
Dec 29 Nathan Hains & Ann Murray. John Messler, Eliz. Dickensheets.
1789
Jan 1 Peter Bell & Magdalena Schmit. Wit: Henrich Gernhardt, Wit: Roth.
Jan 6 Evan Dorsey & Susan Lawrence. Wit: Basil Dorsey, Sr. & Jr.
Jan 9 Daniel Zürrich & Martha Brashears. Wit: Jacob & Johannes Zürrich.
Jan 12 Henry Cecil & Sarah Hinton. Wit: James Smith, Brice Cecil.
Jan 13 Johannes Remsperger & Cath. Thomas. Wit: Geo. Remsperger, Sr. & Jr.
Feb 24 James Irvine & Mary Cole. Wit: Francis McCannel, Jos. Wright
Jan 25 Jacob Wintz & Cath. Fischer. Wit: Geo. Snertzel, Thomas Schley.
Feb 24 Andreas Zeller & Catharina Gunther. Wit: Christian Gunther, Ab. Frey.
Feb 24 Wm. Butler & Delilah Browning. Wit: Thos. Chineth, Jos. Stauder.
Mar 3 John Vion & Catharina Ruf. Wit: Michael Ensminger, Mich. Holon.
Mar 10 Adam Krieger & Susanna Springer. Wit: Edward Springer.
Mar 10 Wm. Moore & Jane Young. Wit: Benjamin Elder.
Mar 31 Georg Remsperger & Cath. Sulzer. Wit: Bernhard Ott, Christoph Zank.
Apr 7 Geo. Remsperger & Christine Peckner. Wit: Joh. Remsperger, Geo. Widerich.
Apr 5 James Wages & Barbara Pool. Wit: -- Pool, Jacob Aurand.
1788
Dec 25 Johannes Baer & Maria Thomas. Wit: Geo. Baer & Wil. Baer.
Mar 31 George Cumberledge & Rachel Barber. Wit: Warren & Sarah Barber.
Apr 7 Geo. Sam. Bager & Catharina Bossert. Wit: Abraham & Adam Bossert.
Apr 12 Peter Heck & Hannah Wäschebach. Wit: --
Apr 14 Jacob Krämer & Cath. Berg. Wit: Geo. Dewelbiss, Joh. Krämer.
Apr 26 Johannes Schaum & Rebecca Whitcraft. Wit: Peter Schaum, -- Wagner.
Apr 26 Peter Brunner & Cath. Sinn. Wit: Joseph Brunner, Elias Brunner.
Apr 28 Christian Hertinger & Julianna Bayer. Wit: Hub. & Peter Bayer.
May 7 Lewis Hon & Eliz. Hagen. Wit: Rev. M. Schneyder, Mr. Dillman.
May 19 Robert Forquhar & Esther Dodson. Wit: Hugh Hogan, John Brightwell.

May 19 Peter Schreyner & Eva Biddel. Wit: Peter Kempf, Joh. Miller.
May 31 Johannes Getzendanner & Cath. Dabler. Wit: Christian Getzendanner, -- Dabler.
Jul 14 John Thomas & Sarah Barber. Wit: Elijah Barber & Thos. Brunkover.
Jul 20 Francis McDonald & Eleonore Hamilton. Wit: Philip Schmit, -- Rau.
Jul 23 Jacob Mohler & Sarah Mathers. Wit: Alex. Haggens, John Patterson.
Aug 4 Ellis Hart & Ann Howard. Wit: James Wood, Joh. Wolffkiehl.
Aug 9 Conradt Miller & Elizabeth McDonald. Wit: Adam Knauf, Wilhelm Miller.
Aug 9 Joh. Walldeck & Susanna Engel. Wit: Henrich Hartman, Joh. Welcking.
Aug 18 Peter Richter & Catharina Grof. Wit: Leon. Storm,David Levy.
Sep 6 Peter Schaun & Sarah Whitcraft. Wit: Peter Hauman, Henrich Streicher.
Sep 1 Joseph Borckhardt & Mary Hansey. Wit: Peter Kempfling & Peter Schreiner.
Sep 1 Elijah Dodson & Mary Karr. Robert Farquaher & Ed. Karr.
Sep 6 Philip Melcher & Esther Fluck. Henrich Fluck, Wendel Melcher.
Sep 17 John Bishop & Hannah Cooper. Wit: Jos. Bishop, Fred. Bucher.
Sep 22 John Slack & Maria Marg. Auman. Wit: Henry Slack, Andreas Auman.
Sep 22 George Lindsay & Elizabeth McDonald. Wit: Jos. Wright, Wm. Leakins
Oct 20 Richard Jacobs & Eleanor Hillary. Wit: John Jacobs, Solomon Norris
Oct 27 Joh. Kuster & Elizabeth Willjard. Wit: Leon. Storm, Eliz. Willjard.
Oct 26 Joseph Wright & Mary Mumford. Wit: Richard Jones, Wm. Merryman.
Nov 3 Joseph West & Anna Mollenecks. Wit: Benj. Todd, Robert Mollenecks.
Nov 3 Joh. Pfeffer & Catharine Schaefer. Joh. Pfeffer, Adam Schaefer.
Dec 1 Levy Thomas & Elizabeth Reeves. Thos. Brookover, James Scags.
Dec 3 Georg Engel & Catharina Jung. Wit: Joh. Freymiller & Elis. Stellinger.
Dec 19 George Harding & Lydia Duhfish. Wit: James Parks & Barbara Brunner.
Dec 20 Michael Luther & Mary Kindle. Wit: Jacob Luther, Robert Hammet.
Dec -- Ashford Dowden & Elizabeth Smith. Wit: John Clower, John Dowden.
Dec 31 William Richards & Katherine Cooper. Wit: Robert & Jos. Cooper.
Dec 31 John Carson & Hannah Haas. Wit: -- Haas, -- Holtzman.
1790
Jan 3 Garret Fitzgerald Lee & Ann Connaway Bannister. Wit: Wm. David, Wm. Lee.
Jan -- Simon Bins & Sarah Wildman. Wit: Ed. Tilly, Ignatio Elkin.
Jan -- John Winter & Martha Long. Wit: Eliz. Ramsey, Cath. Runkel.
Jan 12 Joseph McLean & Susanna Gossling. Wit: Gilbert Parish, Amos Gossling.
Feb 8 Johannes Diel & Catharine Beltz. Wit: Hub. Bayer, Peter Bayer.
Feb 11 Casper Kufer & Christina Schoner. Wit: Johannes Krebs, Joh. Leinbach.
Feb 28 Wm. Hedges & Leah Duffild. Wit: Mat. Schmit, Adam Krieger.
Feb 21 Jacob Delater & Catharine Mahn. Wit: Geo. & Adam Mähn.
Feb 11 Casper Kufer & Christina Schöner. Wit: Joh. Krebs, Joh. Leinbach
Mar 4 John Carter & Ann Thomas. Wit: Cath. & Marg. Runckel.
Mar 9 Henry Pool & Margaret James. Wit: Dan & John James.
Mar 16 Wilhelm Krämer & Marg. Krieger. Peter Krämer & Philip Heintz.

Mar 28 Abraham Faeh & Maria Anna Steiner. Wit: Jacob & Johannes Steiner.
Apr 1 Wm. Leakins & Martha Mumford. Wit: Wm. Merryman, Jos. Wright.
Apr 4 Frantz Geissinger & Sarah Levi. Adam Schreiner, Jacob Levi.
Mar 30 Abraham Lehman & Elisabeth Fluck. Wit: Jacob Fluck & Maria Lehman.
Apr 4 Robert Hill & Maily Fitzgerald. Wit: Benj. Hill, John B. F. Johnson.
Apr 5 Wm. Pippinger & Mary James. Wit: Philip Schmit.
Arp 5 Benjamin White & Susanna Carmack. Wit: --
Apr 5 George Deiwelbiss & Susanna Berg. Wit: Adam Krieger.
Apr 6 John Turner & Martha Luton. Wit: Cath. & Marg. Runckel.
Apr 1 Wm. Leakin & Martha Mumford. Wit: Wm. Merryman, Jos. Wright.
May 2 Francis Davis & Sarah Elliot. Wit: Thos. Elliot, Wm. Davis.
May 2 Wm. McClain & Maria Breusch. Wit: -- Dressler, Joh. Hoffman.
May 4 David Miller & Catherine Kast. Wit: Geo. Kast, Henrich Ascherman.
May 4 James Knight & Ann Williamson. Wit: James Ford, Joshua Knight.
Apr 29 John Thomson & Mary Sellers. Wit: Geo. Sensser, Nico. Dehof.
May 4 Levy Bently & Sarah Harlan. Wit: Abrner Bently, James Harlan.
May 4 Jacob Fluck & Elizabeth Koblentz. Wit: Herman Koblentz, Abraham Lehman.
May 8 Philip Scheelhans & Julianna Hempe. Wit: Hen. Hempe, Hen. Brăm.
May 9 Johannes Stoll & Marg. Dottero. Wit: Geo. Zimmerman, Friedr. Holtzman.
May 31 Conrad Weissman & Marg. Kern. Wit: Jacob Miller, Cath. Dannbach.
May 30 Richard Hardy & Rachel Cressel. Wit: Thos. Crabb, -- Cressel.
Jun 27 Stephan Klein & Marg. Schultz. Wit: Jacob Walter, Cath. Schultz.
Jul 17 John Weyman & Margaret Elliot. Wit: Wm. Noocum, Thos. Bryan.
Jul 25 Ninian Beall & Christina Stoll. Witn at Dehof's house

1790

Jul 28 James McClusky & Henrietta Riggs. Wit: James Foely, Wm. Cutter.
Sep 12 Reinhardt Waltz & Susanna Schotter. Wit: Philip Heintz, Adam Krieger.
Sep 21 Joseph Baily & Susanna Hedges. Wit: Geo. Keller, Sol. Bently.
Sep 20 James Scaggs & Catherine Raeser. Wit: Maria Weiss, Elis. Deiss.
Sep 21 Henrich Schreyer & Maria Ludy. Wit: Geo. Beckenbach, Jacob Schreyer.
Sep 28 Jacob Siess & Maria Schreyer. Wit: Georg & Paul Siess.
Oct 11 Leonard Barnes & Nancy Price. Wit: Ed. Karr, Wm. Barnes.
Oct 31 Jacob Konig & Elis. Froschauer. Wit: Peter Hardt, Phil. Rohr.
Nov 9 Francis Wm. Davis & Elisabeth Parrish. Wit: Sol. Parrish, John Dorsey.
Nov 11 Joseph Plasterer & Nancy Porter. Wit: Aaron Stevens, Peter Gottselig.
Nov 9 Valentin Bucky & Elizabeth Stricker. Wit: Peter Bucky, Joh. Scheibly.
Nov 23 James Walters & Margaret Scholls. Wit: Geo. Borckhardt, Gilbert Parish.
Nov 23 Johannes Keller & Catharina Koblentz. Wit: Herman Koblentz, Friedr. Miller.
Nov 23 Adam Shuman & Cath. Koblentz, of Peter. Wit: Peter Koblentz, Sr. & Jr.

Marriages of the Evangelical Reformed Church in Frederick, Maryland

Nov 28 Solomon Kempf & Barbara Hirschberger. Wit: Peter Kempf, Henrich Hirschberger.
Oct 12 Daniel O'Bryan & Mary Ann Perry. Wit: Even Turner, Geo. King.
Nov 23 Henrich Thomas & Marg. Remsperger. Wit: Joh. Thomas, Geo. Remsperger.
Nov 30 Alexander Lindsey & Rebecca Marsteller. Wit: Jacob Miller, Cath. Dornbach.
Dec 16 Lloyd Bett & Elizabeth Met. Thomas. Wit: Frank Thomas, Wm. Thomas.

1791
Jan 4 Nicolaus Keil & Mary Baggerly. Wit: Lohr. Eberhardt, Ralph Brisco.

1790
Dec 14 Wm. Shreaves & Elizabeth Lawrence. Wit: Jacob Aurand, -- Masfield.

1791
Jan 16 Jediah Waters & Catherine Rapp. Wit: John Bett, Jos. Jones.
Jan 23 Johannes Fuchs & Catherine Fuchs. Wit: Joh. Lack, Geo. Fuchs.
Jan 29 Matthew Hilton & Susanna Wheeler. Wit: Daniel Ehl, Thomas Wheeler.
Jan 30 Georg Bähr & Elizabeth Koblentz. Wit: Peter Koblents, Adam Keller.
Feb 1 Cornelius Vanandy & Rebekah Shagan. Wit: Philip Schmit, Conrad Egler.
Feb 1 Wm. McClaskey & Hannah Hophin. Wit: Joh. Miller, Jacob Schmit.
Feb 20 John Reily & Mary Steel. Wit: James Steel, -- Hays.
Feb 23 Georg Fahly & Maria Wolff, in Loudon, Va. Wit: Adam Wolff, Joh. Krumbach.
Mar 6 Thomas Perrill & Zilpha Calliman. Wit: Moses Calliman, David Davis.
Mar 3 Daniel McClean & Anna Marsteller. Wit: Joseph & Anna Fey.
Mar 15 Johannes Redig & Barbara Zimmerman. Wit: Friedrich Ungefehr, Jacob Eck.
Mar 15 Peter Schnook & Polly Pipinger. Wit: Abraham & Henrich Kreiss.
Mar 13 Levy Phillips & Eleanor Swearingen. Wit: Philips, Geo. Hoffman.
Mar 22 Adam Keil & Elisabetha Martin. Wit: Joh. Brunner, Elias Butter.
Mar 29 Georg Klos & Sarah Linkins. Wit: Robert Attison, Eliz. Burns.
Mar 29 Michael Remsperger & Catherine Wolff. Wit: Jacob Kempf, Peter Herget.
Apr 8 John McMullen & Ann Unglesby. Wit: Duckes Wells, Jos. Rice.
Apr 13 James Harlan & Mary Wood. Wit: Joshua Harlan, James Hall.
May 10 John Camphle & Anne Winegardner. Wit: James Hall, Wm. Ales.
May 10 Daniel Geyer & Maria Brengel. Wit: Friedr. Schittenhelm, Geo. Brengel
May 17 Joshua Rhodes & Catherine Spielman. Wit: Thos. & Jeremiah Gilbert.
May 29 Alexander Perrill & Grace Beaumont. Wit: Jacob Kern, James Watts.
May 31 Philip Schmit & Maria Fuchs. Wit: Joh. Lack, Anthony Bastian.
Jun 12 Horatio Athern & Maria Schaun. Wit: Wilson Athein, Wm. Morland.
Jun 12 Adam Hauser & Sibylla Jantz. Wit: Geo. Hoffman, Michael Braun.
Jun 13 Lakin Israel & Leah Hall. Wit: Nath. Colder, Jos. Hall.
Jun 24 Jacob Bittel & Rachel Todd. Wit: Alexander & Joshua Todd.
Jul 5 Valentin Hoffman & Elisabeth Doll. Wit: Peter Hardt, Geo. Hoffman
Aug 14 Adam Mahn & Margaret Jauzy. Wit: Geo. Mahn, Mat. Collins.

Aug 16 Adam Jacob & Elisabeth Spannseiler. Wit: Jacob Spannseiler, Geo. Wolff.
Aug 22 Jonathan Gess & Rebekah Dowell. Wit: Sam. How, Cath. Dowell.
Sep 22 Philip Matern & Barbara Thomas. Wit: Valentin & Christoph Thomas.
Aug 28 Robert Cooper & Catherine Harlin. Wit: -- Harlin, Bal. Schneider.
Sep 25 David Levy & Maria Sturm. Wit: Nicolaus Deiss, James Smith.
Sep 18 Johannes Schatz & Elisabeth Leschhorn. Wit: Joh. Brunner, Henrich Kempf.
Oct 11 Georg Busch & Elisabeth Grall, thru Mr. Krub. Wit: --
Oct 11 Johannes Miller & Catherine Bayer, thru Mr. Krug.
Oct -- Georg Hoffman & Eleanor Phillips. Wit: -- Philips.
Nov 15 Daniel Bauman & Catherine Let. Wit: Thos. Salmon, Charles Barten.
Nov 22 Jacob Schop & Elisabeth Brengel. Wit: Georg & Jacob Brengel.
Nov 27 Rudolph Rohr & Catherine Lauffer. Wit: Jacob & Philip Rohr.
Dec 1 Henry Wilson & Susanna Farquhar. Wit: James Norrad, Benj. Wilson.
Dec 11 Michael Hutzel & Susanna Miller. Wit: Geo. Hutzel, Catherine Miller.
Dec 22 Frantz P. May & Catherine Gross. Wit: Carl & Phil. Gross.
Dec 29 Isaac Mesmith & Ann Johnson. Wit: Thos. & Benj. Johnson.

1792
Jan 8 Joshua Harlin & Sarah Wood. Wit: Jos. Wood, Joh. Balzel.
Jan 22 Bernhard Wiesenthal & Maria Steiner. Wit: Johannes Steiner, Sr, & Jr.
Jan 19 Johannes Fröhlich & Salome Rothrock. Wit: Ludwig & Maria Rothrock.
Jan 29 Archibald Campbell & Sarah McDonald. Wit: Francis McDonald, Wm. Powell.
Feb 9 Allen Hays & Catherine Bossert. Wit: Andrew Bossert, Hen. Wolff.
Feb 12 David Carl & Barbara Grof. Wit: Joh. Grof, Theobald Wiljard.
Feb 21 Johannes Niemayer & Barbara Stohr. Wit: Lo. Brengel, Jacob Schneider.
Feb 29 Samuel Uhry & Sarah Bayer. Wit: Sam. Dodero, Nico. Eisenberg.
Mar 8 Ralph Briscoe & Sarah Delashmitt. Wit: Elias Butler, Jos. Howard.
Mar 13 Michael Dorsey & Ann Poole. Wit: John James, Henry Poole.
Mar 20 James Mumford & Nancy Fuller. Wit: Jos. Wright, Wm. Mumford.
Apr 9 James Morris & Elizabeth Pittinger. Wit: Philip Heintz, Dan. Ludwig.
Apr 9 Johannes Jendes & Catherine Sauer. Wit: Joh. & Daniel Jendes.
Apr 24 Johannes Schley & Maria Schreiber. Wit: Joh. Stover, Joh. Fischer.
May 29 Gilbert Parish & Ruth Hall. Wit: Solomon Parish, Greenberry Ham.
May 29 Michael Irons & Eve Stripe. Wit: James Sparks, John Irons.
Jul 15 Peter Jager & Marg. Bucky. Wit: Mat. & Joh. Bucky.
Aug 5 Johannes Jost & Julianna Jung. Wit: Conradt Jung, Jacob Eberhardt.
Aug 5 Johannes Filius & Elizabeth Yates. Wit: David Mercky, Conrad Becker.
Aug 14 Georg Hap & Catherine Puderbach. Wit: Adam Schnock, Joh. Guckerle.
Aug 19 Michael Grenier & Sibylla Jendes. Wit: Joh. & Daniel Jendes.
Aug 12 Basil Dorsey & Harriet Harris. Wit: At Mr. Harris's house.
Oct 8 Edward Fields, black, prop of John Develbiss. Minty, prop. of Michael Bayer. Wit: Joh. Bop, Daniel Ehl.
Oct 14 Jacob Eller & Margaretha Willjard. Wit: Geo. Willjard, Esther Eller.

Marriages of the Evangelical Reformed Church in Frederick, Maryland

Oct 9 Adam Küster & Clara Schön. Wit: Len. Storm, — Küster.
Oct 21 Andreas Schmit & Maria Eliz. Stein. Wit: Jacob Kern, Philip Heintz.
Oct 29 Adam Krämer & Apollonia Dewelbiss. Wit: Georg & Peter Krämer
Nov 4 Lancelot Chun & Martha Ridgley. Wit: Thos. Thrasher, John Sergeant.
Nov 11 Andreas Dehaven & Esther Kempf. Wit: Jacob Kern, John Preiss.
Nov 20 Joshua Delaplain & Mary Dern. At Dern's house.
Dec 4 Henrich Herbach & Catherine Reiss.
Dec 9 Isaac Dern & Susanna Berger. at Mr. Dern's house.
Dec 24 Georg Beckebach & Maria Magd. Baulus. Wit: Nicol & Geo. Baulus.
Dec 25 Leonard Stuardt & Elizabeth Perrill. Wit: Thos. Stuardt, Alex. Marshall.
Dec 30 Nathaniel Sute & Elizabetha Grover. Wit: Wm. Evans, Michael Dabler.

1793
Jan 8 Adam Antes & Christina Schmit. Wit: Philip Schmit, Con. Krumbach.
Jan 13 Joshua Collins & Mary Rubey. Wit: Adam Wolff, Mat. Schmit.
Jan 15 Adam Klee & Elizabeth Hardiger. Wit: Ed. Stuardt, Anna Klee.
Jan 20 Dewald Jung & Eliz. Hirschberger. Wit: Bern. Hirschberger & Mat. Schmit.
Jan 22 Lemuel Root & Magdalena Schmit. Wit: Mat. & Joh. Schmit.
Jan 29 John Barker & Elizabeth Mugg. Wit: John Slut, Wm. Meyers.
Jan 29 Thomas Carr & Catharine Gaschauer. Wit: John Cammel, Tob. Schäfer.
Jan 29 Valentin Bucky & Charlotte Remsperger. Wit: John & Mat. Bucky.
Jan 31 Johannes Miller & Elizabeth Hellman. Wit: Henr. Hellman, Joh. Bopp.
Feb 5 John Crum & Rebecca Crum. Wit: John Crum, David Bayer.
Mar 13 Joseph White & Mary Fulton. Wit: Michael Bayer, Daniel Ehl.
May 17 Hezekiah Medcalf & Clarissa Lindon. Wit: Zachariah Lindon, Christopher Ball.
Feb 17 Alexander McIntire & Nancy Chamberlain. Wit: James Chamberlain, John McIntire.
Feb 21 John McWilliams & Elizabeth Hagan. Wit: Robert Crone, John McGary.
Mar 22 William Russell & Elizabeth Randall. Wit: A. Maria Schmit, Catherine Runckel.
Mar 24 David Sauer & Elizabeth Krebill. Wit: Peter Stimmel, Andrew Adam.
Mar 24 Christian Martin & Magd. Helbort. Wit: Peter Stimmel, Andrew Adam.
Mar 28 Thomas Mathers & Elizabeth Cummings. Wit: James Love, Debby Drake.
May 5 Cornelius Shaghan & Anna Maria Mähn. Wit: Geo. Mähn, Joh. Mähn.
May 7 Michael Mosseter & Philippina Jacob. Wit: Mich. Mosseter, Phil. Jacob.
May 19 Wm. Eaton & Nancy Bryan. Wit: Jacob Kern, Joh. Hauck.
Jun 5 John Stevens & Jane Nailer. Wit: John Nailer, James McLane.
Jul 14 Christian Vogel & Nancy Norwood. Wit: Robert Naud, Andrew Schnook.
Jul 25 Thomas Bryan & Masey Plumer. Wit: Robert Ward, Jerome Plumer.
Aug 8 Daniel McHiver & Sarah Ramsey. Wit: Abr. Rauser, Leon. Storm.
Aug 15 James Jervis & Elizabeth Plumer. Wit: Abr. Devereh, Bapt. Ungelsbee.
Sep 15 Carl Sieg & Maria Faut. Wit: Jacob Kern, Joh. Meck.
Aug 25 Henrich Wolff & Elizabeth Haller. Wit: Peter Haller's house.

Sep 6 Philip Schatz & Catharine Bergesser. Wit: David & Jacob Schatz.
Oct 22 Peter Gosnell & Mary Mollahan. Wit: Abr. Gendy, Jos. Gosnell.
Oct 23 Francis Sanders & Margaretha Schley. Wit: Joh. Schley, Joh. Steiner.
Oct 29 Saphenia (Zephaniah?) Harrison & Sarah Biddle. Wit: Jacob Medtard, Henry Nichols.
Oct 29 Basil Grimes & Betsy Picket. Wit: Greenberry Hern, Fred. Grimes.
Nov 12 Jacob Kempf & Marg. Getzedanner. Wit: Jaccb Getzedanner, Ludwig Kempf.
Nov 5 Philip Weiss & Barbara Becker. Wit: Conrad & Philip Becker.
Nov 19 Daniel Frey & Elisabetha Christ. Wit: Joh. Gum, Joh. Gumo.
Dec 3 Thomas Edmorston & Ruth Shekell. Wit. At the bride's father's house.
Dec 1 Archibald Mason & Mary Conner. Wit. at the bride's father's house.
Dec 10 Samuel Harvey & Virlinder Fisher. Wit: Basil Harvey, Thos. Lewis.
Dec 10 Philip Sauer & Sarah Hobelman. Wit: Cath. & Margr. Runckel.
Dec 15 Thomas Bowens & Louise Barnes. Wit: Geo. Pool, Nicholas Jenkins.
Dec 27 John Peck & Betty, blacks. Wit: Cath. & Margr. Runckel.
Dec 24 John Manehan & Mary Hains.. Wit: Dennis Ensey.
Dec 24 Abraham Gandy & Sarah Manihan. Wit: Sophia Ensey.
Dec 29 Wm. Crum & Elizabeth Levy. Wit. at the Poor House.
Dec 26 Zadock Browning & Mary Browning. Wit: James & Walter Purdon.

1794

Jan -- Edward Dowling & Mary Gordon. Wit: Philip Weber, Daniel Mackentire.
Jan 9 Wilhelm Henner & Maria Gert. Kuhns. Wit: Both of the fathers.
Jan 19 Valentin Steckel & Catherine Remsperger. Wit: In the house of the father's bride.
Feb 2 Dennis Pool & Henrietta Gather. In the bride's father's house.
Feb 4 Solomon Parish & Mary Parish. Wit: Wm. Davis, Wm. Parish.
Feb 27 Joseph Jones & Henrietta Cash. Wit: Jos. Plumer, Philip Sissel
Mar 11 Robert Fulton & Barbara Balzell. Henry Jackson, Johannes Schenck.
Mar 18 Georg Bechtel & Esther Eller. Wit: Jacob Wiessman, Peter Haller.
Mar 18 Thomas Lewis & Mary Ellis. Wit: Stephan Lewis, Nicho. Watkins.
Mar 4 Jacob Daub & Elizabeth Merckel. Wit: Abraham König, Joh. Merckel.
Mar 23 Jacob Schmit & Catharine Lefever. Wit: Johann & Carl Schmit.
Mar 30 James Campbell & Sarah Sewell. Wit: Geo. Beckebach, Jacob Christ.
Apr 8 Abraham Konig & Magdalena Merckel. Wit: Jacob Rohr's House.
Apr 13 Valentin Haas & Elizabeth Dodero. Wit: the brothers of the bride.
Apr 13 Johannes Brandenburger & Phoebe Garner. Wit: Joh. Georg Bucky.
Apr 15 George Beeler & Elisabetha Molledor. Wit: Joh. Kast, Joh. Molledor.
Apr 18 Uriah Fox & Grace Sedwith. Wit: Wm. Vanhorn, Asa Fox.
Apr 20 Jacob Matthew & Sophia Strubel. Wit: Joh. Mick, Joh. Jendes.
May 11 Johannes Ott & Maria Schäfer. Wit: Bern. Ott, Adam Schäfer.
May 11 Jacob Stehly & Elisabeth Stehly. Wit: Jos. Doll, Jacob Stehly.
May 11 Jacob Kinsel & Catharina Schmit. Wit: Conrad Doll, Peter Dofler.
Apr 29 Peter Stimmel & Barbara Bossert. Wit: In the house of the bride's father.
May 30 Ebenezer Doly & Mary Philips. Wit: James Sergeant, Marg. Runkel.
Jun 3 Peter Koblentz & Barbara Rübel. Wit: Peter Koblentz, Peter Rubel.

Jun 8 Francis Paster & Stacy Beall. Wit: Joh. Rein, Zephaniah Leisure.
Jun 7 George Fulton & Margaret Hedge. At the bride's father's house.
Jun 10 Carl Balzell & Elizabeth Fulton. Wit: Joh. Balzell, Robert Fulton.
Jun 12 Balthasar Getzedanner & Philippina Stoll. Wit: Jos. Stehly, Marg. Runckel.
Jul 22 Dewalt Stattelmayer & Sabery Downey. Wit: Jacob & Joh. Stattelmayer.
Jul 25 Wendel Traut & Sarah Gebhardt. Wit: Cath. & Marg. Runckel.
Aug 12 Jacob Spitznagel & Maria Schreyer. Wit: Leon. Storm, Michael Jest.
Sep 7 Johannes Molledor & Julianna Kast. Wit: Geo. Kast, David Mollendor.
Sep 28 Johannes Krumbach & Maria Schneider. Wit: At the house of the bride's father.
Oct 2 Aden Coomes & Pamilia Williams. Wit: Sam. Coomes, Martha Adams.
Oct 5 Christoph Berntheisel & Catherine Grof. Wit: Elijah Beatty, Lucas Luckharst.
Nov 6 Joseph Rice & Rebekah Leatch. Wit: Eli Sergeant, Walter Leatch.
Nov 19 Johannes Diel & Maria Eckhardt. Wit: Philip Rohr, Geo. Kuhns.
Nov 25 Walter Tall & Ann Dull. Wit: Loyd Ward, Wm. Tall.
Dec 2 Christian Schneider & Sarah Miller. Wit: Cath. Runkel, Cath. Miller.
Dec 2 Wm. Murphy & Margaret Moore. Wit: Geo. Silber, Geo. Klos.

1795
Jan 13 John Eaton & Rachel Pearsons. Wit: Alex. Perrill, James Watts, Robert Peckins.
Jan 13 Meshac Plummer & Anna Elliot. Wit: Jos. Plummer, Richard Kirk.
Jan 22 Wm. Plummer & Rachel Hobbs. Wit: Capt. Phil. Burgis, Jos. Hobbs.
Feb 12 Benj. Hopkins & Nancy Briscoe. Wit: at the bride's father's house.
Feb 15 James Torrance & Drusilla Simmons. Wit: at the bride's father's house.
Feb 15 Henrich Geyer & Elizabeth Ireland. Wit: Jacob Martin, Jacob Getzedanner.
Feb 17 Alexander Downey & Mary Tucker. Wit: Geo. Spalding, John Brunner.
Mar 3 John Grover & Jemimah Fitzgerald. Wit: Robert Hill, Wm. Evans
Mar 3 Moses Justice & Sophia Sual (Sewall?). Wit: Wm. Justice, Tob. Schafer.
Mar 15 Rezen Simpson & Elizabeth Shekles. at the bride's father's house.
Mar 17 Jacob Jung & Catherine Kern. Wit: Joh. & Jacob Kern.
Mar 26 James Morrisson & Clarissa Gittings. at the bride's father's house.
Mar 31 Joseph Murry & Rachel Crawford. Wit: John Rinkard, Sam. Crawford.
Apr 7 Jacob Krämer & Magdalena Stimmel. Wit: Peter Stimmel, Peter Krämer.
Apr 21 Conrad Specht & Elizabeth Schäfer. Wit: Joh. Ott, Peter Schäfer.
Apr 26 Georg Liess & Elizabeth Teiss. Wit: Nicolaus Teiss, Val. Bruner.
Apr 28 Henrich Schau & Maria Kessler. Wit: Jacob Brunner, Sam. Philips.
Apr 28 Joh. Gittinger & Marg. Hauck. Wit: Joh. Hauck, Stephan Brunner.
May 25 Conradt Becker & Maria Jost. Wit: Lo. Eberhardt, Jacob Jung.
Aug 19 Evan Crum & Sarah Hertzog. Wit: Nicol Hertzog, John Crum.
Aug 23 Adam Ramsour & Mary Purdie. Wit: Geo. Littlejohn, Charles Purdie.
Sep 6 Mattheus Lang & Eva Marg. Rausser. Wit: Joh. & Carl Baltzell.
Sep 10 John Shekel & Mary Burges. Wit: Dan. Hock, Col. Luckit.

Sep 14 Georg Borckhardt & Hannah Hedge. Wit: Isaac & Ruth Hedge.
Sep 22 Zephaniah Hill & Barbara Teschner. Wit: Geo. Teschner, Wm. Evans.
Aug 20 Henrich Kiefer & Rachel Ried. Wit: Joh. & Jacob Ried.
Nov 19 Simon Krumbach & Philippina Deiwelbiss. Wit: Joh. & Georg Deiwelbiss.
Nov 29 Jacob Bixler & Barbara Grebiel. Wit: In the house of the bride's father.
Dec 1 Johannes Samsell & Catharina Bott. Wit: Georg Bott.
Dec 1 James Harson & Rosey Gess. Wit: Jonathan Gess, Israel Maynard.
Dec 8 Peter Drum & Sarah Hansey. Wit; Joshua Cox, Michael Drum.
Dec 6 Peter Hardt & Charlotte Doll. Wit: Jos. Doll, Val. Hoffman.
Dec 20 Beale Owings & Cornelia Harriss. At the bride's father's house.
Dec 13 Brice Poole & Achsa James. Wit: John James, Daniel James.
Dec 24 Johannes Mick & Priscilla Grover. Wit: Joh. Mick, Joh. Bucky.
Dec 25 Georg Jendes & A. Maria Roth. Wit: Maria Cath. Borckhardt, Cath. Diel.
Dec 27 Barth. Murphy Malone & Lydia Bradie. Wit: John Laking, Jacob Wip.
Dec 27 Jacob Rauzahn & Christina Sinn. Wit: Peter Sauer, Wilhelm Schmit.
Dec 29 Thomas Butler & Jane Gittings. Wit: at the bride's father's house
Dec 31 Benjamin Thomson & Charlotte Tripolett. Wit: Greenberry Tripolett, Sam. Singleton.

1796
Feb 4 James Scot & Mary Williams. at the bride's father's house.
Feb 9 John Richards & Ann Waters Williams. at the bride's father's house.
Feb 23 Johannes Breiss & Elizabeth Lefever. Wit: Phil. & Adam Breiss.
Feb 28 John Williams & Catherine Wood. at the bride's father's house.
Mar 6 Friedrich Schlagel & Elizabeth Buteler. at the bride's father's house.
Mar 14 Gibson Kadle & Martha Lemaster. at the bride's father's house.
Mar 15 Robert Anderson & Mary Brashears. at the bride's father's house.
Mar 17 John Myers & Ann Anderson. Wit: Arch. Means, John Craven.
Mar 8 William Beall & Isabella Ramsey. Wit: Mordecai Beall & 2 others.
Mar 15 William Beall & Mary Winroad. Wit: Charles Harry, Fred. Winroad.
Mar 22 Michael Keller & Elizabeth Ebbert. Wit: Philip & Henry Keller.
Mar 22 Benjamin Duppel & Elizabeth Reitenauer. Wit: Isaac Duppel, Joh. Wilheid.
Mar 27 Friedrich Roos & Maria Froschauer. Wit: Jacob Schafer & William Runckel.
Mar 28 John Williams & Julianna Storm. Wit: Phil. Weiss, Peter Jung.
Mar 29 Johannes Oechslein & Maria Bossert. Wit: Dan. & Joh. Bossert.
Apr 10 Friedrich Strassburger & Elizabeth Vanderburg. Wit: Geo. Fuchs & many others.
Apr 12 Arthur Wallis & Maria Greber. Wit: Catherine Greber.
Apr 12 Johannes Schröder & Rosey Killy. Wit: Zach. Condon, Elisha Griffith.
Apr 14 Samuel Brayfield & Jane Pancoast. Wit: Geo. Swan, John Brayfield.
Mar 27 Michael Storm & Catherine Keller. Wit: Jacob Koller, Jacob Storm.
Apr 17 Peter Storm & Susanna Wright. Wit: Jacob Jung, Leon. Storm.
May 1 Robert Macky & Sarah Ragan. Wit: Jacob Levy & Joh. Lingenfelder.
May 1 William Hambleton & Susanna Todd. Wit: Jacob Keller & others.

Marriages of the Evangelical Reformed Church in Frederick, Maryland

May 10 Jacob Balzell & Anna Campbell. Wit: Jacob & Daniel Balzell.
May 15 Henry Thomson & Elizabeth Liess. Wit: Jacob Liess, -- Eder.
May 22 Edward Stevens & Keziah Coale. Wit: Richard Williams, Hugh Luster.
May 22 Heinrich Stuntzer & Elisabeth Roth. Wit: Jeremias Gilbert, Jacob Roth.
May 22 Georg Zieler & Barbara Hauck. Wit: Hen. Zieler, Joh. Hauck.
May 31 Henrich Weber & Elisabetha Trit. Wit: Peter Trit, Jacob Ostertag.
Jun 5 Daniel Lefever & Marg. Sulzer. Wit: Phil. & Johannes Breiss.
Jun 21 Jacob Margartie & Susanna Schon. Wit: Jacob Martin, Joh. Feuerstein.
Jun 22 Henry Allison & Elizabeth Linton. Wit: the bride's two brothers.
Jun 26 Martin Maurer & Margaretha Lenhardt. Wit: Jacob Brunner, & others.
Jun 28 Joshua Carter & Catherine Springer. Wit: Zech. Powel, Jacob Zimmerman.
Jul 17 Henry Mayers & Ann Davis. Wit: Zech. Davis, Wm. Philips.
Aug 10 Charles Stevens & Marg. Waltz. Wit: Joh. Schneider, Reinhardt Waltz.
Aug 18 Peter Gebhardt & Elisabetha Haas. Wit: Christoph Brandt, Val. Hoffman.
Aug 25 Christian Uhry & Catherine Streip. Wit: Sam. Uhry, David Streip.
Aug 30 Jacob Bart & Maria Schmidt. Wit: Philip & Daniel Schmidt.
Sep 4 Johannes Rein & Priscilla Wilson. Wit: at the house of the bride's father.
Sep 11 Johannes Waltz & Elisabeth Borger. Wit: Philip Borger, Sam. Waltz.
Sep 11 Jacob Ostertag & Rachel Landers. Wit: Ludwig Herring, Joh. Landers.
Sep 12 Wm. Peck & Susanna Glasscock. Wit: Sam. Peck & Elijah Karichalbeal.
Sep 27 Michael Dorsey & Elisabeth Poole. Wit: Luke & Henry Poole.
Oct 4 George Sargent & Ann Wells. Wit: John & Daniel Leakins.
Oct 4 Abraham Edwards & Ellen Jones. Wit: Georg & Mary Charly.
Oct 4 Jacob Haard & Mary Dwyer. Wit: Abr. Edwards, Michael Mulvey.
Oct 6 Abraham Magens & Elisabeth Frey. Wit: Johannes & Susanna Frey.
Oct 8 Georg Bucky & Susanna Krieger. Wit: Conrad Krieger, Vall. Bucky.
Oct 11 Jacob Bast & Catherine Heckendorn. Wit: Jacob Bast, -- Bast.
Oct 11 Abednego Plumer & Anna Redman. Wit: John Ball, N. Sissel.
Oct 15 Dennis Vanhorne & Catherine Burns. Wit: Johannes & Michael Haller.
Oct 17 Brice Richards & Elizabeth Hart. Wit: Peter Bucky, El. Hart.
Nov 13 Reuben Davis & Ellen Taylor. Wit: Lev. Davis, Ruth Scaggs.
Nov 22 Warfield Todd & Eleanor Ball. Wit: Wm. Hamelton, Sam. Thomson, Luke Davis.
Nov 24 Richard Taylor & Susanna Riddle. Wit: Adam Deshler & Wm. Runkel, Jr.
Nov 29 Johannes Meiner & Maria Kehl. Wit: Andreas & Cath. Mill.
Dec 6 Mattheus Schweitzer & Catherine Schenck. Wit: Wil. Schmit, Daniel Pimmel.
Dec 14 Richard Osborn & Mary Humphrey. Wit: Thos. Killgore, Jacob Humphrey.
Dec 13 George Swan & Emmy Redman. Wit: Sam. Brayfield, John Lutz.
Dec 13 Henrich Schmit & Anna Maria Stehly. Wit: Jos. Stehly, Andreas Schmit.
Dec 27 Andrew Zimmerman & Ruth Taylor. Wit: Georg Krieger, Hen. Kolp.

Dec 27 Wm. Walling & Elizabeth Delaschmitt. Wit: John & Jos. Walling.
Dec 28 Johannes Bayer & Maria Borckhardt. Wit: Geo. Zimmerman, -- Zimmerman.
Dec 28 John Price & Rebekah Pritchard. Wit: George Rice, -- Clemens.

1797

Jan 5 Hazil Sissel & Lydia Ball. Wit: Christoph Ball, Joh. Beckwith.
Jan 8 John Cain & Maria Geber. Wit: Jacob Person, Henry Bieler.
Jan 10 Griffith Henderson & Hannah Richardson. Wit: Mr. Flanegan, Mr. Richardson.
Jan 10 Jacob Getzedanner & Elisabeth Getzedanner. Wit: Joh. Getzedanner, Christ. Getzedanner.
Jan 17 Benjamin McKay & Rebekah Briscoe. Wit: at the bride's father's house.
Feb 5 Thos. John Hammond & Rachel Gaither. Wit: the bride's father's home.
Feb 7 Joh. Philips & Susanna Finck. Wit: Sal. Finck, Sam. Geber.
Feb 12 Christoph Westenhefer & Mary Downey. Wit: Con. Schäfer & others
Feb 21 Thomas McAboy & Rachel Rilet. Wit: Ed. Rilet, Wm. McAboy.
Feb 28 Wilhelm Schmit & Susanna Renner. Wit: Joh. Lack, Jacob Bastian.
Mar 7 Elijah Medley & Mary Peters. Wit: Jonathan & Thos. Andrews.
Mar 9 Joseph Patterson & Elizabeth Let. Wit: Aaron & John Calleman.
Mar 9 Lot Hammond & Elizabeth Davis. Wit: at the bride's mother's house.
Mar 9 Benjamin Waters & Elisabeth Becker. Wit: at the bride's father's house.
Mar 12 Johannes Hauck & Elizabeth Sinn. Wit: Joh. Melcker, Daniel Balzell.
Apr 6 Johannes Kramer & Catherine Stimmel. Wit: Peter Stimmel, Peter Peter Krainer.
Apr 16 Peter Christ & Margaretha Mang. Wit: Hen. Christ, Jacob Balzell.
Apr 17 Georg Krämer & Maria Hammond. Wit: Johann & Peter Krämer.
Apr 21 Johannes Krämer & Marg. Huber. Wit: David Bayer, Geo. Krämer.
Apr 25 Peter Stehly & Elisabeth Schäfer. Wit: Jacob Stehly, Conrad Schäfer.
Apr 25 Johannes Schenck & Lydia Reynolds. Wit: Geo. Keller, Hen. Berg.
May 7 Michael Hauck & Magdalena Engel. Wit: Peter & Georg Hauck.
May 21 Thomas Castle & Elizabeth Messerle. Wit: Jacob Stehly, Peter Jost.
Jun 1 Jacob Kern & Margaretha Schnook. Wit: Joh. Kern, Daniel Ehl.
May 2 Henrich Spicker & Elizabeth Kupferschmit. Wit: Hen. Kupferschmit, Peter Mayer.
Jul 11 Adam Schwedtner & Eva Lehman. David Lehman, Marg. Adam.
Jun 18 Peter Ewerly & Julianna Messman. Wit: Peter Grof, -- Wissman.
Jul 9 Peter Fluck & Maria Hans. Wit: Phil. Melcher, Mat. Fluck.
Jul 20 Joseph Paxson & Mary Lusty. Wit: Mr. & Mrs. Mabery.
Jul 30 Jacob Keller & Elisabeth Schlägel. Wit: many.
Sep 5 Jacob Schaaf & Marg. Weber. Wit: Geo. Schaaf, Daniel Weber.
Sep 11 James Smith & Atty Evans. Wit: Jos. Pangost, Hannah Pangost.
Sep 12 Arthur Boteler & Eliz. Sweringer. at the bride's mother's house.
Oct 5 Daniel Gant & Lucy Anderson. at the bride's father's house.
Oct 5 Friedrich Nuss & Catherine Dofler. Wit: Joh. Welcker, Georg Hauck.
Oct 10 Dennis Ensey & Elizabeth Crawford. Wit: Sam. Christian Uhry.
Oct 15 Matthias Schley & Maria Drill. in the house of the bride's father.

Nov -- Jos. Gordon & Mary Balton. Wit: Jacob Meddart, -- Idlen.
Oct 2 Zechariah Hobbs & Susanna James. at the bride's mother's house.
Nov 2 Lorentz Schweitzer & Sarah Niecky. Wit: Sam. Niecky.
Nov 14 Conrad Bauer & Elizabeth Schmidt. in the father's house.
Nov 20 Adam Staub & Ann Friet. Wit: Jong Davis, Sisselly Brau.
Nov 21 Isaac Coale & Sarah Ridgely. at Mr. Lynch's.
Dec 4 Daniel Osborn & Rebekah Coplan. Wit: Jeremiah Steward.
Dec 5 Wm. Dall & Ellen Arnold. Wit: Eph. Arnold, Thos. Spurrior.
Dec 5 John Sheppard & Elisabeth Hennighauser. Wit: Levi Storm, -- Shlegel.
Dec 17 John McNeal & Hannah Mahn. in the father's house.
Dec 21 Jos. Ball & Ally Phelps. Wit: Isaiah Phelps, Dan. Ball.

1798
Jan 16 Isaac Schimer & Eliz. Delaschmitt. at the bride's father's.
Jan 14 Jacob Schmit & Elizabeth Butman. Wit: Andrew & Michael Schmit.
Feb 15 Nicholas Philips & Mary Wilson. Wit: Jacob Long.
Mar 15 Joseph Stump & Elizabeth Bogges. Wit:--
Mar 22 Frederick Grimes & Mary Randal. Wit: John Madan, Wm. Clary.
Mar 27 Georg Nicol & Elisabeth Wallis. Wit: Joh. Nicol & others.
Apr 9 Georg Jung & Maria Jost. Wit: Adam Koblentz & others.
Apr 10 Benjamin Zimmerman & Catherine Eppert. Wit: Joh. & Michael Zimmerman.
Apr 15 Joseph Filius & Elizabeth Schlicher. Wit: Jos. Doll, Jacob Schlicher.
Apr 20 Reuben Graham & Rachel Carter. Wit: Georg Rose, Wm. Graham.
May 20 Henrich Jendes & Catherine Jendes. Wit: Joh. & Georg Jendes.
Jun 11 Georg Dofler & Catherine Spannseiler. Wit: Peter Dofler, Jacob Spannseiler.
Jun 17 Daniel Schmit & Barbara Stephanus. Wit: Philip & Wilhelm Schmit.
Jul 8 Johannes Weiss & Eleanor Farthing. Wit: Henrich Derkes.
Jul 23 John King & Margaret Daub. Wit: Val. Bender, Joh. Schley.
Jul 30 Johannes Stattelmayer & Sarah Michael. in the bride''s father's house.
Aug 23 Gregory Noland & Eliz. Dowdle. at John Bucky's house.
Aug 26 Michael Haller & Catherine Rabourne. Wit: George Rein.
Sep 4 Levi James & Rachel Hough. Wit: Isaac Hough, Aret Connor.
Sep 4 Abraham Schmit & Esther Lefever. Wit: Mat. & Johannes Schmit.
Aug 26 Michael Beckebach & Maria Bartholomae. Wit: Joh. Bartholomae, Nicol Klefaber.
Sep 9 Joh. Dewelbiss & Maria Mayer. Wit: in Rocky Hill Kirche.
Sep 11 Daniel Staab & Elisabeth Berg. Wit: Peter & Christian Berg.
Sep 18 Johannes Fuchs & Catherine Simmons. Wit: Adam Simmon, Con. Schafer.
Sep 18 Jacob Battenfeld & Elisabeth Emmerich. Wit: Samuel Battenfeld, Jacob Emmerich.
Sep 22 Georg Wachter & Philippina Beckebach. Wit: Jacob & Samuel Wachter.
Oct 9 Philip Karper & Catherine Drill. at the bride's father's house.
Oct 9 Philip Sinn & Elisabeth Lehr. Wit: Valentin Bruder, Lorentz Brengel.
Oct 15 Abraham Shoemaker & Phoebe Baldwin. Wit: John Baldwin, Jacob Meddardt.

Oct 19 Philip Sommers & Catherine Sauer. Wit: Cath. & Marg. Runckel.
Oct 28 Abraham Ried & Elisabeth Brubacher. Wit: Joh. Ried, Jacob Ried.
Nov 1 Michael Zimmerman & Barbara Taylor. Wit: Geo. Dofler, Weil & others.
Nov 8 Thomas Williams & Susanna Steyer. Wit: Rezin Cooke, Wilhelm Steyer.
Nov 13 Wm. J. Turner & Sarah Harvey. at the bride's father's house.
Nov 1 Peter Gosnell & Emma Hill. Wit: Ludwig Stark, Hen. Gernhardt.
Nov 18 Salomon Steckel & Charlotte Doll. at the bride's father's house.
Nov 18 David Schreyer & Cath. Fleck. Wit: Andrew Hedges, Jacob Krämer.
Nov 19 James Druman & Sarah Starling. Wit: Jos. Disbrow.
Nov 22 David Gruber & Susanna Moore. Wit: Joh. Weber, -- Crabb.
Nov 22 Jonas Porter & Martha Dowlen. Wit: Daniel Schumacher, Marg. Ang. Lehr.
Nov 26 Samuel Lloyd & Henny Hows. Wit: Thos. Lloyd, Elsey Smith.
Dec 3 George Allison & Christina Zimmerman. Wit: at Kleinhardt's, in presence of many.
Dec 25 Zadock Holland & Priscilla Mockabee. Wit: -- Evans & many others.

1799
Jan 1 Henrich Lehr & Maria Dien. Wit: Geo. Fuchs, Lawr. Murphy.
Jan 6 Jacob Springer & Elisabeth Kaufman. Wit: Catherine Runckel & others.
Jan 10 Walter Simpson & Elis. Thomas. at the bride's father's house.
Jan 15 Michael Lauffer & Eva Hirschberger. Wit: Conr. & Sal. Kempf.
Jan 18 Henrich Fuchs & Leah Zimmerman. Wit: Georg Baer, Henr. Kroneiss.
Jan 20 Jacob Bentz & Catherine Steckel. Wit: Joh. & Jacob Remsperger.
Jan 22 Wm. Crumwell & Sarah Groff. Wit: -- Groff, -- Randal.
Feb 26 Jacob Kern & Magdalena Thomas. Wit: Val. Thomas & others.
Mar 7 Friedrich Riehl & Marg. Luckhorst. Wit: Geo. Riehl, -- Sulzer.
Mar 14 Wm. Herd & Phoebe Waltz. Wit: --
Mar 17 Valentin Thomas & Elizabeth Keller. Wit: Jacob Weiss, Leon. Thomas.
Mar 31 Jacob Herman & Marg. Zieler. Wit: Daniel & Georg Hauer.
Apr 7 Adam Schwatner & Anna Cox. Wit: Henrich & Friedr. Kempf.
Apr 9 Wm. Patterson & Susanna Griffin. Wit: Jacob Plymont & Zach. Patterson.
Apr 15 Wm. Colly & Rebekah Braun. Wit: Joh. Schley, Sal. Kester.
Apr 16 James Pearl & Priscilla Adkins. Wit: Alexander & Samuel Pearl.
May 7 Peter Thomas & Barbara Schäfer. Wit: Joh. & Peter Schaefer.
May 14 Johannes Schaefer & Susanna Ott. Wit: Bernhardt & Johannes Ott.
May 14 Owen Lamb & Susanna Grant. Wit: Benjamin Grant, Cath. Leth.
May 22 Johannes Hinckel & Maria Rennels. Wit: Jacob Springer, Wm. Runkel, Jr.
Jun 18 Michael Fries & Catherine Gräbiel. Wit: Peter Wolff, -- Klebsattel.
Aug 20 Peter Engel & Maria Renner. Wit: Georg Engel, Georg Briedy.
Sep 8 Georg Witerich & Catherine Herget. Wit: Peter Herget, Joh. Leder.
Sep 8 Georg Engel & Susanna Jung. Wit: Georg Briedy, Jacob Jung.
Sep 15 Jacob Wiest & Susanna Schenckmayer. Wit: Christian Weber, Philip Rohr.

Mar 11 Georg Doll, s. of John & Cath. Schmit. Wit: Mat. Schmit, Jos. Doll.
Oct 8 Zechariah Danner & Marg. Zayer. Wit: Joh. & Peter Bucky.
Oct 13 Salomon Schuh & Magdalena Kern. Wit: Joh. & Jacob Kern.
Oct 20 Johannes Weber & Maria Garner. Wit: Adam Gayer & wf.
Oct 20 Johannes Dertzebach & Christina Knauff. Wit: Wilhelm & Conrad Miller.
Oct 22 Jacob Weber & Elisabeth Waltz. Wit: Sam. & Reinhardt Waltz.
Oct 22 Enoch Sheigly & Mary Murry. Wit: Andrew Thomson, Francis McKinny
Oct 31 John Boyd & Hannah Smith. Wit: Matthias Hilton, Adam Frantz.
Nov 24 Daniel Balzell & Susanna Gittinger. Wit: Jacob Baltzell, -- Gittinger.
Dec 1 Daniel Delaplane & Sophia Dern. at the bride's father's house.
Dec 3 Jacob Kast & M. Magd. Gross. Wit: Carl Gross, Frantz May.
Dec 3 Peter Tritt & Esther Süss. Wit: Samuel Griffith, Sophia Süss.
Dec 24 Stacy Newman & Sarah Davis. Wit: David Wells, Jos. Woolard.

1800
Jan 12 Abraham Wiljarch & Catharine Beisser. Wit: Jacob Beisser, Peter Wiljarth.
Jan 14 Michael Eckman & Maria Jacob. Wit: Philip & Adam Jacob.
Jan 21 Thomas Andros & Delilah Fisher. Wit: Jon. Andros, Herm. Cecil.
Jan 28 John Simmons & Susanna Knie. Wit: Abr. Nussbaum, Georg Knie.
Jan 30 Lloyd T. Frizzel & Seeny Turner. Wit: Chas. Frizzel, Lilah Turner.
Jan 26 Jacob Miller & Ann Rice. Wit: Wilhelm Miller, Joh. Dertzebach.
Jan 27 George Schneider & Catherine Brunner. Wit: Elias & Charlotte Brunner.
Jan 28 Johannes Doll & Susan Kortz. Wit: Jos. Doll, Sr. & Jr.
Feb 12 Valentin Wissman & Maria Gebhardt. Wit: David Levy, -- Wissman.
Feb 16 Friedrich Steiner & Marg. Sinn. Wit: Henrich & Stephan Steiner.
Apr 1 John Evans & Miranda Owings. at the bride's father's house.
Apr 1 Samuel Tilson & Mary Cooper. Wit: Edward Gound, Aaron Rollins.
Apr 8 Samuel Richardson & Elizabeth Mobberly. at the bride's father's house.
Apr 15 Richard P. Richardson & Sarah Richardson. Wit: Samuel Richardson & others.
Apr 17 Johannes Uhry & Elisabeth Hensey. Wit: Richard Brightwel, John Fatzton.
Apr 17 Henrich Getzedanner & Hannah Becker. Wit: John Wiest, John Campbel.
Mar 4 Sebastian Nagel & Magdalena Schaefer. Wit: Adam Froschauer & another man.
Mar 13 Henry Hall & Mary Turner. Wit: Lewis Hall, Joanna Pierce.
May 3 Christian Steiner & Susanna Remsperger. Wit: Geo. Remsperger, Sr. & Jr.
May 6 David Fortny & Elisabeth Lewis. Wit: Gottfried Borger, -- Wolff.
May 8 Johannes Stehly & Marg. Adams. Wit: Peter & Fredr. Kempf.
May 6 Johannes Wullet & Maria Kupferschmit. Wit: Henry Schickert, Henr. Kuperschmit.
May 8 Michael Battenberg & Maria Jendes. Wit: Henry & Daniel Jendes.
May 20 Jacob Becht & Maria Schenck. Wit: at the bride's father's house.
May 20 Ambrose Davis & Bewly White. Wit: Ed. Henegan & Wm. Smith.

Marriages of the Evangelical Reformed Church in Frederick, Maryland

Jun 19 Benjamin Apollo & Mary Usher. Wit: Mr. Davis & wf. (French)
Jun 28 Peter Staup & Magdalena Eler. Wit: -- Josse & wf.
Jun 20 Joh. Klinck & Elisabeth Gills. Wit: Con. Schaefer, Joh. Beyer.
Jul 30 Joseph Stehly, s. of Jacob & Elis. Stehly, d. of Jos. Wit: Jacob & Jos. Stehly.
Aug 10 Edward Boyd & Maria Hoffman. at the bride's father's house.
Aug 10 Wm Ferrel & Mary Burns. Wit: John Mace & others.
Aug 17 Peter Samsell & Marg. Gilaspie. at the bride's father's house.
Aug 18 Benard Neale & Elisabeth Christian. Wit: John Vain, D. Levy.
Aug 19 James Woodard & Sally Asdell. Wit: Wm. Knoly, Wm. Lewis.
Sep 2 Samuel Davis & Rachel Walls. Wit: Richard Hooken, Henr. Breish.
Sep 16 Peter Fuchs & Bridget Ingen Hall. Wit: Hannah Runkel.
Oct -- Wm. Larkin & Christina Allison. Wit: Zadock Fowler, Jacob Butcher.
Oct 7 Samuel Boden & Susanna Mähn. Wit: Georg Mähn, Wm. Suter.
Oct -- John Fitzgerald & Mary Phelps. Wit: Benj. Barnes, Rachel Fitzgerald.
Oct 12 Philip Huber & Susanna Borckhardt. Wit: Johannes & Margaret Huber.
Oct 28 Ezra Mainard & Hannah Robertson. Wit: Thos. Maccabee, Ann Nelson.
Nov 9 Wm. Curry & Sarah Dean. Wit: Joh. Mosseter, Chas. Curry.
Nov 13 Joseph Stehly, s. of Jos. & Cath. Guthman. Wit: M. Guthman, Jos. Stehly.
Dec 22 Georg Knie & Maria Datz. Wit: Joh. & Abr. Nussbaum.
Dec 21 George Ried & Elisabeth Dofler, at the bride's father's house.
Dec 23 Adam Breiss & Maria Stoll. Wit: Joh. Breiss & Philip Breiss.
Dec 23 Daniel Gedon & Susanna Butler. Wit: John Felton, Benjamin Ogle.
Dec 25 Wilhelm Däbler & Elisabeth Jones. Wit: Wilhelm Däbler & many others.
Dec 29 Nicolas Herman & Margaret Kennedy. Wit: Alexander & Samuel Perrel.

Death Records of Evangelical Reformed Church, Frederick, Maryland

Index of Deaths

"Note - The following obituary notices are transcribed from loose scraps of paper. They were written in German, in the hand-writing of Rev'd William Runckel. (E. W. Reinecke)"

Nov. 25. Thomas Schley, first teacher in this congregation, born Aug. 31 1712 at Mertzheim in Germany, was married to Margaret Wintz (an. 1735), which latter died in June last. They lived in wedlock nearly 55 years, had nine children, of whom 8 are still living. He had been suffering for some time with asthma, but was confined to bed for one day only. He died yesterday morning 10 o clock, aged 78 years, 2 months & 3 days.

1788
Apr. 15 John, son of Valentine Schwartz, aged 27 years
May 3 John, of Thomas Getzendanner, aged 2 months
Jul 28 Jacob, of Nicholas Madery 16 months
May 20 Wife of Thomas Beatty
-- child of Peter Bell

(Ages following names, given in years-months-days)

1789
Mar 8 A. Reitenauer
Mar 7 Stephen Remsberg 77-4-19
Mar 20 George Wintz 64-1-14
Mar 26 Susan, ch. of Jacob Schneider 0-5-2
Apr 12 --- ch. of Ad. Wirtenbecher
May 24 George, son of Tho. Ogle 6-8-5
Jul 3 Jacob Frosh 1-4-15
Jul 20 John Roth 80-2-4
Jul 30 John Kempf 78-10-13
Aug 5 Elizab. ch. of John Faubel 0-7-14
Aug 6 George Jantz 70-6-0
Aug 6(?) Catharine, ch. of John Paltzer 1-2-14
Aug 6(?) William, son of Jac. Baltzel
May 4 Elizabeth, ch. of Henry Kempf
Aug 11 An. Cath. wid. of Peter Berg 63-1-20
Aug 12 Margaret, wife of George Roth 32-5-24
Aug 16 Catharine, wife of Peter Herget 70-6-0
Aug 9 George Frederick, ch. of And. Lohs 0-10-0
Aug 19 Susan, ch. of John Zimmerman 3-1-0
Sep 7 Catharine, wife of Jacob Beisser 64-0-0
Sep 18 Michael, son of John Morgan 0-9-10
Sep 26 William son of John Hoffman 0-8-3
Oct 3 Rebecca, ch. of John Beltz 0-10-14
Oct 7 ("?) Gottseelig 68-0-0
Oct 21 Elizabeth, ch. of Jacob Aurand 6-10-16
Oct 29 Catharine ch. of Jacob Aurand 2-3-9
Oct 23 Catherine, ch. of Geo. Reinhard 1-1-21
Nov 11 Elizabeth, ch. of David Schultz 4-3-6
Nov 24 Philip Christ 87-5-10
Nov 17 Mary, ch. of George Hoffman 0-10-0
Nov 18 Peter, son of Peter Gebhardt 12-9-3

Nov 2 Elizabeth, ch. of Andrew Loh 1-0-23
Dec 1 Barbara, ch. of John Bockins 3-2-8
Dec 4 Elizabeth, ch. of John Remsperger 1-10-14
Nov 2 Anna Barb. ch. of St. Brunner 0-8-5

1790
Jan 13 Blantina, wife of John Holtz 35-2-0
Jan 25 Mary, ch. of Frantz Kleinard 0-11-10
Jan 27 Michael, son of Nicholas Deisz 20-2-21
Jan 27 Caspar Beckebach 68-6-7
Feb 1 Christian, son of Henry Hartman 11-8-1
Feb 10 Christopher Stoll 48-1-9
Feb 20 Stephan, son of Stephan Brunner 3-0-21
Feb 23 Elizabeth Keller 14-0-0
Mar 2 Margaret, d. of Edward Woodward 6-0-3
Mar 8 Anna Cath. wife of Sebast. Doerr 50-9-21
Feb 28 Mary Ann, widow of Ad'm Steckel 47-2-9
Apr 3 Anna Barb., wife of Melchior Stehly 63-3-8
Sep 3 Mary, ch. of Jacob Kast 3-3-5
Sep 25 Daniel, son of Elias Brunner 2-9-1
Sep 30 Jacob son of John Schaefer 12-10-27
Sep 31 Agnes, d. of Philip Schmit 5-1-0
Oct 11 William Krum 59-6-4
Oct 12 Valentine Adam 63-0-9

1791
Jan 2 Anna Mary, d. of Lewis Kern 1-0-21
Jan 10 Catharine, wife of Wm Crum 49-0-0
Jan 14 Jacob, son of Joseph Doll 10-11-1
Feb 10 Anna Marg. wife of Christoph Eckhart 56-4-6
Mar 1 Caspar Mantz 72-11-11
Mar 16 John, son of John & Rebec. Leshhorn 0-8-15
Mar 20 Philip Lehmer 90-9-17
Mar 21 Melchior Stehly 71-9-16
Mar 2 Michael, son of Jacob Traut 7-1-8
Mar 30 David, of Jac. & Sus. Gombe 1-0-27
Mar 31 Barbara, of Martin & Barb. Tschudi 8 yrs minus 8 days
Jun 8 Henry Bruder 46-3-3
Jul 12 Mary Julianna, cons. of Balth. Fuchs 42-2-21
Oct 3 Henry Schober, from Erlebach, Gy. 74-6-0
Oct 11 Anna Barb., w. of George Josz; nearly 67
Oct 13 Charlotte, w. of Geo. Gerlach 30-5-27
Oct 19 George Doffler
Nov 7 Jacob Balzel 80-2-0
Nov 16 Henry Krass 38-0-0
Nov 18 Michael Christ 55-2-0
Dec 2 Johanna Elenor, wid. of Geo. Niecky 78

1792
Jan 1 George Bernhardt Kessler 80-1-0
Jan 4 Mary Magd. wid of Geo. Dertzebach 69-
Jan 29 Cath. Elizab., w. of John Steiner 53-7-0

Death Records of Evangelical Reformed Church, Frederick, Maryland

Feb 1 Barbara, wid. of Conrad Roth 68-11-
Feb 10 Ott's child
Mar 17 John, son of John Zimmerman 11-1-16
Apr 4 John Klein (unmarried) 34-3-15
May 24 Benedict Holtz 75-2-2
Jun 27 Elizabeth, d. of John Schaefer 7-3-0
Jun 29 John, son of Christian Balzel 4-6-8
Jun 30 Christian Stauder 68-5-8
Jul 1 Jacob Hauck 76-
Jul 17 Conrad, of Jacob & Cath. Schneider 0-9-16
Jul 24 --- Bernesius (an excom. Swiss minister)(the funeral service was performed by the teacher)
Jul 24 Daniel, of George & Mary Hofman (age too indistinct)
Jul 31 Peter Schaefer 64-0-0
Aug 5 Elizabeth, wid. of John Keintz 78-1-0
Aug 15 Jacob Vollweiler 57-0-0
Aug 24 Ann Eliz'th, d. of Daniel Grim 2-6-0
Sep 17 Elizabeth, d. of Frantz Germayer 1-5-0
Sep 20 John, son of George Bentz 1-3-0
Oct 19 Valentine May 17-2-5
Oct 29 Jacob, son of Balthasar Getzedanner 21-9
Oct 29 David, son of John Wallen 1-1-21
Nov 12 Jacob Roth 52-1-1
Dec 3 Henry, son of Adam Klee 16-
Dec 17 Andrew Dehaven 22-
Dec 19 Anna Catharine Dofler 67-
Dec 30 Nicholas Wollenschlager 73-

1793
Jan 5 Peter, son of Eckh. Gills 0-7-0
Jan 19 George Mich'l Beckebach 63-10-0
Jan 22 Magdalen, of Bened. & An. B. Steiner 13-11-0
Jan 23 The wife of Mr. Cammel, at Rocky hill
Feb 16 The widow Hoffman at the English Church
Mar 11 Jacob, son of Mich'l Weber 2-
Apr 19 John, son of Jacob Keller 2-3-23
May 8 George, son of Jac. Getzedanner 5-2-4
May 13 Elizabeth, w. of John Crum 58-0-0
May 14 Eva, w. of Peter Stimmel 40-1-0
May 19 Adam Schaefer 60-
Jun 15 Adam Reeb 50-1-0
Jun 26 William of Jacob & Elizabeth Steiner 2-0-0
Jun 30 Mary, of Adam & Syb. Hausser 1-2-0
Jul 12 Ann, w. of Balthas. Getzedanner 52-6-6
Jul 23 Mary, of Jacob & Elizab. Poley 1-6-0
Jul 27 Mary Salome, w. of Mich'l Veist 51-3-2
Jul 31 Elizabeth Hintzig 12-
Aug 2 Jacob Christ 54-4-1 and his wife 51-/Both were buried in the same grave
Aug 5 William, of John & Gertr. Heintz 4-0-0
Aug 6 Daughter of Mr. Campbel, at Rocky hill
Aug 6 Mary, w. of Jos. Borckhardt 26-0-0

Aug 13 Lewis, of Lewis & Eliz. Kramer 0-6-16
Aug 14 Peter, of Peter & Cath. Wolf 1-1-13
Aug 27 Michael, of Mich'l & Chris. Kern 7-2-0
Aug 28 Elizabeth, of David & Sus. Ehly 12-0-1
Sep 2 Mary Cath., w. of Pet. Engels 65-4-0
Sep 9 Catharine, wid. of Lewis Wissinger 74-0-0
Sep 13 Charles, of Mich'l & Marg. Lingenfelder 2-7-0
Sep 27 Mathew, of Jacob & Elizab. Traut 7-0-0
Sep 27 Ann Barb., w. of Jacob Stehly 40-
Sep 28 Catharine, of Henry & Marg. Kuhns 1-1-16
Sep 29 Catharine, wid. of G. Jantz 52-0-20
Sep 30 George, of John & Sus. Morgan 1-7-0
Oct 2 William, of Mich'l & Cath. Weber 5-
Oct 2 Sybilla, wid. of Valent. Steckel 73-0-16
Oct 10 Jacob, son of John Meyer 10-
Oct 10 David, son of John Meyer 5-
Oct 9 Anna Mary, w. of Andr. Derner 35-8-0
Oct 19 Julianna, wid. of John:Diel: Berg 69-1-23
Oct 21 Eva Mary, w. of Christ. Schryack 54-9-13
Oct 24 George, son of Sebastian Doerr 16-6-7
Oct 26 William, of Conr. & Sus. Reitmay 3-7-0
Oct 28 Elizabeth, of Peter & Cath. Fleck 2-
Nov 5 Peter Engels 75-
Nov 18 John Rohr (of, or from, Pen. Bucks) 22-
Nov 28 Valentine, son of Jacob Traut 9 weeks
Dec 27 Theobald Kuhns 71 years
Dec 31 George Mertz 50 years

1794
Jan 8 William, son of Wm McClane 1-24-0
Jan 13 William Allbach 70-10-5
Jan 14 Margaret, w. of Mich'l Hafner 31-11-0
Jan 16 Balthasar Hemp 73-10-0
Jan 19 Gabriel Thomas 73-7-12
Jan 30 Margaret, of Jacob & Cath. Rohr 1-11-6
Jan 31 Mary Cath., Fred. Wm Handshu's wife 26-1-6
Feb 6 Jerome Hildebrandt 69-0-24
Feb 26 Jesse, a stranger, at J.Traut's 30-
Feb 28 Jacob Kempf 29-2-19
Mar 7 Ann Marg., wid. of Henry Hemp 64-0-1
Apr 3 Adam Knauf 33-
Apr 7 William, son of John Crum 0-5-0
Apr 12 John Schenckmayer 71-0
Jun 2 Peter Salethe 79-
Jun 6 Mary Elizabeth Witmer 77-9-0
Jul 15 Christina, daught. of Mr. Brine 6-0-0
Jul 23 Sister of Mrs. Holiday
Jul 25 Anna, daught. of Just. Gerecht 0-10-0
Jul 27 Mr. Campbell
Jul 30 Barbara, daught. of Geo. Daub 19-7-3
Jul 31 George, son of Henry Smith 6-6-0
Aug 3 Daughter of Mr. Jacobs

Aug 6 Magdalen, w. of Conrad Becker 45-0-0
Aug 7 William Marshall, s. of wid. Marshall
Aug 14 Susan, daught. of George Daub 9-0-0
Aug 15 Elizabeth, daught. of Geo. Lieblick 0-11-0
Aug 16 Jacob, son of Adam Schaefer 17-0-0
Aug 24 Jacob Schmit 69-2-0
Sep 5 Adam Schaefer 54-5-0
Sep 5 Jacob, son of George Nicols 2-8-0
Sep 5 Christina, daught. of John Thomas 1-1-0
Sep 18 Christina, daught. Bernard Ott 1-0-7
Oct 4 John Dean 45-
Oct 5 Math. Bucky 66-5-18
Oct 5 Elizabeth, daught. of Mich'l Kern 0-9-4
Oct 8 A Daughter of Wm Dewall, age unknown
Oct 8 A man's wife, age unknown
Oct 9 w. of --- Grafft 50-0-0
Dec 22 Henry, son of Henry Fehling 4-8-10

1795
Jan 8 Dorothy, w. of John Ried 55-0-0
Feb 4 Charles, son of Mat. Ami 22-
Feb 5 Gabriel Thomas 42-9-21
Feb 15 Daniel Mades 75-8-18
Feb 16 Elizabeth, d. of Elias Brunner 0-2-14
Feb 16 Elizabeth, d. of Frederick Hafner 43-0-0
Jan 24 Jacob Storm 30-8-0
Mar 16 Widow Elizabeth Stehly 76-9-9
Mar 23 William, son of John Wallen 1-6-0
Apr 20 Elizabeth, d. of Henry Bantz 0-7-0
Apr 22 Charles, son of Wm Springer 1-6-0
May 9 Henry Jung 46-
Jun 7 Anna Mary, wid. of Pet. Baltzell 83-3-0
Jun 20 John Adam Eberly 72-11-1
Jul 11 Joseph, son of John Getzendanner 0-8-0
Jul 21 John Schaefer 85-10-27
Aug 8 Widow Elizabeth Dibuss 81-11-16
Aug 18 Margaret, wid. of John Schaefer 70-0-0
Aug 22 Naomi, daught. of Banj. Hull 3-0-0
Aug 23 John, son of Benj. Hull 15-0-0
Aug 26 Valentine Thomas 70-1-4
Aug 31 Benjamin, son of Benj. Hull 10-0-0
Sep 5 Widow Gottselig 80 - nearly
Sep 11 Elizabeth, w. of Jacob Schaefer 35-0-0
Sep 12 Catharine, w. of Jac'b Getzedanner 57-6-25
Sep 12 Julianna, d. of Jac.'b Schaefer 1-10-0
Oct 1 Mrs. Tustin
Oct 5 Mr. Tustin
Oct 7 George Zimmerman, Sr. 81-7-0
Oct 9 Henry, son of Henry Fehling 0-7-0
Oct 22 Mary Elizab. wid of Jno. Schenkmeyer 69-
Nov 12 Ann Elizabeth, d. of Mat. Haux 3-0-0
Dec 21 Charles Hedge 83-

Death Records of Evangelical Reformed Church, Frederick, Maryland

Dec 24 Ann Dorothy, w. of Paul Leschhorn 67-
Dec 10 Margaret, w. of Ad. Wolff (Virg) 27-10-0

1796 Mar 24 William Henry Brandenburger 73-7-0
Apr 6 John Thomas 38-10
Apr 12 Elizabeth, d. of John Kramer 0-5-0
May 24 John Peter, son of John Thomas 5-2-21
Jun 14 Henry, son of Henry Kempf 0-4-0
Jun 20 Abraham, son of Charles Lang 0-10-0
Jul 2 Mary, daught. of Jacob Eder 5-2-1
Jul 23 Ann Cath. w. of Bal. Riehm 77-7-0
Aug 10 Mrs. Linton 70-
Sep 1 George Kramer 58-3-0
Sep 19 Widow Elizabeth Huber 45-0-0
Sep 20 Mary Huber 22-0-0
Sep 21 Catharine, d. of Jacob Wiest 1-2-0
Sep 26 John Engelbert, s. of Ph. Morgenstern 13-0-0
Oct 6 Peter, son of Peter Stimmel 20-0-0
Oct 9 Anna Barbara Bergesser 80-0-10
Oct 10 George Frederick Draxel 55-0-0
Nov 21 Esra, Jacob Kramer's son 2-2-0
Nov 28 John Ried, Sr. 67-0-0
Dec 4 --- McKinsey
Dec 15 John Keller 83-10-11
Dec 30 Valentine Steckel 23-11-0

1797
Jan 19 Susan, daugh. of Ephr. Crumm
Apr 16 Susan, daugh. of John Schaefer 2-
May 4 Eva, w. of John Bockins 47-5-0
May 12 George, son of Andr. Hedges
Jun 22 Elizabeth, Val. Steckel's daugh. 0-8-21
Jun 29 John, son of Peter Stimmel 9-8-0
Aug 4 Mary Ann Barb., of Dav. Levig 0-10-21
Aug 17 M. Magdalen, d. of Hen. Hemp 5-9-11
Aug 22 Anna Mary, d. of John Holtz 3-8-
Aug 29 Peter Jauzy 71-0-17
Aug 31 William, son of Henry Otto 3-
Sep 5 A. Margaret, w. of Geo. Schneider 68-9-2
Sep 7 Elizabeth, d. of John Keplinger 1-8-12
Sep 9 Frederick, son of Henry Otto 0-5-8
Sep 9 John, son of George Briedy 0-5-5
Sep 22 Frederick, a foundling 0-3-0
Oct 17 Elizabeth, d. of Andr. Hedges 2-6-4
Nov 15 Mary Elizab., w. of John Breisz 84-2-2
Dec 13 William, son of John Crum 11-
Dec 17 A son of Mr. Marlow
Feb 4 Philip Weber (1798?) 58- (Note. The year here is not given. The original order is observed)
Feb 14 James, Mr.Campble's son
Mar 10 Widow Morgenstern
Mar 19 Anne, w. of John Farrin 49-7-21

Mar 29 Mary Salome, w. of Elias Lafeber 49-
Apr 8 Mary Magd., w. of Jacob Levi 24-3-0
Apr 11 Balthasar Simmon 75-2-21
Apr 13 Mrs. Mackie

1798
Apr 22 Lucas Luckhorst 44-0-5
May 20 Michael, son of Chr. Getzendanner 6-11-8
May 31 Sus. Holtz, w. of Will'm Benedict 76-3-28
Jun 7 Eva Elizab. d. of Mich'l Eberhard 7-4-23
Jun 27 Mary, wid. of William Crum 51-0-0
Jun 28 Adam, son of Adam Knauf 3-8-20
Jul 22 Peter Hauck 63-2-0
Jul 30 Willable, son of George Berg 1-10-4
Aug 20 John Weiss, son of Jac. Beringer 9-9-20
Aug 29 Mary, w. of George Briedy 38-1-24
Sep 5 Elizabeth, w. of David Schreyer 34-3-18
Sep 11 Elizabeth, d. of George Beck 0-7-0
Sep 21 Dorothy, w. of Phil. Stober 41-9-0
Oct 13 Anna Mary, w. of Conrad Doll 53-7-0
Oct 20 Rebecca, d. of John Rickert 3-4-14
Oct 31 Lewis Kramer 50
Nov 11 Anna Susan Dabler 40-10-3
Nov 21 George Daug 66-
Nov 24 Catharine, w. of Henry Richter 36-1-3

1799
Feb 10 Melchior Geisser 110-
Mar 6 Philip, son of Conrad Becker 23-1-19
Apr 8 Attended the funeral of Mr. Beckwith
Apr 10 Andrew Spannseiler 77-0-0
May 14 Mrs. Duwall
May 16 Magdalen, d. of John Schaefer 8-4-0
Jun 10 Daniel, of Sim. Schnook 16-etc.
Jun 17 Mr. Cample
Jun 18 Eva Catharine, w. of Jac. Wiest 44-0-0
Jun 21 Henry, son of Henry Kempf 1-&c
Jun 28 Geo. Elias 57-3-11
Jul 11 Catharine, w. of George Engel 28-10-20
Jul 20 Daniel, son of Jacob Rohr 0-4-
Jul 24 Samuel, son of Jac. Getzedanner 1-0-11
Aug 3 Arthur, son of Mr. Dorsey 0-8-0
Aug 23 John, son of Adam Koblenz 3-6-21
Sep 13 Mary, d. of George Briedy 8-10-11
Sep 13 Sarah, w. of Peter Schaun 28-6-0
Sep 17 Margaret, wid. of Balth. Simmon 81-0-0
Sep 23 William Umbach 47
Oct 24 Margaret, w. of Frederick Riehl 31-9-7
Oct 28 Mary Albertina, wid.of Andr. Bastian 91-
Oct 29 Nicholas Deisz (Tice) 57-0-17
Dec 11 Nicholas Hauer 66-4-3

Death Records of Evangelical Reformed Church, Frederick, Maryland

1800
Jan 15 Widow Anna Mary Bucky 62-1-22
Jan 16 Conrad Miller 33-8-13
Mar 11 Christina, w. of Andr. Hedges 24-11-3
Mar 25 Leonhard Huber 69-4-17
Apr 5 Catharine, d. of John Reischwein 1-8-0
Apr 8 Widow Johanna M. Magd. Storm 81-10-5
Apr 15 Widow Elizabeth Spannseiler 79-7-0
Apr 17 Widow Anna Schober 76-7-0
Jun 20 Hubertus Bayer 71-2-10
Jun 20 Lewis Hauer 29-6-27
Jun 24 Jacob Schneider 67-0-20
Jul 7 Margaret, w. of Peter Fuchs 64-
Jul 21 Jacob, son of Jacob Jung 2-2-20
Jul 22 John, son of Michael Holtz 5-0-22
Aug 8 Henry, son of Henry Hering 19-
Aug 24 Henry Kempf 41-2-1
Aug 31 Henry, son of John Hauck 1-3-25
Oct 21 Mary, d. of John Carny 0-10-
Oct 25 Jacob, son of Michael Holtz 3-0-0
Oct 28 John, son of George Schneider 0-5-24
Oct 27 Catharine, w. of Peter Berg 32-10-7
Oct 30 Widow Anna Mary Hildebrand 59-10-21
Oct 30 John Breisz 77-3-16
Nov 12 John Spohn 24-3-24
Nov 17 Henry Wolff 74
Nov 23 Jacob Friederick (Frederick) 27-6-14
Nov 29 Anna Mary, w. of John Schamly 68-
Dec 9 Frantz Becker 57-

INDEX

INDEX

INDEX

INDEX

INDEX

INDEX

INDEX

INDEX

INDEX

INDEX

INDEX

INDEX

INDEX

INDEX

INDEX

INDEX

INDEX

INDEX

INDEX

INDEX

INDEX

INDEX

INDEX

INDEX

INDEX

INDEX

No surnames given (Negroes)

www.ingramcontent.com/pod-product-compliance
Ingram Content Group UK Ltd.
Pitfield, Milton Keynes, MK11 3LW, UK
UKHW020133250726
13967UKWH00002B/622

9 781585 490950